BIG MONEY

BIG MONEY

2.5 BILLION DOLLARS, ONE SUSPICIOUS VEHICLE, AND A PIMP— ON THE TRAIL OF THE ULTRA-RICH HIJACKING AMERICAN POLITICS

Kenneth P. Vogel

PUBLICAFFAIRS

A MEMBER OF THE PERSEUS BOOKS GROUP

New York

Book Design by Cynthia Young

Library of Congress Cataloging-in-Publication Data
Vogel, Kenneth P., 1975–
    Big money : 2.5 billion dollars, one suspicious vehicle, and a pimp-on the
trail of the ultra-rich hijacking American politics / Kenneth P. Vogel.
        pages cm
    Includes bibliographical references and index.
    ISBN 978-1-61039-338-6 (hardback) — ISBN 978-1-61039-339-3 (e-book)
    1. Campaign funds—United States.   2. Campaign funds—Law and
legislation—United States.   3. Presidents—United States—Election—
Finance.   4. United States. Congress—Elections—Finance. 5. Citizens
United—Trials, litigation, etc.   I. Title.
    JK1991.V65 2014
    324.7'80973—dc23

                                                            2014004954

First Edition

10 9 8 7 6 5 4 3 2 1

Contents

Preface

It was a dreary Pacific Northwest evening in February 2012, and President Barack Obama's mood matched the weather. Despite being among supporters who had gathered in a stunning modernist mansion in Seattle's eastern suburbs, he seemed irritated. Pacing in front of towering twenty-five-foot-high windows that offered a sweeping view of a rain-spattered Lake Washington, he rattled through a short pro forma speech about how his administration was working to help struggling Americans through "the toughest three years economically since the Great Depression."

Tickets for the speech—a fund-raiser for Obama's reelection campaign—cost $17,900 apiece, so it was unlikely anyone in the small crowd was going to end up in a breadline anytime soon. In the Medina, Washington, living room of the hosts, Costco cofounder Jeff Brotman and his wife, Susan, Microsoft founder Bill Gates—the richest man in the country—leaned against a black grand piano, while others, including fellow Microsoft billionaire Steve Ballmer, were scattered about, some standing with their backs to muted off-white walls decorated with colorful bursts of abstract expressionist art. They listened attentively to Obama's speech, which lasted all of sixteen minutes. But they really perked up when he finished and the traveling press pool was escorted from the room, which allowed them to talk candidly with the president.

In their private question-and-answer session, Obama let his guard down and eventually shared some thoughts that revealed more about his view of American politics than perhaps anything he said publicly during the entire campaign. Election Day was still more than eight months away. But Obama, in a previously unreported riff, signaled surrender on one of the fights that had drawn him to politics in the first place: the effort to limit the flow of big money. It was a remarkable concession, one that would have stunned the campaign volunteers who believed so deeply in his promise to change the way politics works. It wasn't just that he was admitting that his own election prospects would be disproportionately influenced by super-rich donors like those he was addressing. He had already done that eleven days earlier, when he blessed a so-called super PAC collecting million-dollar checks to boost his reelection. What really distinguished his remarks to Gates and company from his carefully calibrated official position was the admission that the grassroots, people-powered politics he had long glorified might never again trump the swelling political buying power of the very richest donors in presidential campaigns in 2016 and beyond.

"You now have the potential of 200 people deciding who ends up being elected president every single time," Obama told the group in response to a question about the 2010 Supreme Court ruling in a case called *Citizens United vs. Federal Election Commission* that gutted campaign finance restrictions and marked the beginning of a new big-money era in American politics.*

Unless things changed dramatically, Obama predicted, "I may be the last presidential candidate who could win the way I won, which was coming out without a lot of special-interest support, without a handful of big corporate supporters, who was able to mobilize and had the time and the space to mobilize a grassroots effort, and then eventually got a lot of big donors, but started off small and was able to build. I think the capacity for somebody to do that is going to be much harder." He continued, "In this election, I will be able to, hopefully, match whatever check the Koch brothers want to write," referring to the billionaire industrialists Charles and David Koch. "But I'm an incumbent president who already had this huge network of support all across the country and millions of donors. I'm not sure that the next candidate after me is going to be able to compete in that same way." Obama turned to face Gates, who stood awkwardly, his hands stuffed in his suit pants pockets. "And at that point, you genuinely have a situation where ten people—hey, you know, Bill could write a check." And, Obama pointed out, it wasn't just Gates, whose fortune, then estimated at $61 billion,

_____

*Obama's remarks were detailed to me by a source familiar with the event.

Democrats had been hoping to tap in a big way. "Actually, there are probably five or six people in this room," Obama said, gesturing to Ballmer and others, as nervous laughter spread through the crowd. Obama plowed ahead insistently, eyebrows raised, his voice rising with agitation as he stepped toward the donors. "I mean, there are five or six people in this room *tonight* that could simply make a decision this will be the next president and probably at least get a nomination, if ultimately the person didn't win. And that's not the way things are supposed to work."

It was jarring to hear such a blunt assessment from a politician who had built so much of his identity around the idea that average people could band together to change the world, partly by taking politics back from moneyed special interests. When he had formally announced his unlikely presidential bid almost exactly five years before the Medina fund-raiser, Obama had boldly declared that it was time to take government back from "the cynics, and the lobbyists, and the special interests who've turned our government into a game only they can afford to play."[1] Now, as the leader of the free world, Obama was admitting that was no longer achievable in the current system—that American politics had fundamentally changed in a way that made it, at the highest levels, a game for the ultra-rich.

Of course, the richest Americans have always used their fortunes to try to tilt the nation's political landscape to their liking. The robber barons spent unknown millions financing William McKinley's 1896 presidential election. Insurance magnate W. Clement Stone invested $4.8 million helping Richard Nixon win the White House—twice.[2] And billionaire currency trader George Soros spent $27 million trying to elect John Kerry in 2004.

Having tracked the flow of money into politics as a reporter for more than a dozen years, I'd heard plenty of hyperbolic predictions from self-styled reformers like Obama. From their perspective, the latest developments in campaign finance law always seemed to be threatening the very fabric of American democracy by empowering rich donors or special interests. Mostly, though, the system self-corrected, and American democracy continued more or less unaltered. If moneyed interests pumped too much cash through a particular loophole and it resulted in a scandal, Congress, regulators, or judges would close it down, only to see the cycle begin anew with a fresh avenue for spending.

But the cresting wave of big money sparked by the *Citizens United* decision was truly altering the very character of American politics. Sure, there were still potential marginal changes that could come from lawsuits, court rulings, bills, and regulatory processes that were pending even as this book was going to press. But Obama's judgment was sound: a new political reality was here to stay.

It's not just that the total sums pouring into our politics are greater than they've been at any other time in our nation's history—though that is undeniably true. Rather, it's that the spending is fundamentally changing how campaigns are run, which issues are debated, and which candidates represent their parties. In past elections, most major donors boosted candidates or causes closely aligned with the Democratic or Republican establishments. Now it's just as likely that the biggest checks will be spent bucking the system. At a time when wealth is increasingly coalescing in the bank accounts of the richest 1 percent of American citizens, members of this mega-donor community—and the consultants who spur them on—are wresting control from the political parties and their proxies, which once combined to dominate politics. A tightly choreographed hierarchy controlled by party insiders is being replaced by a chaotic one where even those with no political experience can buy in. In a perverse kind of way, the new system is more democratic, but only for those with the cash to buy in. Anyone with enough net worth can become a player in the new big-money politics, and the country's ultra-rich have lined up to get in the game. They are—in a very real and entirely legal way—hijacking American democracy.

The 2012 election was a tipping point in this evolution—the first in the modern campaign finance era[3] in which independent groups like those powered by the mega-donors spent more money, $2.5 billion, than the political parties themselves (which spent $1.6 billion).[4] Some of the implications of this trend will likely take years to become apparent, but it has already profoundly reshaped the political landscape. The parties are losing the ability to pick their candidates and set their agendas, as fewer and fewer politicians are reliant on the financial support of their party to win. In fact, it can be preferable to have the backing of a sugar daddy donor or a group with deeper pockets willing to spend unlimited cash to fight the party.

To date, this dynamic has played itself out more fully on the right. Rich Republicans leapt to take advantage of the new Wild West–like landscape. Their huge checks helped harness the energy of the anti-establishment tea party movement and lift the GOP to control of the House of Representatives in 2010. But that widened sectarian rifts between the party and factions of its base that regarded party leaders as insufficiently conservative on fiscal or social issues. The new tea party wing of the House majority quickly became an albatross, calling public attention to noisy internecine disagreements that resulted in disputes over national fiscal policy, expensive and damaging primaries in 2010 and 2012, and a disastrous government shutdown in 2013 that left party elders dreading another big-money demolition derby in the 2014 primaries.

Rich Democrats mostly sat on their wallets early in the big-money era. They were sidelined by apathy toward Obama and other party leaders, and by queasiness about the impact of big money on democracy. The famous "shellacking" they took at the ballot box in the 2010 midterms helped them get over their qualms. Once they joined the game, they managed to play it more skillfully than Republicans, taking advantage of their relative ideological unity to adhere to the same playbook, and attracting plenty of million-dollar checks to help reelect Obama and protect his Democratic allies in Congress. But with Obama's presidency coming to an end and disagreements percolating over the direction and leadership of the party, it seemed only a matter of time before wealthy Democrats found themselves at odds and battling one another with their checkbooks, just like the Republicans before them. Already a coalition of rich partisans was trying to avoid this plight by aligning behind a prospective Hillary Clinton 2016 presidential campaign. But a sect of more liberal donors was quietly searching for a more progressive alternative to support with their own super PAC mega-checks.

As Obama said in Medina, it no longer requires an army of supporters to make a serious presidential candidate—just a handful with enough zeros in their net worth. Heck, it only took one sugar daddy apiece to allow Rick Santorum and Newt Gingrich to make a messy and prolonged race out of the 2012 Republican presidential primary.

Neither White House hopeful had assembled the basic trappings of
a credible presidential campaign, but that doesn't matter as much in
the big-money era. It used to be that a viable presidential campaign
meant spending years building lists of small donors, traveling to county
fairs, endorsing state legislative candidates, and schmoozing local party
chairmen in their Iowa, New Hampshire, and South Carolina living
rooms and rec centers. That still has its place, of course. Now, though,
you can be competitive with minimal commitment to that kind of retail politicking, as long as you have one billionaire who's able to stroke
seven- or eight-figure checks. And while a single mega-donor can now
subsidize a politician through any given election or even for an entire
career, no class of people benefits from the new big-money political
economy as much as the consultants who keep it all going. They solicit
and spend the money, earning fat commissions on the cash as it comes
in and then again when it gets spent, regardless of their results in any
given election. As long as they keep the mega-donors happy, the money
keeps flowing.

So just what is it that drives these donors to keep giving? Among the
motivations of these guys—and they are mostly men, mostly older, and
largely white—are passion, ego, and in some cases financial self-interest,
though the new big-money politics is no way to boost profits. In fact,
most of the mega-donors whose areas of business are closely regulated
by government also spend heavily—and more efficiently—on lobbying.
One uniting factor in this gilded club is a political junkie's love of the
game. They may be true believers in a cause or a candidate, but politics
is also their hobby, just like the Washington cabbie whose radio is glued
to NPR or the uncle at Thanksgiving dinner who can't stop quoting
Bill O'Reilly.

At first blush, they may seem like conniving robber baron arche-
types trying to buy government favor, but they remind me more of the
wealthy class of sports junkies who plunk down hundreds of millions
of dollars to buy a professional team. In fact, there's a good bit of
overlap between team owners and political donors. Los Angeles Kings
investor Phil Anschutz and Arizona Diamondbacks owner Ken Kend-
rick regularly attend secretive mega-donor conferences organized by the
Koch brothers, while New York Jets owner Woody Johnson is a leading

GOP donor, as is Joe Ricketts, whose family bought the Chicago Cubs in 2009. Big Democratic donors include Peter Angelos, who owns the Baltimore Orioles, and George Soros, who owns a stake in Manchester United and tried to buy the Washington Nationals.

Like their fellow 1-percenters playing the political field, it's usually not enough for sports patrons to merely cut the checks. Many seem almost pathologically compelled to try their hand at managing aspects of the team better left to professionals. It's as if the newly minted owners are impatient to show that the same acumen they demonstrated in business can be applied to sports. Often it can't. History is rife with examples of sports owners whose meddling has kept their teams mired in chaos near the bottom of the standings. The mega-donors playing the political field have in many ways wrought chaos on American politics, but that seems only to have emboldened them to dig deeper to try to get their way in the next election. While some politicians and consultants privately grumble about the impact on the process, many more are queuing up to try to tap into the cash flow. The big-money game is only just getting started. This is the story of that game—how it came to be, the donors who underwrite it, the consultants and politicians who play it—and how it's changing American politics.

CHAPTER 1

The Billionaires' Club

It was 105 degrees on a late April afternoon in the California desert town of Indian Wells. A blazing sun was beating down on the manicured grounds of the Renaissance Esmeralda Resort. A contingent of several dozen guests trickled into the hotel from the broiling outdoors wearing slacks and long sleeves, the women in silk blouses, the men sweating under sport coats. They were older and almost entirely white, and they had that well-kempt look that only privilege can bring. It was clear they were all together, both because they wore small black tags engraved only with their names and because they stuck out conspicuously from another set of guests who were about a third their age and were toned, tanned, tattooed, and quite fond of the poolside bar.

The boozier crowd was in town for the spring 2013 Stagecoach country music festival. The more groomed group had been invited by the billionaire industrialists Charles and David Koch to attend the latest in a running series of secretive political gatherings of the big-money conservative elite. Since 2003, twice a year the Koch brothers have brought together some of the top Republican politicians in the country, leading political operatives, and a hundred or more of the party's most generous donors for closed-door "seminars" on how, as an invitation to Indian Wells put it, "to advance a plan to defend our free-enterprise system." I had decided to travel to the California desert to try to get as close as I could to some of the most important—but least known—donors and operatives in politics. My aim was to get a sense of whether the Kochs and their donors were discouraged by the 2012 election six months earlier. After all, their political network had spent an estimated $400 million—an astounding and historic sum—in the run-up to Election Day, mostly beating up on President Barack Obama and his Democratic allies in Congress. Yet Obama had won handily and the Democrats gained seats in Congress.

But the election seemed not to be weighing on the Koch guests congregating in the hotel's eight-story atrium lobby before the seminar's opening dinner. One after another they made their way down a grand, curved double staircase built of tropical African hardwood, as if arriving for their coronation into politics' most elite ranks. A few hours later, with the Stagecoach posse mostly off-site, the Koch invitees had the run of the place. Some rimmed the lobby bar, while others gathered in a private lounge. Hotel and Koch security roamed the lobby anxiously and stood sentry by the double glass doors to the lounge, talking through earpieces and watching over their prized guests. State troopers buzzed about—a sure sign that governors were present. I tried my best to blend in, pulling up a seat at the bar next to a middle-aged fellow with the creased tan skin and shaggy blond hair of an aging beach bum. He was not, in my best estimation, a likely Koch seminar participant. Turns out he was a marketing executive for Toyota, the main sponsor of Stagecoach, and he wasn't particularly talkative. We watched the end of an NBA playoff game between the Oklahoma City Thunder and Houston Rockets, and I tried to make small talk during breaks in the action while keeping my eyes peeled for any circling big-name Republicans. I feigned disinterest in a conversation that Sen. Ron Johnson of Wisconsin was having with a group of donors as they walked by. Ken Ellegard, an Arizona car dealer and Republican donor, sidled up to the bar next to the Toyota marketing guy and me and ordered a vodka soda with a splash of cranberry. The conservative pundit Erick Erickson pulled up a seat at the far end of the bar and ordered food. Behind us, South Carolina governor Nikki Haley joined a small group at a high-top table near the bar. Nursing a glass of red wine, she held court for an hour about politics and stock car racing.

"That's the governor of South Carolina," I informed the Toyota guy in hushed tones, perhaps out of a subconscious desire to enlist an ally in my reconnaissance. I told him he was surrounded by masters of the universe, whose wealth the Koch brothers hoped to tap to reshape American politics, and that I was a reporter hoping to learn about their exclusive world. "The only Koch I know is Coca-Cola," the Toyota guy said, shaking his head and chuckling (the brothers' last name is pronounced "Coke." Turning back to his cabernet, he conceded it was a relief to find out why everyone else was so much better dressed than he.

Not all the Koch summit attendees had followed the business casual dress code for daytime sessions. Billionaire tech entrepreneur Rob Ryan ambled through the Renaissance lobby in a rumpled white polo shirt, wrinkled khakis, and scuffed white sneakers. Rick Sharp, the former chairman of Crocs, Inc. and a regular at Koch seminars, regularly sported the ultra-casual, ultra-comfortable, and ultra-dorky foam clogs manufactured by the company at seminars. The point of the dress code is to suggest the aesthetic of an investors' conference. And that's pretty much what the Koch seminars are—political investors' conferences. Prospective donors sit through jargon-laden presentations and get up close with politicians and operatives in whom they might invest money. The summits are designed to help donors "effectively achieve what we believe to be your policy, political and philanthropic goals," as an email sent to attendees two months prior by senior Koch aide Kevin Gentry put it.[1] Gentry promised an exclusive opportunity to engage with "several hundred of America's top business owners and CEOs" to discuss "short-term policy threats in 2013 while building toward free-market gains in 2014 and beyond."

The seminars are a brilliant way to raise political cash. For politicians and operatives, invitations are coveted. You got the closest thing to an endorsement from Koch World, plus a chance to go fishing in a stocked pond full of some the biggest donors in the land. It is the Kochs' ability to pool donations from wealthy attendees—rather than just Charles's and David's personal fortunes (estimated at $36 billion each in 2013)[2]—that has put them among the leading forces in the increasingly competitive world of big-money politics. The more cash the

Koch political network could raise in Indian Wells, the more influence it would have in setting the course for the then-rudderless Republican Party. Among the attendees at Indian Wells were Sens. Ted Cruz of Texas and Rand Paul of Kentucky and Govs. Bobby Jindal of Louisiana and John Kasich of Ohio, all prospective contenders for the party's 2016 presidential nomination.

Just like an investor conference, the Indian Wells gathering included presentations from experts on a range of subjects: How to use elaborate databases to mobilize voters. How to craft messages that appeal to young, female, and Hispanic voters (though in Indian Wells those demographics appeared to be represented primarily by the hotel staff). How to recruit and train candidates who adhere to the Kochs' small-government, anti-regulation philosophy.

Before the Kochs could shape the future of American politics, though, they needed to convince donors that they had learned from the bust that was 2012. That was perhaps the major task at Indian Wells. And it was the one facing all the well-funded operations on the right, from the Republican National Committee (RNC) to the groups powering the anti-establishment tea party to Koch World's most direct rival for big-money supremacy—the American Crossroads operation, steered by veteran GOP operative Karl Rove.

The Democrats had their own issues. They had nowhere near the big-money network that the conservative side did. Rich liberals like George Soros and Peter Lewis had spent more than $200 million a decade earlier trying to elect John Kerry president, and after that failure, many remained leery about tossing their millions into electoral politics. Democrats were trying to rally the major donors they did have into a cohesive group that could keep the party united post-Obama, or at least avoid the toxic factionalism being fueled by deep-pocketed conservative groups. It wasn't going to be easy. Lone-wolf liberal billionaires such as Michael Bloomberg and Tom Steyer were signaling a willingness to challenge the Democratic Party and its candidates on tricky issues like gun control and energy production. Some of the left's most influential leaders were trying to head off deeper divisions by uniting the deepest Democratic pockets behind Hillary Clinton, but several major donors were bristling at the idea that Hillary represented the future of the party. They were signaling willingness to invest serious cash to boost a more progressive alternative to carry the party's banner in 2016—and were actively looking for such a candidate.

The big-money jockeying on both sides would go a long way toward determining the shape of American politics for years to come. It was a striking departure from recent political history. A few dozen rich donors were now helping set the course of the two major political parties, challenging the power of elected and appointed party leaders who for decades had ruled politics with an iron grip. It used to be that if the party thought a particular politician would be a good soldier for them in Washington, they could use their recruiting, fund-raising, and networking infrastructure to propel that person to victory, if not in every case, then in many. Now, all it took to throw that into disarray was one affluent activist with a favorite candidate different from the party's. Things could really get messy if multiple wealthy partisans had different ideas about the best candidate.

The historic conservative big-money spending spree in the 2012 election and its aftermath provided the first real glimpse of the chaos that this new reality could bring. Yet none of the participants wanted to take the blame, since it would play into the hands of their rivals. If donors decided the Koch operation had squandered their cash in 2012, it could mean more money in 2014 for Rove's operation—or vice versa. Rove, who made his name as former president George W. Bush's political guru, had emerged in the new world as sort of the shadow boss of the business-backed GOP establishment. That put him at odds with an increasingly influential cluster of fiscal hard-liner groups eager to raid his donor base, as well as with some parts of the Koch operation, which had come to represent the strain of uncompromising fiscal conservatism that spurred the anti-establishment tea party movement to major wins in the 2010 midterm election. The Kochs' political team had entered into a tenuous collaboration with Rove's Crossroads network in 2010 and again in 2012. But Rove had not attended any recent Koch summits, and the distrust between the two camps ran deep.[3] Some in Koch World viewed Rove as representative of a philosophically compromised brand of pocket-padding big-government conservatism, while Rove's allies regarded the Kochs as uncooperative ideologues willing to sacrifice the good in futile pursuit of the perfect. The tentative alliance was showing signs of fraying after 2012, when Rove's operation suggested that tea party groups and candidates were hurting the GOP. With so much money at stake and so many fingers pointing following the 2012 disaster, the rivalry had never been fiercer.

At Indian Wells, the Kochs' operatives and allies were trying to walk a fine line between contrition and self-preservation as they assessed the election for their donors. Conservatives had a lot to learn from Obama's campaign and its well-funded allies, they said. Liberals had spent their cash more effectively than conservatives on campaign advertising, messaging, and voter mobilization, asserted presenters, who showed the donors comparisons of television ads to make the point. But the most effective groups on the right were those funded by the Kochs' network, according to the Koch-allied operatives giving the presentations. Additionally, the Kochs' main political operation, Americans for Prosperity (AFP), which spent $179 million during the 2012 campaign cycle,[4] had a far more effective voter mobilization force than either Mitt Romney's Republican presidential campaign or the Republican National Committee, donors were told. The takeaway was unmistakable: the Koch operation was a better steward of the donors' cash than either the official Republican Party or rival private groups such as Rove's.

The philosophical divide between the business conservatives and the fiscal hard-liners erupted during another panel in Indian Wells moderated by Greta van Susteren, a top host on the conservative Fox News network. It featured Govs. Nikki Haley, Bobby Jindal, and John Kasich. Kasich found himself on the defensive over his support for a government health care expansion for hundreds of thousands of low-income Ohioans. Jindal, Haley, and several of the donors opposed the expansion, made possible by Obama's signature health care reform law—Obamacare—and Kasich took some heat from the crowd.

The argument dovetailed with a larger debate conservatives were having about the direction of the Republican Party after its 2012 chastening. More centrist figures, including Kasich and Rove, seemed to want to broaden the party's appeal by dialing down its fiery rhetoric on lightning-rod issues like immigration reform, abortion rights, and gay marriage while stepping up its outreach to young, working-class, and minority voters. When one donor at the summit declared that the party needed to fight the perception that it was "the all-white party," the Indian American Jindal quipped, "We can't be the all–Indian American party, either." Then there were the fiscal conservative purists like the Kochs, who opposed the minimum wage and social programs that appealed to working-class voters, but mostly shied away from social issues. And, of course, there was still a prominent core of well-funded religious conservatives who wanted the GOP to focus more attention on opposing gay marriage and abortion rights. After 2012, when their issues were blamed for key Republican losses, they began actively recruiting new big donors to stave off what they felt was an increasing push by the better-funded Rove and Koch operations to marginalize them.[5] These were delicate debates that once would have been hashed out by elected officials within the party apparatus, sometimes in rounds of platform committee votes, other times behind closed doors, but usually with some measure of accountability. Now, the new rules of money and politics allowed the ultra-rich a seat at the head of the table for these debates—often without the public ever knowing that the debate had even occurred.

The Koch operation, in particular, has prided itself on keeping the seminars—and Koch political activities generally—shrouded in secrecy and beyond access to reporters like me, ostensibly to make publicity-averse donors feel comfortable. As seminar emcee Kevin Gentry put it while coaxing donors to open their checkbooks at a 2011 gathering, "There is anonymity that we can protect." Ironically, his remarks and others from that seminar were recorded and leaked to the press.[6] Eager to avoid any more of that, Koch operatives at Indian Wells conducted background checks on the Renaissance Esmeralda waitstaff and collected smartphones, iPads, and other electronics before many sessions. Attendees were told to protect their meeting materials and not post anything on blogs, Facebook, or Twitter. No one did. Nor did I get anywhere near the formal sessions. What I learned came from various sources who were in the sessions or had access to people who were.

Usually at their seminars, the Kochs would have rented out all the hotel rooms, allowing them to more easily bar reporters or other unwanted interlopers from entering the premises. When I tried to crash their winter 2011 seminar, held at another tony California desert resort six miles down the road in Rancho Mirage, California, I was informed not long after entering the hotel that the grounds were closed for a private function, and I was escorted outside by security. Guards wearing gold lapel pins bearing Koch Industries' *K* logo threatened "a citizen's arrest" and a "night in the Riverside County jail" if I continued asking questions and taking photographs.[7]

So I was elated to have gotten inside the Renaissance Esmeralda during the April 2013 seminar—if only to spend two days hanging out by the lobby bar, on the massage table, or at the pool bar, soaking up Miller Lites and bits of conversation. I diligently avoided eye contact with Koch officials and operatives who knew me by sight. There were a few close calls, such as when I entered the lobby men's room and spotted Americans for Prosperity president Tim Phillips at the urinals, prompting me to turn on my heel in retreat.

By the time I drove my rented Chevy Impala from the Holiday Inn Express, where I was staying, to the gates of the Renaissance Esmeralda on the final full day of the seminar, it was clear something had changed. There was a security checkpoint manned by several guards in the driveway outside. The driver in front of me slowed, rolled down the window, gave a knowing nod, and was waved through without even a cursory check of a clipboard that presumably held a list of approved guests. I figured I'd try the same and—surprisingly—got the same result. The hotel lobby was quieter than it had been. Stagecoach, it seemed, had pulled out of town. It was all Koch donors and operatives now, including several who I knew would recognize me. There was nowhere to hide, and I imagined I would soon be thrown out—or worse. I noticed Sen. Johnson schmoozing two donors at a poolside cabana. I'd heard someone who attended these seminars describe Johnson as the Kochs' "model legislator." Figuring I had to make my last few moments count, I walked over and sat down nearby. It was just me, the Kochs' model senator, and the two wealthy backers he was talking to, identified by their name tags as Ned Diefenthal and Rob Ryan.

Diefenthal, it turns out, is a Louisiana metal titan, and he was complaining to Johnson about the incompetence of the Republican National Committee. Johnson did not reject Diefenthal's complaint, instead suggesting that RNC chairman Reince Priebus was aware of the weakness Diefenthal had flagged, but also implying that the Kochs might be a viable alternative to the RNC—at least for the function in question. "That's what they're trying to do here and that's what Reince is trying to do," Johnson said. But Diefenthal, whose family over the years had donated more than $280,000 to the RNC, was riled up. Priebus "keeps sending me letters asking for money. I'm not giving him any money. He doesn't know what to do with it," said Diefenthal, suggesting that he considered the Koch political network a better investment.[8] By this point I was subtly trying to interrupt the conversation to introduce myself. But Diefenthal was on a rant and wasn't leaving any gaps where I could interject. When he finally paused for a breath, I jumped in. I explained that I was a reporter—a declaration that journalistic standards required me to make before conducting an interview—and then led with a blunt question: do big donors and outside groups like those at the seminar have too much influence in politics?

Before I finished my question, Johnson rose from the cabana couch and stepped around me. "It's—it's—it's pretty hot," he stammered, marching toward the nearby doors to the hotel lobby, donors in tow. Ryan, a tech billionaire, started to follow, but pivoted toward me. Pointing a stubby finger in my face, he scolded, "That's pretty rude, you know? You interrupted a private conversation," which, of course, I had. I didn't disagree, and apologized again.

I caught up with Johnson a few months later, and repeated my question about whether big donors and outside groups had too much influence in politics. Johnson said he encourages business owners like those at the Koch seminar to become more politically engaged and argued they'd do well to avail themselves of new channels for spending big money in elections. "People feel they have to influence the political process because the federal government is doing so much harm to them personally, to their personal freedoms, to their organizations, to their businesses, to their ability to create jobs," he said. Johnson also stressed that during the conversation I'd overheard in Indian Wells, he hadn't been criticizing Priebus, a fellow Wisconsinite, but rather allowing Diefenthal and Ryan to vent their frustrations. "That's just sort of the process. People got to get things off their chest," said Johnson. Johnson's only criticisms were that the Republican Party, its congressional delegation, and the various conservative outside groups didn't coordinate their messages—an argument he'd made during a seminar panel moderated by media entrepreneur Tucker Carlson—and that they didn't employ strategic planning like that common in business. "A lot of that doesn't exist within the political realm, and it's frustrating for me and it's frustrating to people like those two gentlemen who you overheard at least part of that conversation," he said. He and the donors had gone to a hotel room to continue their conversation after my interruption, he told me, adding, "Those seminars are supposed to be totally confidential, and I respect that. They weren't real happy with you sittin' down."

I assumed the jig was up. Surely one of them would alert security that their sanctum had been breached. So I found the nearest Koch security guard, figuring it was better to present myself as an honorable member of the fourth estate than to be tracked down like a fugitive. I handed him my business card, explained that I was a reporter, and told him that I was hoping to talk to Rob Tappan, a Koch public relations guy I had spotted earlier. I was ushered to the head of Koch security, Larry Moorman, and the head of hotel security, Armando Limon. How had I gotten past the checkpoint at the entrance? Limon asked. I'd just driven in, I explained. "That's surprising," Limon said, looking down while flicking my business card with his thumb.

I was expecting an unpleasant exchange with Tappan, who had done a stint flacking for the mercenary military firm Blackwater[9] and was now the pointed spear of Koch Industries' antagonistic Washington public affairs shop. I'd covered plenty of politicians and companies that took a bare-knuckle approach toward dealing with the press—from the scandal-plagued Hartford County (Connecticut) sheriff's office to Hillary Clinton's 2008 presidential campaign to Fox News—but none of it had quite prepared me for Koch Industries. Its PR team seemed to revel in publicly shaming journalists, pitting them against the outlets that carried their journalism,[10] and accusing them of bias and of colluding with an anti-Koch liberal conspiracy. Their pushback ratcheted into high gear in 2010, when scrutiny increased after the Koch political network started seeding the tea party movement. They denied that the Koch brothers, their companies, or their foundations had ever given any money "specifically to support the tea parties"[11]—the word *specifically* a conspicuous bit of plausible deniability—and became particularly virulent over an exposé in the *New Yorker* by reporter Jane Mayer. She asserted that the Kochs' political activity supported policies that boosted their profits at the expense of the environment. Koch Industries assailed Mayer's reputation with tough Web ads and letters to her editors and to the judges of awards for which she had applied. She soon found herself the subject of unfounded plagiarism claims, while the website Gawker reported on rumors that a private investigator "was hired to dig up dirt on Mayer in the wake of the Koch brothers story"[12]—though neither was traced back to Koch Industries.

When I emailed Tappan links to stories in the *New York Post* and on Gawker chronicling the plagiarism claims and the private-eye rumor and asked whether there was any connection to Koch, he responded, "I don't know what you are referring to"[13]—though he did point out that Koch Industries had raised questions[14] about Mayer's reliance on the work of a liberal blogger "which she failed to acknowledge." In fact, Mayer *had* acknowledged the blogger's work. When she was asked years later, while receiving a journalism award, about "the most serious threat" she'd received from the government in the course of a career's worth of reporting on sensitive military and intelligence matters, Mayer said it wasn't from the government. "It was the story I did about a couple of billionaires who fund politics, the Koch brothers," she said, recalling that while she was working on the story, "maybe just coincidentally, I became the subject of a private eye's investigation into everything in my life. Looking into legal files, former romances, you name it. Everything was turned over. Every story I'd written, books I'd written. They put all my writing through some kind of forensic program that looks for plagiarism, and were hoping to try to expose me in some way or another. And that was actually pretty threatening, and scary."[15]

The Kochs also had turned their ire on me. They once wrote a top editor at Politico, where I work, to suggest I be barred from covering the Kochs because I had once, a decade earlier, worked for a non-profit journalism outlet backed partly by grants from liberal billionaire George Soros's foundation,[16] which also had funded advocacy groups that seized on the Kochs as poster children for the corruptive power of big money in politics. The outlet was so removed from any influence by its funders that I had no idea Soros was among them until years afterward. Another time, Koch Industries posted my emails with Tappan and various Koch-linked operatives on its corporate website in an item accusing me of journalistic misconduct.[17] The item, and the Kochs' aggressive media strategy more generally, reflected poorly on the company, concluded the well-respected blogger Dave Weigel, who has defended the Kochs against unfair press coverage but also called out their PR shop for lying.[18] Yet when Tappan greeted me in Indian Wells, he was all sunshine and smiles. He wondered why I hadn't given him "advanced warning" of my plans to swing by and asked if I had "self-identified" or talked to any Koch guests. "The hotel is pretty much locked down now," he told me almost apologetically, before signaling to Limon, Moorman, and another security guard that it was time to escort me out. As the cavalry walked me to my car, Tappan asked me casually where I was staying during the summit. "Just down the road," I offered.

"In Palm Springs?"

"No, in Rancho Mirage," I said, "close to the hotel that hosted the 2011 conference"— from which I'd also been escorted. Driving off the hotel property under their watchful gaze, past the same security guards I'd seen on the way in, I wondered why Tappan was curious about my accommodations. Oh, well, at least I'd gotten some good stuff and wasn't in jail, I thought, tweeting later that I had been "politely escorted" from the Koch conference by Koch and hotel security.[19] Apparently proud of his handiwork, Limon retweeted me.

My good cheer faded when I returned to the Holiday Inn Express and was startled by the ring of my hotel room phone. I picked it up, and the line went dead. I called the front desk asking if the hotel was trying to get in touch. Nope, the clerk said, it was a man who had asked for me but didn't identify himself. I hadn't told a soul—not even my wife—where I was staying, so I racked my brain for plausible explanations. The front desk said they couldn't track the number, so that was out. I tried to dismiss it as a wrong number. But given my and others' history with the Kochs and the fact that the caller had my name, I couldn't let it go. So I called my wife, hoping she'd convince me it was nothing. Instead, she suggested I either get on an earlier flight home or change hotels. Heeding her advice, I started to pack, but I also figured I might try to put my concerns to rest by emailing Tappan for a possible explanation. "Sorry to bug you again," I wrote, "but I received an odd hang-up phone call to my hotel room a little before 8 pm, and—since you're literally the only person who has any clue where I'm staying—I was wondering if you were trying to get in touch with me."

Not waiting for a response, I packed up the car and headed toward the airport, but I didn't get far before I got a call from the rental car company's emergency assistance team. My car had been reported as "suspicious or abandoned" to the Riverside County sheriff. So, at the urging of the rental car representative, I dialed a Riverside County sheriff's deputy named Sean Patrick, who told me that either "hotel security or the client"—the Kochs—had called him out to the hotel, where they provided the license plate number and asked him to investigate why the car was on the property. But my car was no longer on the property—I had been gone for more than two hours by the time Patrick arrived at the hotel and was provided the plate number, according to Riverside County sheriff's office dispatch logs I obtained later under the California Public Records Act. Patrick conceded it was "kind of weird" that the hotel or Koch officials would still want to report a long-gone car. And when I told him I felt kind of intimidated and wondered if I should be concerned, the deputy suggested I provide my social security number and birth date, just in case anything should happen to me.

By this time, Tappan had emailed me back. "I didn't ring you this evening—don't know where you are staying." Huh. "So weird," I responded. "Other than telling you I was in a hotel right near the resort that hosted the 2011 Koch conference, no one had any idea of even the town in which I was staying. Kind of spooked me a bit, in combination with the Riverside County sheriff telling me that my rental car was reported abandoned after I left the hotel. Odd stuff." Tappan replied, "I don't want to belabor this, but just to reiterate, I didn't call you at your hotel, and I still don't know which hotel where you were staying at."

Trying to get to the bottom of this mystery later, I asked a public relations executive at Marriott, which owns the Renaissance Esmeralda, if hotel security had reported my rental car as suspicious. They hadn't.

So I asked Tappan if someone affiliated with Koch had done so, and why he'd asked me where I was staying. "No one did any such thing," he said of the call to the sheriff. As for the questions about where I was staying, "I don't remember discussing that with you, but to the extent I did, it was just idle conversation," Tappan said.

That's the thing about the Kochs' style. Maybe Tappan didn't know who reported my rental car. Maybe his inquiries about my hotel were just chitchat. But the Koch operation's aggressive approach and penchant for plausible deniability always keep you wondering.

A day later, the Kochs wrapped up their April 2013 seminar without me, and donors participated in a fitting—and fittingly effective—ritual that has marked the conclusion of most of their confabs. After a closing speech about the importance of unburdening business from governmental interference, the donors were encouraged to make pledges to a pool of cash that Koch operatives distribute to a constellation of handpicked groups, many of which are represented at the seminars. While quite a number of donors make their end-of-seminar pledges privately, others stand up and announce them, giving the pledge session an auction-like feel, with donors trying to outdo one another. The final tally can be an effective gauge of enthusiasm. That sum—like much about the Kochs' political activity—is usually a tightly held secret. "You never know how much they raise, because they don't tell you," billionaire Minnesota media mogul Stan Hubbard, a regular attendee, told me.[20] But occasionally the number leaks out, and I thought it might be especially telling after Indian Wells, given that Republicans were coming off a bruising defeat and the Koch operation was facing its share of questions about what it had done with the $400 million it had raised for its 2012 efforts.[21] I expected the pledge tally to reflect some dampened enthusiasm. Only it didn't. A source told me later that they raised $70 million. That's 43 percent more than they raised at the conference after their first high-profile, and highly productive, big-money spending spree, in the 2010 midterm elections. Coming out of Indian Wells, they were on pace to far surpass both their 2010 midterm effort and their $400 million 2012 effort—meaning the checkbooks of political billionaires weren't closing over one bad election. In a letter to the brothers on "what we might have done better and what we might do better for the next election," Hubbard spoke for many of the donors in the Koch network when he pledged his ongoing support. "Charles and David, please know that you can count on me, my wife and our family to stand foursquare with your ongoing efforts to preserve our unique American way of life," he wrote.[22]

Indian Wells was a snapshot of an extraordinary shift: the reordering of the political system by an elite fraternity of the superrich and a small brain trust of consultants who cater to them. Starting in 2010, a few dozen of the wealthiest donors turned on a gusher of mega-checks that have made them more important than the thousands of grassroots activists, small individual donors, and even party leaders put together. Together, these donors have injected into campaigns sums that were once unimaginable, even as recently as the 2008 presidential election. During that election cycle, so-called outside spending of the sort that can be funded by massive checks totaled $338 million. In 2012, it was $1 billion,[23] and that didn't include hundreds of millions in additional spending by more secretive groups like those in the Koch network that don't have to disclose as much information to the Federal Election Commission (FEC).

Intentionally or not, this new system has eroded the power of the official parties that have rigidly controlled modern politics for decades by doling out or withholding pork-barrel spending earmarks and campaign cash. Suddenly, party leaders have none of the former to offer (the result of symbolic belt-tightening reforms), and far less of the latter than big donors operating outside the party system. The result is the privatization of a system that we'd always thought of as public—a hijacking of American politics by the ultra-rich.

The foundation of this new system was laid ten years before the 2012 election, ironically by those working to *diminish* the role of big money in politics. These legislators and activists had pushed through a 2002 bill limiting mega-checks—parties could no longer accept them, and political committees could no longer spend them on certain campaign ads. That sparked a brief period in which bold donors and operatives steered money further outside the system, into groups that spent on ads and political organizing (some of which drew legal scrutiny). Then in 2010, a pair of federal court decisions came down that freed the ultra-rich to legally spend with even more impunity, and secrecy, than they'd had even before 2002. The catch was, they couldn't give the unlimited money directly to candidates or political parties. It had to go to independent groups that aren't allowed to coordinate their efforts with politicians or parties. The most impactful of the decisions was the Supreme Court's now-famous January 2010 ruling in a case called *Citizens United vs. Federal Election Commission* that struck down restrictions on corporate- and union-funded political ads. The restrictions, which had been reinforced by the 2002 law, had limited how explicit ads could be in supporting or attacking candidates. But a 5–4 majority of justices ruled the restrictions to be an unconstitutional infringement on free speech, and without such limitations, corporations and labor unions could spend as much as they wanted on aggressive campaign advertising. Two months later, the D.C. Circuit Court of Appeals issued a decision that was lower-profile but profound in impact. It allowed individuals (as well as unions and corporations) to give as much as they wanted to a new breed of independent political committee that came to be known as a super PAC, which could spend unlimited sums boosting or attacking candidates—again, as long as those new groups remained separate from the candidates' campaigns and parties.

The result? In 2012, the amount parties and candidates could accept was downright insignificant compared to what the super PACs and other big-money groups were allowed to take. The most an individual or group could donate was $5,000 to candidates and $30,800 to the national party committees. That may not sound paltry, but it was nothing compared with the unlimited checks pouring into the super PACs and other outside groups empowered by the court decisions. *Citizens United* did more than change the rules. It changed the mind-set of big donors and big-money operatives. Perhaps more importantly, it introduced the idea that a single ultra-donor, or a well-connected consultant with the ears of a handful of mega-donors, could fundamentally shift a campaign for the US presidency, not to mention a handful of Senate or governors' races or dozens of House races.

It's not just the politicians who've benefited from the mega-donors. The gusher of checks has sparked a gold rush among Washington's private political class. All manner of consultants jockey to tap this new vein of big money coursing into the system, knowing that all it takes to succeed is the ear of a single donor. Those who rise to the top gain wealth and power, pretty much irrespective of how their candidates fare. This secretive and hypercompetitive world, largely unregulated, has attracted a mix of accomplished political operators and young innovators offering new services, along with a fair number of scammers. The common thread is this: almost everyone now recognizes that the action—and the money—is outside the party system.

Perhaps no one personified this change more than Karl Rove. He had risen to the pinnacle of the official party system, only to step aside in disgrace, then build a big-money shadow party of sorts that made him more powerful than ever. The left had no real analogue of Rove, though its elite operatives were increasingly becoming super PAC players in their own right. There was more power outside the official Democratic Party structure for folks like Harold Ickes, whose long connections to Bill and Hillary Clinton gave him access to the party's deepest pockets, and David Brock, whose compelling biography and fleet of bare-knuckle nonprofit attack groups made him a golden boy among rich Democrats. They'd done well for themselves, too. Ickes's companies have reaped millions in payments from big-money groups and campaigns. Brock's various groups have raised $95 million since 2003,[24] and they paid him a handsome $428,000 in 2012[25]—a sum that, given his fund-raising prowess, probably underrepresented his value in the new big-money politics. Jim Messina, who managed Obama's reelection campaign, was also building a power base outside the party. Rove, the right's undisputed fund-raising king, has gone out of his way to insist that he doesn't earn a dime from the Crossroads outfit he fronts. But his close relationships with donors and his multiplatform media presence have afforded him a comfortable lifestyle nonetheless. I learned that one mega-donor Rove advised, Steve Wynn, in 2012 flew Rove and his new wife aboard Wynn's 737 to Italy for their honeymoon, where they cruised the Mediterranean on Wynn's 184-foot yacht.

Below shadow-party chieftains like Rove, Messina, Ickes, and Brock is a younger generation that before the new political economy made its debut might have followed a path from government to traditional party or campaign consulting. These are people like Bill Burton, who left Obama's White House press office to start a super PAC that raised $80 million for Obama's reelection. Soon after Election Day, he found himself in a plush consultancy. What is called the operational side— the folks who spend this big money—has attracted some of the most ambitious and innovative operators, and they have done well for themselves. Among the breakout GOP stars of 2012 were Michael Dubke, Carl Forti, and Zac Moffatt, who were forty-two, forty, and thirty-three years old, respectively, on Election Day 2012. In recent years they all started their own consultancies, which rode the big-money wave and landed each of the men in gleaming new million-dollar homes soon after the voting ended.

Washington political lawyers are also fishing in this pond. Their job is to advise big donors, outside groups, parties, and candidates on what they can and can't do in the ever-shifting legal landscape. They get paid hefty fees for doing it. Perkins Coie, the firm that represents top Democrats including Obama and Harry Reid, as well as the super PACs and party committees supporting them, has been paid more than $20 million since 2009, according to FEC records. The lawyer for Crossroads, a former FEC chairman named Tom Josefiak, begins each meeting of outside groups with a "legal invocation," as it's called by operatives. But they're not making fun. He was once praised in a meeting with donors as "the guy who keeps us from ever having to wear orange jumpsuits."[26]

In another corner of the marketplace, you have a group whose primary function is to act as gatekeepers for the rich, screening potential recipients of their client's largesse to see if they're worthy. This group includes Michael Vachon, who advises George Soros on political giving; Andy Abboud, who counsels the Las Vegas casino billionaire Sheldon Adelson; Mike Britt, advising rival casino titan Steve Wynn; and Andy Spahn, who serves Jeffrey Katzenberg. Mere access to these advisors is a valuable commodity for fund-raisers and super PAC operatives, so the gatekeepers are often players in their own right. The more the boss gives, the higher the gatekeeper's stature.

The effect on the politicians has been to force the most ambitious among them to engage in a marathon mating dance in which they look to pair up with mega-donors who might subsidize their careers. Just a week after Election Day 2012, a couple of Republican governors mentioned as centrist candidates for the party's 2016 presidential nomination, Bobby Jindal of Louisiana and John Kasich of Ohio, each made a pilgrimage to meet privately in Las Vegas with the biggest single known 2012 whale, Sheldon Adelson, who spent upward of $100 million on that year's elections.[27] The Kochs' August 2013 summit, held on the outskirts of Albuquerque, drew a handful of top 2014 Senate candidates from across the political spectrum, including Tom Cotton of Arkansas, Steve Daines of Montana, Joni Ernst of Iowa, and Mike McFadden of Minnesota. The more centrist among them—Cotton, Daines, and McFadden—also attended an October 2013 Crossroads summit hosted by Rove. His summit drew a number of other Chamber of Commerce–type GOP Senate hopefuls, including Thom Tillis of North Carolina and Reps. Shelley Moore Capito of West Virginia and Bill Cassidy of Louisiana—and featured talk among business donors about how to defeat tea party candidates. On the other side of the aisle, 2014 Texas gubernatorial candidate Wendy Davis, a rising liberal star, and Massachusetts senator Elizabeth Warren, often discussed as a liberal 2016 presidential alternative to Hillary Clinton, quietly huddled with some of the richest liberal donors at a November 2013 meeting at Washington's posh Mandarin Oriental hotel.

If you're trying to raise money, the data prove there's no better strategy than chasing the wealthiest people. In the 2012 election all told, roughly eight million small donors gave a total of about $500 million to Obama, Romney, and the main groups that backed them.[28] It took only forty-six hundred big donors to match that tally. In other words, in a presidential campaign that centered on the question of who would better represent the middle class, the top 0.04 percent of donors gave about as much as the bottom 68 percent.[29]

After the 2012 election, I set out to determine to what extent the new big money had altered American politics. So I visited with a range of veteran party operatives and fund-raisers whose resumes went back a few decades. On the day after my run-in with Koch security, for instance, I headed to an airy modern condo in the hills above Palm Springs, California, to meet with a pair of old hands in GOP fund-raising, Keith Coplen and Brian Kraft. Now mostly retired, Coplen and Kraft are credited with pioneering big-donor maintenance programs starting in the late 1960s while raising money for various state and national party committees and candidates, including Richard Nixon and Ronald Reagan. "Back in those days, donors gave so much less, and the consultants weren't getting rich," said Kraft as orchestral music rode a warm desert breeze wafting through the patio's glass doors. "There was no such thing as a professional campaign class or industry prior to somewhere in the mid-1960s."

But even then, recalled Coplen, donors craved the feeling of being insiders. So Coplen and Kraft created a big-donor club for the California GOP called the Golden Circle of California, and made John Wayne the chairman. The annual dues were $1,000, for which donors received a heavy wood-mounted bronze plaque declaring them "one of California's most distinguished and dedicated citizens," as well as access to periodic briefings and shindigs. "The annual party was on John Wayne's yacht with the movie stars—it was unbelievable, the donors loved it," said Coplen. "Who doesn't want to be one of California's most distinguished and dedicated citizens?" he cracked, showing me his own plaque demonstrating that he had paid his dues through 1975. The club—which they ramped up during Reagan's governorship and augmented during his presidency through his national Citizens for the Republic PAC—created an illusion. That illusion, said Kraft, "was that, every morning, Ronnie woke up and turned to Nancy and said, 'Honey, did Brian renew his Golden Circle dues?' Because that was how it was played—all smoke and mirrors."

Today, the biggest donors give way more, and the perks they get are way better. A $1,000 donor is now considered on the low end of the middle tier and can expect attention roughly commensurate with what members of Coplen and Kraft's Golden Circle got back in the 1970s, when $1,000 was considered a major donation. People who give the federal maximum to a candidate—$5,200 in 2014—are solidly in the middle tier, but they get actual face time with candidates or at least advisors. And today's biggest donors, those who give millions through the new channels, get real say in advertising campaigns and strategy. In other words, what used to be an illusion is now real.

What donors want, exactly, tends to vary. Some crave the feeling of being "in the room" with powerful politicians crafting strategy, even if their actual input is minimal, limited to the "smoke and mirrors" described by Kraft. Others want to put their imprint on the campaign. Some prefer to do it all anonymously, like many of those at the Koch conference in Indian Wells. Others love the attention—for themselves, their ideas, or both. Foster Friess, the mega-donor whose millions buoyed Rick Santorum, could barely contain his enthusiasm when I interviewed him after the super PAC he funded helped lift his candidate to victory in Iowa. "I'm so excited about becoming this instant celebrity with all you guys calling me. I mean, gosh, CNN, *New York Times,* Reuters, the Associated Press, I can't believe it," he gushed. "I was a pretty obscure eighteen-handicap golfer out here in Jackson Hole. Now I'm getting all this attention."

Friess's main issues—fighting what he calls "Islamofacism" and increasing the place of religion in public life—had little to do with his business. In fact, Friess no longer had much in the way of active business, and once told me he was proud to have "paid the full load" of taxes for his entire life. Of course, there are cases where donors' political giving does overlap with their financial interests. But it's a tricky matter to determine which came first. Dallas leveraged-buyout billionaire Harold Simmons, a top GOP donor who died in December 2013, believed regulations generally stifled business. He also specifically opposed federal regulatory roadblocks that could have limited the earning potential of his pension fund investments and planned nuclear waste dump in west Texas. Yet when Simmons was warned about the scrutiny that could accompany his $30 million political spending spree[30] in the run-up to the 2012 election, he replied, "I want President Obama to know my name."[31] Hollywood producer Jeffrey Katzenberg, one of Obama's top donors and fund-raisers, gave or steered more than $3 million to boost the president's reelection effort. He was invited to lunch in 2012 in Washington with Vice President Joe Biden, Secretary of State Hillary Clinton, and Chinese president-in-waiting Xi Jinping, whose personal approval Katzenberg was seeking in order to create a studio in the hugely lucrative Chinese market. Xi flew to Los Angeles to meet with Katzenberg soon after the lunch, and within a few days a deal was announced, though a Katzenberg spokesman insisted it wasn't secured using his ties to the Obama administration.[32]

Though I'd spent years watching deep-pocketed interests interface with government, big giving never struck me as a particularly effective way for billionaires to get what they wanted. Savvy CEOs with major interests before government consider lobbying a more effective way to boost or protect their interests. Lobbying, in other words, is for financial gain, while big campaign contributions are mostly for passion or ego. The data back up this assessment. A 2012 analysis of hundreds of publicly traded companies found that for every 10 percent increase in corporate lobbying spending, corporate incomes rose by more than 0.5 percent; that may seem tiny, but it can mean hundreds of thousands of dollars for even medium-sized companies.[33] By contrast, the casino mogul Sheldon Adelson in 2012 steered tens of millions of dollars to super PACs expressly devoted to boosting nine different candidates. Only one of them won on Election Day, and there wasn't much that politician could do for Adelson unilaterally.[34] It was a pretty paltry rate of return.

Sure, a liberal study estimated that Adelson, who was worth $28.5 billion in 2013,[35] could have benefited to the tune of an estimated $2 billion from Mitt Romney's tax plan,[36] but that assumes that controversial elements of such an initiative could clear Congress—a big assumption. And Adelson's own explanations for the spending spree were no less baffling. He suggested, for instance, that he believed the Obama administration was punishing him with a bribery investigation against his Las Vegas Sands company, and predicted that a second Obama term would bring "vilification of people that were against him."[37] But if Adelson was worried about being targeted by the federal government, his flashy campaign spending to defeat Obama was the least wise way to protect himself, according to disgraced lobbyist Jack Abramoff.

"That's an astonishingly naive comment," said Abramoff, who was sentenced to six years in prison for conspiring to bribe public officials.[38] "That isn't gonna help you. Look, take it from me. I was prosecuted by the Bush Justice Department—the *Bush* Justice Department, all right?—and I gave them plenty of money. They went out of their way to show they weren't playing favorites." Adelson's giving shouldn't be looked at as transactional, Abramoff asserted. "He's the kingmaker of the Republican Party. He doesn't have to win races. It's irrelevant to him. This is his toy."

Money has made everyone headstrong rather than wise. As veteran Republican Party fund-raiser Brian Kraft put it to me during our conversation in Palm Springs, there used to be dire consequences for bucking your party leaders. "As a congressman, you went against the Speaker or you went against the party structure? Forget it. You wouldn't get funded, and if you got reelected, they'd lock you out of the bathroom. They can't do that anymore. Now everybody is an independent actor. Everybody has their own funding, and you'll get even more if you tweet 'Boehner just lowered the boom on me and I told him to go fuck himself.' He doesn't even have a bridge in your district he can throw you anymore."[39]

Democrats have so far mostly avoided the big-money havoc uprooting the Republicans, but that's unlikely to last. Steve Mostyn, a Houston trial lawyer and major Democratic donor, told me a few weeks after the 2012 election that many on the left were bracing for possible conflict on their side.[40] "There is a possibility of the same type of demolition derby on both sides," he said.[41]

The way the new big-money politics was shaping up, such derbies seemed inevitable.

CHAPTER 2

The Pony

Robert Michael Duncan had been immersed in the machinery of politics since before Watergate, specializing in the money that fuels it. Both a walking encyclopedia of campaign finance and a master forecaster of what was coming next, he preferred to remain mostly in the shadows, where the real political money business was transacted.

Duncan, who always went by Mike, got his first taste of politics when he was still in elementary school. His father, Bobby Duncan, owned a general store in rural Kentucky, and the family lived in back of it for the first four years of Mike's life. The store was near the state's southern border, and the family owned a working cattle farm on the Tennessee side of the line. But when it was time to send the kids to school, Bobby Duncan built the family house in Scott County, Tennessee, where Mike and his younger sister could get a better education.

Mike was a curious boy with ambitions beyond the horses and ponies he and his sister coveted. At age eight, he threw himself into an uncle's campaign for Scott County superintendent of schools. Young Mike spent weeks knocking on his neighbors' doors with Uncle Clarence, distributing campaign cards with Clarence Smith's platform. Mike and Clarence each would take a side of the street, and whenever the youngster was asked a question that was too hard or wasn't covered by the cards, he would signal for Uncle Clarence to come help. His uncle lost by fewer than twenty votes. The next Sunday at church, when Mike was rehashing the campaign, he discovered that several of his relatives hadn't voted. The experience taught him the value of not only communicating a message but also mobilizing supporters—both of which take resources and, at higher levels, money. That would come later. For now, all Duncan knew was that he was hooked on politics.

About a dozen years later, Duncan entered the big leagues, at least fleetingly. As a newlywed law student, he took a semester off to serve as Kentucky youth director for the president of the United States, Richard Nixon, who was running for reelection. Back then, "cash was king in politics," he recalled nostalgically in his soft honey drawl.[1] Duncan has an incredible recall of numbers and details from decades-old campaigns, and his political war stories unfold in an understated matter-of-fact progression. The only hints that he enjoys the tales are a sly little smile and an almost mischievous glint in his eyes when he reaches an amusing moment. "Frankly, in the 1972 campaign with Nixon, we had more money than we knew what to do with, so we wasted a lot of it," Duncan said, eyes glinting, "Some of that wound up in Kentucky."

Nixon primarily used his massive war chest—including $20 million raised in secret before new disclosure laws went into effect[2]—to run what amounted to the first modern presidential campaign. Sophisticated polling shaped a devastatingly effective two-pronged advertising strategy that softened Nixon's humorless image while portraying his Democratic foe, George McGovern, as a dangerous liberal extremist. Nixon barely hit the hustings himself, making only eight campaign outings the entire fall.[3] One of the trips, though, took the president to the declining coal town of Ashland, Kentucky, where Duncan had done the advance work for a rally that drew an overflow crowd of thirty-five hundred to a local high school gym. Only once that night did Nixon allude to his opposition, and he made no mention of the Watergate scandal, which by the time of the rally had been revealed as a vast plot involving political espionage and huge sums of cash. In the weeks before the Ashland rally, the *Washington Post* reported links between Nixon's administration and the burglars who had broken into the Democratic Party's headquarters in the Watergate complex. The paper revealed that Nixon's attorney general controlled a secret slush fund that was used to spy on Democrats.

But Nixon's team was acting as if there was nothing to it, and Duncan was only tangentially aware of it during the campaign. After the rally, as a reward for his stellar work organizing it, Duncan got five minutes with the president in a holding area behind the stage. Nixon gave him a pair of gold cufflinks with the presidential seal in blue, and answered a question the young law student asked about foreign policy.

Although twelve days later Nixon won in a landslide, not long after that the Watergate scandal started swallowing his presidency. But Duncan's most enduring memory was the spigot of cash that Nixon had at his disposal. At least $1.65 million turned out to be illegal,[4] but the campaign was better funded than any Duncan had seen before or since. Duncan was a witness not only to the power of political cash but also to what was at the time regarded—wrongly, as it turns out—to be the end of the Wild West era of campaign cash. Just ahead was the beginning of a new, highly regulated world, of which Duncan would become a preeminent navigator.

Watergate spurred Congress to create a host of new campaign restrictions, setting new limits on how much individuals, political parties, and political committees could give to campaigns. It also set in place a public financing system for presidential campaigns and established the Federal Election Commission to enforce it all.

Just around the time Nixon resigned, Duncan was settling in with his new wife, Joanne, whom he had met in law school, and embarking on a lifelong career in banking. The couple had honeymooned at the 1972 GOP convention in Miami, so there could be little doubt that a life of politics, in some fashion, was before them. They moved to the tiny eastern Kentucky mining town of Inez, where Joanne's father owned about a third of a community bank. Mike went to work for him, and he and Joanne had a son. When his father-in-law died, Mike took over, becoming the youngest bank CEO in the state. Duncan and his wife borrowed money to gain control of the bank, and they launched a modest financial empire. Before long, they had acquired another bank and opened more branches. The banks' assets—along with the family's—kept growing. Mike, who had kept a foot in politics by raising money for Kentucky Republicans including the powerful Sen. Mitch McConnell, began thinking about a return to national politics.

In 1989, with the bank thriving and his son in his teens, Duncan took a sabbatical to go to Washington for a yearlong fellowship in President George H. W. Bush's administration. The program enabled accomplished private sector executives to serve in high-ranking administration posts. Bush abolished it in 1991 amid charges that executives were chosen for political reasons and were lavished with expensive taxpayer-funded European trips, jewelry, and other perks.[5] Duncan had left before the controversy hit, and was not implicated in it. When he returned to Kentucky, he decorated his office at the bank with photos of himself with the president,[6] then set his mind to what seemed an improbable task for a community banker: becoming a top player in national GOP circles. He soon became finance chairman of the Kentucky Republican Party and was a national committeeman on the RNC. A few years later, he chaired Congressman Jim Bunning's successful 1998 campaign for Senate. He even toyed with the idea of mounting what would have been an uphill race for governor himself in 1999[7] but decided against it, citing family, business, and political considerations.[8]

Instead, he accepted a volunteer gig as a regional chairman for George W. Bush's 2000 presidential campaign. Bush, a storied bestower of nicknames, dubbed him "Dunc"—as sure a sign as any that Duncan had arrived as a bona fide national player. When Bush won, he tapped Dunc as RNC treasurer, giving him oversight of the national party's bank accounts, including about $30 million left over from Bush's campaign. "Hold on to that, I'm going to need it later and I want my interest," the new president told Duncan.[9] The job was unpaid and required him to commute from Kentucky to Washington, sometimes driving over the Appalachian Mountains in his black SUV, but Duncan threw himself into it.

He had arrived in the top tier of national politics just as another earthquake was about to rock the world of campaign money. Until February 2002, party committees like the RNC and the Democratic National Committee (DNC) and the congressional campaign committees could accept massive checks from individuals, corporations, and (in the case of Democrats) labor unions. This so-called soft money was the only stream of unlimited funds the parties had left after the Watergate-era reforms, and it was essential to funding the national parties' efforts on behalf of their presidential and congressional candidates. So valuable was this soft money that President Bill Clinton famously welcomed major donors to the party into the White House for coffees and sleepovers in the Lincoln Bedroom—an unseemly practice that was nonetheless incredibly effective in getting rich Democrats to cough up mega-checks. What was so critical about this cash is not just its impact on who won but the power it gave to the individual political party committees. More than a third of the $5.2 billion the parties raised between 1991 and 2002 came from soft money.[10] That bounty allowed the parties to maintain tight control of their messages, platforms, and even candidates.

But by the time Duncan pulled into town, the parties were facing the very real prospect of watching the soft-money spigot go dry. Congress was on the verge of passing the McCain-Feingold bill, which would ban soft-money donations to the parties and also restrict the types of cash that could be used to fund costly advertisements in the weeks before an election. The bill passed the House on Valentine's Day in 2002. Duncan, out to dinner that night with a senior White House official and several congressmen, begged the White House official to stop Bush from signing the legislation.[11] A month later, it passed the Senate. In a decision that rankled Republicans, Bush signed it into law, then almost immediately skipped town on a fund-raising jag to collect as many big checks as possible before the law took effect. Duncan was morose. "As treasurer of the party, I saw my life flash in front of me," he recalled later.[12] "I saw 40 percent of my revenue going out the door with that legislation."[13]

Not long after Bush had signed the bill, Duncan quietly went to the White House and told the president that the RNC was contemplating a lawsuit against the bill. It was a bizarre twist, but it showed how critical these large donations had become: in order to keep the money flowing, the president's own party would publicly challenge a law he had just signed. "To the credit of the White House, the president said," Duncan recalled, paraphrasing Bush, "some of this legislation may be unconstitutional, so have at it."[14] And so the president's party, with the stealthy okay of the president, sued to overturn it.

As Republicans pinned their hopes on fighting the law, the Democrats put their chips on finding a way around it. So Clinton acolytes like

Harold Ickes and John Podesta joined with well-funded labor unions to form a network of nonprofit groups that would raise huge sums from rich donors for advertisements and organizing activities supporting Democratic candidates. About two months before the Supreme Court even heard arguments in the McCain-Feingold challenge, the billionaire currency trader George Soros hosted a dozen or so donors and fifteen Democratic operatives (including Ickes, Podesta, and labor leader Steve Rosenthal) at his $27 million Hamptons beach home for a two-day strategy session about using these new groups to defeat George W. Bush in 2004. Before the confab adjourned, Soros and billionaire insurance mogul Peter Lewis had made the first of their big pledges.[15] They would eventually combine to donate the lion's share of the then-unprecedented $200 million raised by a suite of political nonprofit groups to elect Democratic presidential candidate John Kerry.[16]

Duncan and other Republican Party leaders, meanwhile, were urging their big donors to stand down. They wanted to make sure that the official party committees continued getting their share, and they were also still fuzzy on the legalities of this new landscape, despite the fact that other well-placed Republicans were pushing their rich supporters to give to new soft-money groups, including a controversial Kerry smear group called Swift Boat Veterans for Truth. "Our donors were confused," Duncan recalled. "And while we were doing that—sending a confused signal to our donors—the Democrats, to their credit, were out organizing and doing a very good job, and I give a tip of the hat to Harold Ickes and John Podesta. Both of them started immediately."[17]

The Democratic nonprofit groups combined to outspend their Republican counterparts three to one during the 2004 campaign[18]—to no avail, since Bush eked out a narrow victory, helped greatly by a devastatingly effective Swift Boat Veterans campaign that raised doubts about Kerry's military service in Vietnam. It also demonstrated to Duncan and other Republicans the stunning potential of mega-checks channeled to groups outside the party infrastructure.

In the months after Election Day, the Federal Election Commission went after the Swift Boat group and the major Soros-funded groups for flouting the new restrictions. The agency alleged that those groups and others violated the McCain-Feingold law by trying to influence the presidential race without properly registering. Had they registered, they would have been prevented from accepting such huge contributions. The ensuing investigations included talk of subpoenaing the big donors, which had a chilling impact on the big-money flow. The most active of the groups folded up shop, and the big-money sector of the political economy essentially went dark. After 2004, few major operatives were publicly pushing big-money election spending, and few major donors wanted the legal trouble that seemed to come with it. On the left, there were further disappointments. The failure to sway the election despite what was, at the time, a record spending spree left Soros, Lewis, and some top Democratic funders convinced that there had to be a better way to influence American politics.

So liberals and conservatives set out on different courses after 2004. The left shifted its money toward think tanks and advocacy groups that were less focused on elections. Big-dollar conservatives already supported a strong think tank network, so Republican Party officials like Duncan focused on building wider and deeper networks of big donors, urging them to give the maximum allowable contribution to the party committees—during the 2006 campaign it was $26,700 per year,[19] and the amount was increased incrementally for inflation in each subsequent cycle.

By the 2006 midterm election, fatigue with George W. Bush and war weariness helped Democrats take control of Congress for the first time since 1994. Looking to stabilize the Republican Party and its base of big donors, Bush tapped Duncan to cochair the RNC with Sen. Mel Martinez of Florida. Martinez was to be the public face of the committee, with Duncan running the operations. But Martinez stepped aside within a year, leaving Duncan alone at the helm. He had risen to the most prominent position he had ever held, but he was inheriting another crisis. Instead of diving into a Scrooge McDuck–style vault of soft money, he was scrambling to secure precious capped hard-dollar contributions ahead of a tough 2008 election cycle. Duncan rented an apartment just around the corner from the RNC headquarters and spent three or four hours every day making cold calls to big donors.[20] With Bush's help and without competition from the mostly mothballed big-money outside groups, Duncan's RNC was able to raise enough to subsidize the 2008 campaign of the Republican nominee to replace Bush, Arizona senator John McCain. McCain not only was an unenthusiastic fund-raiser personally but, as one of the two architects of the 2002 bill, had helped crush the parties' fund-raising ability. Still, Duncan's committee, relying on a carefully cultivated network of big donors, overwhelmed the DNC in fund-raising during the 2008 election cycle, $445 million to $278 million.

Yet fund-raising was changing again, and this time there was nothing Duncan and the Republican Party could do to keep up. Their haul wasn't nearly enough to help McCain offset the pioneering small-donor-powered fund-raising of Barack Obama's presidential campaign. Fueled by an anti-Washington message that capitalized on public weariness with Bush as well as the historic prospect of electing the nation's first African American president, Obama's tech-savvy campaign raised a record $750 million. That dwarfed the $204 million brought in by McCain,[21] though he also received $84 million through a Watergate-era public financing program that Obama declined to participate in. Obama handily won the presidency and took office pledging to empower regular folks over deep-pocketed interests that had long had an outsized voice in politics.

Obama's unprecedented success tapping the often modest bank accounts of grassroots supporters left many Republican activists wondering whether the old-boy big-donor model represented by people like Mike Duncan was outdated. A few months after the election, Duncan lost his bid for another term as RNC chairman to a relative outsider named Michael Steele. The first African American to assume the post, Steele cast himself as a breath of fresh air who was going to broaden the party's appeal and fund-raising base from the wealthy Bush crew to minorities and grassroots activists. The race left some ill will between the new chairman and Duncan's allies (including Karl Rove), who suddenly found themselves without access to the party reins for the first time in twenty years.

Duncan packed up his apartment in Washington, D.C., crossed back over the Blue Ridge Mountains, and returned to the family bank. It seemed his high-flying Washington days were a thing of the past. He wasn't expected back in the capital anytime soon. He did, however, still chat fairly regularly with the old Bush crew—including Rove. Duncan and Rove knew each other from way back in their College Republican days, and they had worked together while Rove was in the White House and Duncan was at the RNC. A regular topic of conversation in the weeks and months after Steele's election was the new chairman's dereliction of the big-donor network built and maintained by Bush, Rove, and Duncan. Duncan and Rove knew they needed to find a way to raise big checks outside the party structure, to supplement the RNC's donor cash and compete with the political muscle that well-funded labor, environmental, and abortion rights groups supplied to Democrats. But the conversations were still abstract, and it wasn't clear when something official might happen.

Then came *Citizens United*.

A few months after the Supreme Court decision, Duncan found himself sitting before several dozen election lawyers and operatives from both parties who had convened in the wood-paneled downtown Washington conference room of a top political law firm. These were his people, which perhaps explained why he had consented to a rare post-RNC public speaking appearance as the main attraction on the panel. I had agreed to moderate. The subject was both simple and complicated: what did *Citizens United* mean for the political world—operatives, lawyers, donors, candidates, party committees, and interest groups?

Duncan, of course, had lots of insight on the subject, but he started with a story about his childhood, going back to his days on the family farm in Scott County, Tennessee. When he and his younger sister were kids, they were given calves as pets to look after until they were full-grown and sent off to slaughter. But what they really wanted were "horses and ponies and things like that," Duncan told the group, momentarily baffling me. Where was he was going with the childhood recollections?

"I remember the year that she got the pony," Duncan continued, taking off his glasses and placing them on the table in front of him. "And I was really happy for her. But," he went on, "I was envious of my sister, because I believed that I should have had that pony." Then he got to his point: back when he was at the RNC, Duncan said, the pony he had wanted was for the Supreme Court to overturn the soft-money ban in McCain-Feingold. But the justices rejected Duncan's lawsuit seeking that result. With the *Citizens United* case—which challenged the other major part of McCain-Feingold, the restrictions on outside advertising—Duncan said, "I was also hoping that my turn would come next." That, Duncan said, was "the way I felt when I heard about *Citizens United*. I'm happy for the First Amendment rights. I think it was the correct decision. I'm a proponent of lots of money in politics and full disclosure in politics." Duncan, in other words, had finally gotten his pony.

It was more than just a philosophical victory. He was ready to act. Three months after the Supreme Court's decision in *Citizens United,* a lower federal court issued a ruling in a complementary case called *SpeechNow.org vs. Federal Election Commission* that paved the way for a new breed of political committee. The new groups, which came to be known as super PACs, allowed individuals (as well as unions and corporations) to spend as much as they wanted backing or opposing candidates as long as they didn't coordinate with the candidates. Three days after the *SpeechNow* decision came down, Duncan's name appeared on an Internal Revenue Service (IRS) filing as director of American Crossroads. It was the realization of the conversations Duncan had been having with Rove, and it was conceived as the flagship of a massive fund-raising, organizing, and advertising machine to be launched in time to influence the 2010 midterm elections.[22] Besides Duncan, the other main folks behind it were Rove, former Bush-era RNC chairman Ed Gillespie, and a former US Chamber of Commerce official named Steven Law. On the very morning of the panel where Duncan waxed metaphorical about ponies and *Citizens United,* a colleague and I had published a front-page story in Politico about American Crossroads, and Duncan was carrying the print edition with him. "I hope you get a chance to look at that," he said, holding it up proudly for the assembled operatives. American Crossroads, the story said, was "based on the model assembled by Democrats early in the decade, and with the same ambitious goal—to recapture Congress and the White House."

The new landscape, Duncan predicted, would give rise to a new class of "cause donors"—businesspeople "who are going to give above and beyond. They can give to the parties and they can also give to some of these third party organizations." He paused to stress that he wasn't out to cannibalize the party or extract revenge on the man who had ousted him as RNC chairman, Michael Steele. "I lament, as a former party chairman and someone who's been involved in the party literally all my life, the relative decline of the party structure in this country. . . . So I lament the fact that we're in this situation, but I recognize that we have to do something about it. And so we have created an organization—and a series of organizations, as you reported on—that will be highly transparent, that will be above and beyond what the party system does. We want the parties to continue to prosper. But we want it to be above and beyond."[23]

The Crossroads team's level of commitment to Duncan's two assertions—that he wouldn't undermine the party and that he wouldn't hide the names of donors from the public—would soon be tested.

Duncan's successor as RNC chairman, Michael Steele, was wary of Crossroads and allied groups from the beginning. He saw them as a power grab, a cynical ploy to create a shadow party that would snatch control and cash away from the official Republican Party and redirect it to a small group of well-connected operatives including Duncan and Rove. "Karl Rove and his crew—Ed Gillespie and a sitting member of the [Republican National] Committee, former chairman Mike Duncan—form American Crossroads," Steele complained to me.[24] "Where are they going to go to get some of that money from? They are going to go to the base that they've cultivated for the last fifteen or twenty years. And that largely rests in the base of the RNC," Steele went on. It was partly business, Steele contended, but also partly personal. "I know some of that was to ding me."[25]

Then again, Steele's struggles to win over big donors helped create a new niche for Duncan, Rove, and their allies. As the influential conservative blogger Erick Erickson told me at the time, "If Michael Steele weren't swallowing his foot on a weekly basis, they wouldn't be able to do what they're doing."[26]

CHAPTER 3

The New Boss

Almost none of the experts who follow campaign finance forecast that the *Citizens United* decision would crown a bunch of billionaires and their operatives the new kings of politics. Even after the decision was issued, President Obama—a former constitutional law professor who once taught campaign finance—badly misjudged its impact. He warned ominously that big corporations, including "foreign entities,"[1] would be the ones taking advantage, not homegrown billionaires.

But one man seemed to envision the world that would be created by *Citizens United* even before the case was filed. Around noon on an August day in 2007—about two and a half years before the Supreme Court would hand down its decision—Karl Rove was already positioning himself to become a leader in the big-money revolution. He was in a lunch meeting offering his thoughts on how a group of billionaires could help his boss at the time, President George W. Bush, sell his military escalation in Iraq. They met in Rove's West Wing office, the den from which he'd ruled politics for the last six and a half years, ever since he guided Bush into office predicting a fundamental realignment of politics.

At the time of the meeting, Rove looked to outsiders like a man on the ropes. He'd been blamed for the sweeping Republican losses in the 2006 congressional midterm elections and was being battered by controversy. He'd been called to testify multiple times before a grand jury investigating one Bush scandal and faced the threat of subpoenas over another.[2] Then on August 13, 2007, he suddenly gave Bush his notice. Even as he was preparing to leave the White House, though, he was laying the groundwork for a new chapter in which he would have another chance to lead a different kind of Republican realignment.

His August 2007 lunch meeting was with a GOP operative and former Bush White House official named Bradley Blakeman. Rove had quietly summoned Blakeman to his office to congratulate him on having been tapped a few weeks prior to run a new nonprofit group formed at the urging—and with the money—of a handful of extremely wealthy Republicans, including Las Vegas casino mogul Sheldon Adelson. The group was planning a $15 million advocacy campaign to build support for the "surge," as the troop-level increase became known. Over lunch, Rove offered Blakeman advice about messaging and timing for the campaign, according to a knowledgeable source. The group, which would be called Freedom's Watch, had yet to be unveiled publicly, but Rove already knew about it. He made it his business to keep tabs on what the right's biggest donors were up to. And he was already quietly helping to shape the group. Having a hand in Freedom's Watch could be very useful to Rove both in the final days of his current job, where he was trying to sell the surge, and in the post–White House reinvention on which he was soon to embark.

The Freedom's Watch plan played into one of Rove's core political beliefs: that big-money spent outside the party system had the power to deeply influence the political debate. The left had proven as much, Rove liked to point out, with its cash-rich labor unions and—since 2004—its klatch of billionaires. If a Republican operative could mount something similar, that person would become immensely powerful, perhaps more so than even the billionaires themselves. But it would take a certain type of operative to devise and execute such a plan. It would require someone who had a track record of winning elections, who had the trust of both elected officials and donors, and who had a personal brand and wasn't afraid to use it. An operative, in other words, just like Karl Rove.

Not long after Rove's lunch with Blakeman, Freedom's Watch made a grand public debut, vowing to become just what Rove craved, "a never-ending campaign—a stable, credible voice of reason on generational issues that won't rise and fall with election cycles," as Blakeman put it at the time.[3] More than a few Republican groups had made similar pledges but failed to raise the money for their vision, or disappeared after one election cycle. Freedom's Watch appeared to have the financial side, at least, nailed down. It quickly executed its initial $15 million campaign[4] aimed at pressuring vulnerable members of Congress to back the surge. Some insiders quietly predicted the group's total budget for the 2008 campaign could soar to $200 million—roughly the same amount spent boosting Democrats four years earlier by the Soros-Lewis vehicles.

Nine days after Freedom's Watch launched, Rove officially left his job at the White House. His public plans included lounging on a beach, writing his memoirs, and hanging with his second wife, Darby, at their home in the Texas hill country. But he couldn't resist the lure of a political landscape that appeared on the verge of a major shift. After all, he had come with Bush to Washington promising to usher in a "durable Republican majority." Back then, he invited comparisons between himself and Mark Hanna, the turn-of-the-century iron and coal magnate turned operative who was credited with leveraging massive contributions from the so-called robber baron industrialists to engineer William McKinley's election and, with it, a decades-long era of Republican dominance. What Hanna launched with McKinley's 1896 ascension to the White House, Rove hoped to replicate with Bush's win in 2000. But his grand plan for enduring Republican dominance hadn't borne fruit. Now Bush was limping across the finish line, and Rove was limping out the door. The emerging big-money world offered Rove another chance, and one that eerily echoed Hanna's famous words: "There are two things that are important in politics. The first is money and I can't remember what the second one is."

Rove continued periodically consulting—albeit informally and secretly—with Freedom's Watch[5] and Adelson, its lead donor, though there are differing accounts of the extent of his involvement. He did stop by the lavish downtown Washington offices that Freedom's Watch had sublet from the previous occupant, the Washington Capitals hockey team. Adelson and the other donors spared no expense when it came to Freedom's Watch. Its state-of-the-art computer systems, huge staff, and sprawling offices were the envy of GOP operatives around town.

Staffers called the oval-shaped conference room where meetings were held "the penalty box," because the Capitals had designed it to look like a hockey rink, complete with glass-topped faux boards around the perimeter, and face-off circles and other ice markings painted on the concrete floor. The group cut big checks to top vendors, including $1.6 million to a direct mail company that Rove had helped found, though he'd sold his interest in the company in 1999. Rove did not draw a salary from Freedom's Watch, and neither he, Adelson, nor the group went public with his association.

It was critical that Rove not be linked to Freedom's Watch. Democrats would have gone nuts had they found fingerprints from "the architect"—as Bush called Rove—anywhere near a group they believed was using shadowy cash to do the White House's dirty work. The Bush administration denied any coordination, which could have created legal problems under rules barring government officials from planning certain types of advertising campaigns with soft-money groups. Given the looseness of the coordination ban, as the applicable election law provision was known, it's certainly possible that Rove and other Bush administration officials could have talked to Freedom's Watch officials about general messaging without discussing specific advertising spending, which would not have triggered a violation. Still, those nuances likely wouldn't have mattered much to Democrats. Rove was among their most reviled bogeymen, and if they had any evidence that he had advised the group—starting when he worked in the White House, no less—it surely would have made its way into one of the many complaints they filed against Freedom's Watch with the FEC and IRS.[6] None of those complaints resulted in sanctions, although the IRS later conducted an extensive audit of the organization and five of its donors, requiring it to pay a piddling $12,000 in owed taxes.[7] The audit cost the group hundreds of thousands of dollars in legal fees. And while Adelson was not among those audited, Blakeman called the audits "political targeting" designed to "intimidate" donors from writing future big checks.[8]

The controversy never touched Rove. So discreet was his involvement that even some of the members of the group's board professed to be unaware of his link. Ari Fleischer, a member of the Freedom's Watch board, said it "goes too far" to call Rove even an "informal advisor" to the group. "Some people at Freedom's Watch may have been in touch with him, like a Carl Forti, you know, and bounce things off of him, like any smart person in politics would do," said Fleischer, referring to a Rove protégé who would go on to become an integral player in Rove's subsequent forays into big-money politics.

Whether or not Fleischer or others at Freedom's Watch knew it, Rove was starting to mutate into a new force, one with the potential to shape American politics even more profoundly than the muscular White House political shop he had built. In his new world, Rove could be the architect of a political operation where money was unlimited, accountability was minimal, and ties to the richest donors were paramount. Freedom's Watch was the ideal beta test for such an operation.

Freedom's Watch had some success building congressional support for the surge,[9] despite rising public war weariness. But in March 2008, about six months after the group went live, the board shifted tack. Blakeman left. Forti—who would later be dubbed "Karl Rove's Karl Rove"[10]—became the lead strategist, and the group moved from pure issue advocacy to a more electorally focused brand of politics of the sort Rove relished. Forti led the Freedom's Watch forays into House races, while its Senate efforts were handled by another Rove acolyte, Tony Feather, whose firm was paid $790,000 for direct marketing,[11] and a Feather protégé named Zac Moffatt. Many of the new Freedom's Watch players would go on to become key figures in the big-money empire Rove would build. And some insiders saw Rove's fingerprints on the shakeup, suggesting it gave him more say in the direction of things.

A few months after the shift, Freedom's Watch secretly made another move that dovetailed with Rove's vision, an innovation he would later deploy to astonishing effect within his own Crossroads empire: the convening of regular closed-door strategy sessions of big-money conservative groups. The idea was to coordinate advertising and voter mobilization strategies to avoid the duplicative efforts that had plagued past Republican groups. Why have three groups airing ads at the same time attacking Democratic candidate X, when you could agree to let one group take on X while the others go after Y and Z? It sounds simple, but it had never been done before on the right, where operatives tended to view others on the same side as competitors for donations and credit.

The clandestine meetings, not previously reported, marked a sea change in conservative big-money politics—the first attempt at a broad-based collaboration uniting sometimes feuding factions. In fact, the Freedom's Watch meetings may be most significant for how they foreshadowed the Koch brothers' political expansion.

Until then, the Kochs' network had steered the bulk of its cash toward think tanks and advocacy groups that favored more quixotic libertarian-leaning causes, as opposed to groups that identified primarily as GOP allies. The sprawling network linked to the billionaire brothers Charles and David Koch had a reputation for not playing well with establishment GOP political actors. Yet Koch political operatives, through their until-now-unknown control of a nonprofit group called the Wellspring Committee, took a leading role in the Freedom's Watch meetings, coordinating both with libertarian-leaning groups like the Club for Growth and also—for the first time—with more mainstream conservative players from the Rove wing, like Freedom's Watch. Wellspring's operatives even met with the political team from the US Chamber of Commerce. And a representative from Wellspring attended meetings at Freedom's Watch's offices, where Wellspring shared opposition research files that it had prepared about Democratic Senate candidates, and coordinated advertising and direct mail campaigns targeting Democrats. The coalition discussions focused on congressional races because, as someone familiar with the Wellspring effort told me, donors believed Republicans had a good chance of taking back the US Senate in 2008. According to the Wellspring source, "It really was like the first professional effort where you had these third-party groups—and there weren't many of them back then—but we all got together once a week and kind of laid our cards on the table."

Election Day 2008 was a major letdown for this stealth armada. Not only did Barack Obama handily defeat John McCain, but Democrats increased their majorities in both chambers of Congress—including victories by several candidates targeted by the Republican groups. The Koch operation cut its ties to Wellspring, while Freedom's Watch abruptly announced plans to close up shop at the end of the year.[12] It wouldn't become the "never-ending campaign" Blakeman had predicted, nor would it get anywhere near the rumored revenue goal of $200 million. By the time all the bills were paid, its tax filings showed, it had spent $56 million.

Insiders offered a range of explanations for the collapse of a group that had been hailed mere months earlier as the right's great salvation. Some asserted Rove discouraged donors by sharing qualms about Freedom's Watch. Others said there was crippling infighting on the staff and board, or that Adelson had micromanaged the organization or soured on it.[13] Still others pointed to a recession that tightened the belts of its small group of donors. Adelson alone lost an astonishing $22 billion in 2008.[14]

As the group was shutting down a few months after Election Day 2008, Adelson got wind that officials there were liquidating at bargain-basement prices all the expensive equipment they'd purchased. So he dispatched an aide to Washington to claim some of the pricier computer hardware, including servers—a move that puzzled even allies, who wondered what a billionaire needed with used computer hardware. It was as if he was making sure no one else could scavenge the choicest remains of his smashed toy. Freedom' staff received help finding new jobs, and the officers were left to deal with the IRS audit.

The Freedom's Watch experiment was seen as a major disappointment in some Republican circles. But it served as a valuable road map for Rove and others still intent on launching a shadow party network of their own. "Freedom's Watch was like the MySpace of IEs," board member Matt Brooks told me, comparing the group's role in the universe of "independent expenditures" (spending by outside groups not affiliated with a campaign or party) to the early social network that was overtaken by Facebook. Freedom's Watch "provided a model for Crossroads and everything that came later," Brooks said. Indeed, it helped train a whole class of operatives who would form the brain trust of Rove's Crossroads empire and also become very wealthy from it. It highlighted traps to avoid—opinionated donors with a voice on the board, huge staff payrolls, and other costly overhead—and also proved the value of coordinating with other groups like the Wellspring effort.

Rove also had the benefit of escaping the Freedom's Watch collapse with no scars. "The chips fell exactly in the right place," said a Republican who worked with Freedom's Watch. "He got none of the blame, but he got the opportunity to then reconstitute a group under his own brand."[15]

Before Rove would put his imprimatur on a big-money group, though, he set about creating some revenue streams for himself. He was facing significant legal bills from the various controversies that dogged him from his time in the Bush administration. And despite his plan to rededicate himself to his family after leaving the White House, a divorce from his second wife, Darby, would soon be under way and cost him more than half of his assets.[16] Rove connected with Bob Barnett, arguably the most politically connected lawyer in Washington, to get help creating the financial foundations for a new life. Barnett negotiated a $1.5 million deal for a memoir that would give Rove's version of the Bush years, a *Wall Street Journal* column, and a $400,000-a-year contract to be a contributor with Fox News.[17] It was the perfect role for Rove, made from the ashes of his old life. He now had a lucrative and prominent public platform that would allow him to build his cachet among donors while speaking directly to conservative voters and continuing to bait liberals, all without sacrificing his autonomy. On the side, he was quietly building up the donor network, rubbing shoulders with—and offering political advice to—mega-donors like the casino moguls Sheldon Adelson and Steve Wynn.

There was something of a running debate in conservative politics about whether Rove was driven more by power or by money. If you look back at his life, even before he personally possessed either power or wealth, he always had an uncanny knack for getting close to both. And yet for someone whose political power would become so closely intertwined with his connections to the very rich, Rove had a complicated relationship with wealth. He grew up on what he would call in his memoir "the genteel fringes of the middle class," in a family where "there didn't seem to be enough money,"[18] and dropped out of college. He has long condemned his critics and opponents as elitists, yet he hitched himself to the patrician Bush clan. In 1973, George H. W. Bush chose Rove to chair the College Republicans, then hired him to be a special assistant to the RNC, where he ran errands for Bush. One day, Rove was asked to deliver car keys to Bush's son George W. Bush, who was visiting Washington during a break from Harvard Business School and reportedly wanted the car to cruise around Washington's preppy Georgetown neighborhood. W., with his family pedigree and folksy charm, made an immediate impression on Rove, who recalled years later being taken with Bush's "swagger, cowboy boots, flight jacket, wonderful smile, just charisma—you know, wow."[19]

Rove began dating a Houston socialite whose family was friendly with the Bushes[20] and who he initially thought was "way out of my league."[21] They married in an extravagant ceremony[22] and moved to Texas to be near her family.[23] He began raising money in preparation for both George W.'s 1978 congressional campaign and George H. W.'s 1980 presidential bid. Both campaigns failed, as did Rove's marriage. Soon afterward, Rove's mother, who had been prone to erratic behavior since Rove's childhood and had long since deserted the family,[24] killed herself. Rove was stunned, though he later wrote that "at some deep level I had always known she was capable of this."[25] Amid the catastrophes, Rove threw himself into Texas politics, building a direct mail business that would make him the state's premier Republican operative and put him in close contact with its biggest donors. Rove seemed acutely attuned to—and fond of—the private planes, sprawling ranches, yachts, and other trappings of wealth that surrounded the rich Republicans he courted. When he moved to Washington after guiding Bush into the Oval Office, he drove a titanium-colored Jaguar to the White House,[26] and he and his second wife, Darby, bought a five-bedroom brick colonial in a prestigious neighborhood in northwest Washington, where Rove made it his business to know the value of every home on his block of Weaver Terrace.[27]

Pat Caddell, a pollster and fellow Fox News pundit, sees Rove as having understood and pursued the nexus of power and money from early on. "I'm telling you, I know Karl, and Karl is in the business of power," Caddell told me. "The money is incidental to it. It's how you have power. It's how Mark Hanna had power, except with Karl, it's more of the donors' money. This is a long-term process with him, as he has seeded and developed these people."[28]

Even after the 2006 midterm shellacking, the White House scandals, and the long, inglorious diminuendo of the Bush presidency, Rove's brand was still golden among many rich, establishment Republicans. But it was tainted among the broader public, where he had only a 23 percent favorability rating two years after leaving the White House.[29] Perhaps more troubling for his political prospects, he was reviled by the activists of the anti-establishment tea party. It aimed to realign the GOP around a more libertarian version of conservatism that emphasized fiscal restraint and limited government over social issues and nation building. It was a Goldwateresque philosophy that matched the ideology of the Koch brothers more closely than that of Rove and the Republican Party establishment.

Many tea party activists I talked to during the movement's rapid rise in 2009 and 2010 considered Rove "antithetical to everything the tea party stands for," as one Wisconsin tea party leader told me.[30] A top tea party group sent out a fund-raising email urging its supporters to "wipe the smirk off Karl Rove's face" and featuring a Photoshopped image of Rove in a Nazi SS uniform. (It later apologized for the image, blaming it on a production error.)[31] The tea party was a threat to Rove's reemergence, and he seemed intent on undercutting the movement, calling its adherents "relatively unsophisticated"[32] and criticizing one of its highest-profile candidates as unimpressive and unelectable.[33]

What was bad for Rove was good for the Kochs. To them, the tea party was a boon. Its activists, many new to politics, looked to well-funded groups like the Koch-backed Americans for Prosperity to help them mobilize against the proposed Democratic health care overhaul. The Koch political operation saw a window and took advantage. Americans for Prosperity's budget, supplied partly by attendees at Koch seminars, soared from $2 million when it was created in 2004 to $40 million in 2010, and it hired scores of organizers in key states and districts with an eye toward harnessing the tea party wave headed into the 2010 midterms. Suddenly the Koch network had battalions of ground troops to go along with its robust infrastructure. The Koch operatives saw the tea partiers, with their passionate opposition to most taxes and government spending, as kindred spirits. Many in Koch World also shared the tea party's distrust of Rove and sense that he personified the pocket-padding Beltway elite.

But just as the tea party's grassroots activists were mobilizing, so too were the big donors Rove had been cultivating. "There's a lot of people who think that Obama is not good for the country, and I'm one of them," Sheldon Adelson once told me.[34] To him, Obama had "socialist leanings" that he said had one of his associates "seriously considering moving away from the country." Republican donors were ready to give big to fight Obama and congressional Democrats, but they were also looking for new outlets for their cash, thanks partly to doubts, stoked by Rove and his allies, about Steele's leadership at the RNC.

Rove had the donors almost exactly where he wanted them. The courts did the rest. Rove and his old buddy Mike Duncan—along with a small group of elite establishment Republicans—had been planning their big-money play for months. And when the court decisions came, they snapped into high gear. Three weeks after *Citizens United*—but before their flagship American Crossroads group was publicly unveiled—Rove hit the road with former RNC chairman Ed Gillespie, top GOP fund-raiser Fred Malek, and former Minnesota senator Norm Coleman to raise seed funding. Over a February 2010 lunch at the swanky Dallas Petroleum Club before about twenty Republican billionaires and multimillionaires, the foursome laid out their blueprint for a sort of shadow party that would be the realization of Rove's grand vision.

It was complicated, calling for an alphabet soup coalition of unlimited-money nonprofit groups that would work together to boost Republicans in the 2010 elections and beyond, each filling a different niche:

- *American Crossroads.* It would eventually be registered as a super PAC, the new breed of political committee that emerged from the lower court decision, and would focus on television ads hitting Democratic congressional candidates. It would be chaired by Duncan and run on a daily basis by former Chamber of Commerce operative Steven Law, along with Forti.
- *American Action Network.* Unlike American Crossroads, American Action Network was registered under a section of the tax code,

501(c)(4), that allowed donors to give anonymously. It would focus
on issue-based ads in Senate races and would be chaired by Malek
and run by Coleman and a former Hill staffer named Rob Collins.

- *Resurgent Republic.* Cofounded by Gillespie, it would conduct
  polling and message testing for the groups in the coalition and
  other Republican outfits.
- *Republican State Leadership Committee.* Registered under section
  527 of the tax code, it was the only group in the coalition that
  existed before the 2010 campaign, but it was being revamped by
  Gillespie, who envisioned it as an aggressive campaign arm for
  state races that would extend the coalition's reach down ballots.

The groups would embrace the collaborative approach pioneered by
Freedom's Watch and Wellspring but would learn from the mistakes.
There would be a deeper pool of mega-donors, so the groups wouldn't
rise or fall on the fortunes of a single patron. Instead of huge full-time
staffs, they would contract out much of the strategic work to a small
group of consultants, some of whom had worked for Freedom's Watch,
with big payments going to the firms started by Carl Forti and Zac Moffatt. The consultants would form a sort of privatized brain trust, taking the shadow party's decision making even further out of the remit of
elected and party officials and distinguishing the shadow network from
the struggling RNC. This was the donors' chance to really shape the future of Republican politics for a long time to come, Rove, Gillespie, Coleman, and Malek told the moneymen at the Dallas Petroleum Club.

"People call us a vast right-wing conspiracy, but we're really a
half-assed right-wing conspiracy. Now, it's time to get serious," Rove
had been saying in these group meetings. It was the duty of the assembled billionaires to dig deep, Rove suggested, telling them that "all
of us are responsible for the kind of country we have."[35] The Dallas
group included donors like T. Boone Pickens, Harlan Crow, and Harold Simmons. There were also newer players like Ross Perot Jr. and
Robert Rowling. Before the briefing wrapped up, Simmons got up to
leave, explaining he had another commitment. But on the way out the
door he said, "I like this, I'm in for five"—as in $5 million.[36] His early
support sent an important signal in the mega-donor community. Other

commitments came after the meeting, and more resulted from a donor pitch session a month later in New York by Gillespie, Malek, and Coleman.

A few days later, American Crossroads filed its incorporation papers in Virginia and started spreading the word among the GOP consultant class that it had received $30 million in pledged contributions. Though the checks themselves were slow in arriving, Rove and his crew began wrangling other big-money groups to join their coalition—which would quickly, and with good reason, come to be regarded as Rove's network. Gillespie emailed a few dozen Republican operatives representing various other conservative groups, inviting them to Rove's house on Weaver Terrace for an "informal discussion of the 2010 political landscape."[37] That was a little coy, it turned out. Rove's plan was already well along. His purpose was less chitchat than recruiting the other groups—almost all with longer track records than Crossroads—to join his shadow alliance.

And so on April 21, 2010, exactly three months after the Supreme Court handed down its decision in *Citizens United,* a group of about twenty Republican operatives convened at Rove's. Karl and Darby had recently split and would soon sell the house for $1.4 million,[38] but on that April day, 4925 Weaver Terrace was the birthplace of a new Republican Party—one steered by just a handful of unelected operatives who answered only to the richest activists who funded them. The turnout was a testament to Rove's clout. The crowd spilled over from the living room[39] and into the adjacent kitchen. There were representatives from corporate heavyweights like the US Chamber of Commerce, new organizations like American Crossroads and the American Action Network, and star vehicles like Keep America Safe, which was spearheaded by the daughter of former vice president Dick Cheney. They munched on a lunch of takeout chicken pot pies, which Malek said left something to be desired. "It's not what a group of our distinction expected, but probably what we deserved," he joked to me later. On a serious note, another attendee, Bill Miller, who at the time was national political director of the US Chamber of Commerce, told me, "It really took people with the stature of Karl and Ed to personally invite all of these political operators at different organizations and groups who were used to working individually—groups that in some cases were not always aligned. Not just anybody could have convened a group like that to get them to see the kind of results that were possible by working together." Several attendees "went so they could tell their friends that they went to Karl Rove's house," said Steven Law,[40] who had been tapped a few weeks prior to run American Crossroads on a day-to-day basis. "That's why I went."[41]

Crossroads would later protest any characterization that implied it was Rove's group, even sending a stern legal letter to a website requesting that an article stating that Rove and Gillespie "formed" American Crossroads "be immediately corrected."[42] But it was clear to almost everyone involved from the moment of that first meeting on Weaver Terrace that Rove would be right in the middle of it.

The meeting kicked off with a detailed briefing from Crossroads lawyer Tom Josefiak about how, thanks to *Citizens United,* the unlimited-money groups could air ads explicitly attacking Democratic candidates and could even coordinate their advertising strategies with one another. The one caveat: they couldn't coordinate with the candidates or the party committees they were trying to help, or else they'd be courting potentially serious penalties. "To me, it was something of a revelation that we could collaborate. That was a very important thing to learn. I didn't know that we could," Malek told me. Subsequent meetings were held at the downtown Washington office suite that the American Action Network shared with American Crossroads, in a modern midrise at 1401 New York Avenue, NW—a couple of blocks from the White House—but the gatherings were still referred to as meetings of the Weaver Terrace Group, ensuring that Rove would be forever seen as the godfather of the coalition.

The meetings on New York Avenue soon came to be regarded as the nerve center of the alternative Republican Party. Its operatives cultivated an aura of mystery around who actually attended and what was discussed. Invitees weren't supposed to talk about the meetings, but invitations were coveted by all manner of groups and operatives, including some that would seem odd bedfellows for the Rove crew.

Once I visited the lobby of the building while the group was meeting and perused the guest sign-in book at the security desk. I was surprised to see the names of a pair of representatives from Koch Industries, including one of the Koch brothers' lead operatives, Marc Short. Another time, an American Crossroads spokesman emailed attendees alerting them that I was "calling folks up asking who attends the Weaver Terrace meetings. Just wanted to give you a heads up in case he calls you." The "rules of the road," the spokesman wrote, were—perhaps ironically—the same as those of the fictional anti-corporate underground organization in the 1999 cult movie *Fight Club* as articulated by a character played by actor Brad Pitt: "The first rule of Fight Club is: You do not talk about Fight Club. The second rule of Fight Club is: You do not talk about Fight Club."[43]

It wasn't immediately clear if the groups would be able to raise the huge sums necessary to pull off their ambitious plans. In the weeks after the first Weaver Terrace meeting, American Crossroads struggled to collect its big pledges. One person who was asked to donate relayed that Republican donors were leery of empowering Rove again and also "truly afraid that the Obama administration is going to target them" if their donations were disclosed.[44] During the month after the first Weaver Terrace Group meeting at Rove's house, for instance, American Crossroads raised a mere $200. When I reported that figure, noting as well that the group said it had $30 million in pledges on the way,[45] the story embarrassed Rove, setting off speculation that he had overplayed—or at least overhyped—his hand. In the new political economy, where the trust of donors was perhaps *the* most bankable asset and where projecting confidence was vital, such negative attention can be debilitating. Even after Rove collected many of those pledges and had secured his place as the unquestioned king of outside money, the story, along with a few others I had written about Crossroads, deeply bothered him.

I learned just how much in a chance encounter months later outside the Capitol Hill building that houses Fox News's Washington studios. I had pulled up to the curb in the backseat of a black town car taking me to a scheduled appearance on another network. Rove didn't see me behind the tinted glass and, apparently thinking the car was there to pick him up, approached the rear door. We nearly knocked heads as I climbed out. Reintroducing myself, I used the chance encounter to ask how Crossroads's fund-raising was going. That's typically the point at which a less combative subject would end an ambush interview—even an accidental one on a sidewalk. Not Rove. "You counted me out," he replied angrily, referring to the early stories.[46] When I explained I was just reporting on publicly available financial reports, he leaned in close to me, his voice rising. "We had $45 million in pledges," he fumed. I reminded him that my story had included the claim about pledged donations, but that only seemed to set him off further. "You're a moron," he spat out, shaking with rage, jabbing a pudgy index finger within an inch of my chest, and adding for good measure that I was "a shitty reporter." Such name-calling was "unprofessional," I told him, to which he responded, with no trace of irony, "You need to develop a thicker skin." I'd heard stories of his eruptions and had been on the receiving end of a few truculent arguments with him, but I'd never witnessed such a fit of insecurity from someone so powerful.

Only two days after the end of the group's $200 month, the American Crossroads team quietly created a sister group called Crossroads Grassroots Policy Strategies. The move seemed a tacit acknowledgment that they needed to do something to loosen donor purse strings, but it was also an abandonment of one of the guiding principles Duncan had set forth for the new venture—"full disclosure." Only one month earlier he had explained, "I believe in the transparency. And when we had the board discussion, we talked about the fact that we were going to be ahead of the curve on this." Yet the new offshoot was registered as a nonprofit under section 501(c)(4) of the tax code. That allowed it to accept anonymous donations—unlike American Crossroads. Secrecy turned out to be a fund-raising boon for the new group, which was called Crossroads GPS for short (its first contribution form played off the satellite navigation system, promising that the new group would chart "the course for a new direction for America"). Donors gave more in secret money to Crossroads GPS than in disclosed money to American Crossroads. Together, the Crossroads groups raised more than $70 million for their 2010 effort, with most of it—$43 million—going to the nondisclosing Crossroads GPS.[47] When I asked why the Crossroads team had deviated from Duncan's commitment to transparency, Carl Forti told me, "You know, disclosure was very important for us, which is why the 527 was created. But some donors didn't want to be disclosed, and therefore a (c)4 was created."[48]

Not that all efforts to keep donors' identities secret were successful. I learned, for instance, that Las Vegas casino owner Steve Wynn, after an assiduous courtship by Rove, became the biggest donor to Crossroads GPS, giving at least $10.1 million sometime between the beginning of June 2010 and the end of May 2011.[49] The two men would attend each other's nuptials—Wynn's gala second wedding in Vegas in April 2011, and Rove's comparatively intimate third wedding in Austin in 2012. Rove's wedding, which fell on the same day the Supreme Court upheld Obamacare (Rove actually did a Fox News hit on the ruling that morning, hours before his ceremony), was attended by former president George W. Bush and multiple mega-donors. It was held on the upper deck of Westwood Country Club and featured a performance from the Grammy Award–winning Austin swing band Asleep at the Wheel. Afterward, Rove, Wynn, and their new wives flew together aboard Wynn's Boeing 737 to Naples, Italy, where they boarded Wynn's massive yacht and cruised the Mediterranean, stopping for Bellinis one night at the lavish Grand Hotel Quisisana on the isle of Capri.[50]

The secret cash flow from Wynn and others affirmed that Rove still had the touch. Crossroads was raising so much money that it was able to pass some of it along to other groups in the Weaver Terrace coalition. It became a bank of sorts for the shadow party.[51] As the 2010 midterms approached, the coalition was functioning just as Rove had envisioned. The Koch network groups had come to the table in a major way, with a top operative named Sean Noble attending the Rove-led meetings at the 1401 New York Avenue office of Crossroads. "We were tracking about 120 House races, and the Koch organization, 60 Plus, Americans for Prosperity, American Action Network all took some, and Crossroads came in and invested heavily at the end," a strategist who participated in some of the meetings told me, adding, "It was very coordinated. There wasn't one race in which there were multiple groups airing ads at the same time."

In the weeks before the midterms, polls of congressional races were starting to register the results of the rising dissatisfaction with Obamacare, combined with the surging wave of tea party activism.

Massive advertising campaigns from the Koch-backed groups, Cross-roads, the Chamber of Commerce, and other Weaver Terrace partici-pants capitalized on the mood, pushing Republican candidates in close races into the lead. It was looking good for Republicans. Democrats, meanwhile, were coming to the realization that they were in trouble, and they began searching for someone to blame.

Obama's political guru, David Axelrod, ripped the Koch brothers as "billionaire oilmen secretly underwriting what the public has been told is a grass-roots movement for change in Washington."[52] A Democratic National Committee ad the month before the election accused Rove and the Chamber of "stealing our democracy," while Sen. John Kerry wrote in a fund-raising appeal for Democratic Senate candidates being targeted by Crossroads ads, "Karl Rove is back—like an even worse sequel to a movie panned by the critics."

The Democrat attacks actually accelerated Crossroads's fund-rais-ing, Rove taunted. "The president, by attacking American Crossroads, has helped drive people to our website and has helped to raise the amount of money that we received," he said in an appearance on Fox News. American Crossroads and Crossroads GPS in the weeks before the election raised their combined fund-raising goal from $52 million to $65 million.

Rove seemed to be relishing his return to center stage, even the barbs that accompanied it. "I'm having a lot of fun," he told me defiantly a week before the election, rejecting suggestions that Democrats might be able to leverage his unpopularity to hurt Republicans. "It certainly hasn't seemed to help them up until now, has it?" he gloated.

A week later, Republicans recaptured control of the US House of Representatives from Democrats and picked up six US Senate seats, six governorships, and 680 state legislative seats.

The architect was back.

CHAPTER 4

The Barrel of a Gun

The mood was somewhere between an Ivy League reunion and a shiva when rich Democrats arrived at Washington's Mandarin Oriental hotel two weeks after their party lost control of the House in the 2010 congressional elections. They had flown to Washington from all over the country and were catching up over tea in the foyer outside the hotel's main ballroom. But when the talk turned to the Republican takeover and the explosion of conservative money since the *Citizens United* ruling, the mood became somber. It might only get worse, invited operatives warned. The Koch brothers and Karl Rove were just getting started, and if the Democratic donors at the Mandarin didn't dig deep, President Obama and the Democratic majority in the Senate would be next to fall.

I was sitting on a plush bench off to the side, nervously taking in the spectacle from the corner of my eye. There was no way I could pass myself off as one of the mega-donors—people like billionaire currency trader George Soros, children's shoe mogul Arnold Hiatt, and San Francisco lawyer Steve Phillips—but I told myself that despite my lack of a name tag, I could plausibly be mistaken for one of the invited fund-raisers hoping to score a six- or seven-figure check for my candidate or cause. My goal was to gauge whether these donors, many of whom had sat on their wallets during the past few election cycles, were ready to open them again. Would they respond in kind to the GOP big-money wave that had just drowned the Democrats, or would they retreat further to the sidelines?

The Mandarin gathering was the 2010 winter meeting of the Democracy Alliance, a club of about a hundred wealthy Democrats who get together twice a year for multiday conferences at lavish hotels to talk about how to divvy up their millions to make America a more progressive place. The meetings were the left's equivalent of the Koch brothers' seminars, only the Democracy Alliance versions had a little more of a party vibe, featuring after-dinner dancing like the oft-discussed night when George Soros boogied away with a much younger woman he was dating at the time. There's also a crowd of donors known for doing tequila shots at the conferences, not to mention the group that partakes in informal late-night weed-smoking sessions. Views are mixed on the DA, as the group is known. Several prominent Democrats I spoke to regard the members as self-important, high-maintenance limousine liberals who expect politicians to kiss their rings in exchange for support. Before the Mandarin meeting, a previous attendee described the group to me as "a liberal country club" composed of "dilettantes" who "care more about having dinner with a senator than about building something that's lasting and that can help the lives of regular people."

But no halfway savvy Democratic operative or politician would express such a sentiment publicly for fear of losing access to the political ATM that is the Democracy Alliance. Since its founding in 2005, the DA has steered $500 million from its members to liberal causes.[1] And, perhaps more important from the perspective of nervous Democrats, DA donors had demonstrated in 2004 that they were capable of underwriting an entire presidential election—if so motivated. After the Democrats' 2012 electoral chastening, Obama's top operatives hoped to scare the DA into reloading its big-money campaign artillery. Their message: Karl Rove and the Koch brothers were preparing to wage an expensive advertising battle, and the president needed the support of the DA partners (as the group calls its members) to mount a counterattack.

As one of the operatives at the Mandarin put it rather succinctly: "Nothing focuses the mind like the barrel of a gun." A week before the Mandarin meeting, the president's political guru, David Axelrod, laid the groundwork by signaling in an interview that, for the first time, his boss wouldn't be opposed if rich Democrats wanted to start writing big checks to super PACs. It was another step in an evolution that would have been unthinkable a few years prior for Obama, who had made his name in politics crusading against the corrupting influence of big money. Less than ten months earlier, he had brazenly—and misleadingly, as it turns out—chastised the Supreme Court justices to their faces for the *Citizens United* decision.* But now he wanted to make sure the donors at the Mandarin understood that he was dropping his opposition to big money. So the White House dispatched a top staffer, Jim Messina, to the Mandarin to schmooze the donors. It was an open secret at the time that Messina was preparing to leave the administration to head the reelection campaign, and his appearance at the Democracy Alliance meeting was intended to get its donors onboard.

It was not going to be an easy sell. Not only had many of the donors decided they were done with campaigns, but some had gravitated to the opposite extreme, advocating for tougher laws to limit the flow of big money into politics. Many DA partners were appalled by the *Citizens United* decision, didn't want to participate in the world it was spawning, and saw themselves as fundamentally different from the Koch brothers and their crowd, whose political activism they believed was animated by a desire to boost their corporate profits. Even those DA partners who got a thrill out of the big-money campaign game weren't particularly fond of Obama, who hadn't given them the time of day. The president

----

*In his January 27, 2010, State of the Union address, Obama asserted that the *Citizens United* decision "reversed a century of law that I believe will open the floodgates for special interests—including foreign corporations— to spend without limit in our elections." The century-old law to which he seemed to be referring, the 1907 Tillman Act, banned the use of corporate money for direct contributions to federal candidates—not for the independent expenditures that were the subject of *Citizens United*. The ban on corporate and union independent expenditures came forty years later, while the actual provision overturned by the Court wasn't enacted until 2002. Also, the nonpartisan fact-checking outfit Politifact concluded that Obama "overstated the ruling's immediate impact on foreign companies' ability to spend unlimited money in U.S. political campaigns."

had steadfastly refused to participate in the type of ego stroking many big donors required, and both he and his vice president, Joe Biden, had turned down invitations to speak at Democracy Alliance conferences. Once Obama even ignored a request to meet with Soros in the White House, leading a Soros confidant to grumble privately that the Obama team "pissed on" the billionaire financier.[2] Beyond the hurt feelings, many Democracy Alliance partners were disappointed in Obama's policies. Unlike a majority of Americans,[3] DA members thought Obama hadn't been aggressively liberal enough.

So, even before these liberal donors grappled with their views on money's role in politics, they first had to answer a more foundational question: was Obama worth saving? There was no ringing consensus at the Mandarin. In fact, one attendee told me that Messina was given a less-than-warm welcome and was peppered with questions about what the donors perceived as Obama's shortcomings on their pet issues and insufficient support for the party's congressional candidates. Another attendee, a Utah-based hedge fund manager named Art Lipson who had supported Obama in 2008, later told me that Obama had proven himself "certainly the least competent president of the twentieth or twenty-first century. I don't know much about the 1900s. I know some of those guys were pretty bad."[4]

There was a wing of the DA that defended Obama, led by the group's chairman, Taco Bell heir Rob McKay. The lanky Californian had long been willing to use his family's fortune, which years earlier he'd casually estimated at "a couple hundred million,"[5] to play at the top levels of politics. He was among the earliest to get on board with Soros and Lewis against Bush in 2004. But the Democracy Alliance was so divided on Obama that not even McKay and his wife saw eye to eye. Anna Hawken McKay had refused to write Obama a single check unless he took a stand against the pending Keystone XL oil pipeline, opposed by environmentalists.[6]

The donor everyone at the Mandarin most wanted to hear from—the one whose support could make or break any colossal money effort—was Soros. A Hungarian-born Jew, he had ridden out the Holocaust in Budapest, fleeing after World War II to London, where he worked as a railway porter and waiter while studying economics. At the time of the Mandarin meeting, Soros was eighty years old, slightly stooped but a sharp and commanding presence, one who happened to be worth an estimated $22 billion.[7] That made him by far the richest DA partner. He was considered a bellwether for big Democratic money as a whole, and Messina and his allies believed that if they could win over Soros, scores of other wealthy Democrats would follow. Soros had resisted entreaties to give big in the months before Election Day 2010. Asked three weeks before the election if the prospect of the GOP winning control of Congress concerned him, Soros said, "It does, because I think they are pushing the wrong policies, but I'm not in a position to stop it." He added, "I don't believe in standing in the way of an avalanche."[8]

After the avalanche left Republicans in control of the House of Representatives, the Democrats realized they needed folks like Soros back in the game to prevent them from being buried a second time. Soros prided himself on his ability to deftly adapt to shifting conditions in both his financial and political investing. "His ideology, to the extent that he has one," his political advisor, Michael Vachon, once explained to me, is "the idea that the ultimate truth is unattainable and therefore you must always hold yourself out for improvement. Critical thinking is key. Soros's investment style and his philanthropy reflect that. It is very responsive to reality."[9]

When Soros arrived at the Mandarin, not even those closest to him seemed to know what he was thinking. An even more private meeting was informally convened by the most affluent of the affluent, in a suite away from the official conference proceedings. The room fell quiet as Soros began to speak.

"We have just lost this election, we need to draw a line," Soros declared in his sometimes quavering, heavily accented voice. "And if this president can't do what we need, it is time to start looking somewhere else."[10]

Needless to point out, I wasn't inside this secret meeting. I pieced it together from sources who talked to me and the Huffington Post, which was first to report what Soros said. When news of Soros's comments got out, it set off frenzied speculation among Democratic operatives. Was the most influential donor on the left signaling that rich Democrats should consider supporting a 2012 primary challenge to Obama?

Or was he, as one operative in the meeting told me, calling for wealthy liberals to focus their giving on groups that could push Obama and congressional Democrats to the left on liberal legislative priorities, rather than groups supporting specific candidates? It was telling that Soros had the hubris to stand up and suggest that it was time for a handful of ultra-rich donors to challenge a sitting president of their own party, whether it was on the issues or at the ballot box. Even more telling, though, was the reality that in the new big-money world, Soros and his crew of DA donors could, in fact, underwrite either a leftward shift of the party or a viable presidential primary challenge.

A source in the meeting told me Soros was advocating the latter and that no one in the meeting was particularly surprised. Lipson, the Utah hedge funder, was less forthcoming, describing it only as "an off-the-record meeting of DA members who expressed a lot of dissatisfaction with Obama. I'll go that far."[11] He conceded there were discussions among big Democratic donors soon after the 2010 midterms about a primary challenge to Obama, but said, "I don't know how much any discussions along those lines were realistic or a pipe dream. You say you'd like to do it, but who is going to run against him? He's the president. He's in there. He's got the machine." Still, Lipson said, "if there had been a halfway decent challenger, I definitely would have supported him. And that's just halfway decent."

San Francisco lawyer Guy Saperstein, a former Democracy Alliance member, took it a step further, trying to enlist Hillary Clinton's 2008 presidential campaign pollster, Geoff Garin, to help build support for a 2012 Clinton challenge to Obama. Saperstein wanted to pay Garin to do some poll testing regarding how Clinton would fare, relative to Obama, in a 2012 general election versus various Republicans. Garin declined and later went to work for the pro-Obama super PAC.

Soros's political advisor, Vachon, who sits on the Democracy Alliance board, quickly tried to quash the idea that his boss was leading an anybody-but-Obama boomlet. Instead, Vachon told me, Soros's message at the Mandarin was that "liberals need to be more forceful and should create pressure from the left" to keep their issues on the legislative radar. That's all he would say, reminding me that the conversation—like the DA conference as a whole—was strictly private.

Don't I know it. An off-duty cop at the Mandarin, who noticed I wasn't wearing a DA-issued name tag, approached and explained that I was not welcome at the event. As an Alliance spokeswoman ushered me through the lobby and into the brisk Washington winter afternoon, she peppered me with questions about what—and whom—I had seen. The Democracy Alliance carefully protects its members' privacy, she told me, asking that I not name any of the donors I had spotted—people like Hiatt, hedge fund financier Donald Sussman, electronics pioneer Bill Budinger, real estate developer Wayne Jordan, and Suzanne Hess, the wife of real estate mogul Lawrence Hess.

As I stood with the valets by the circular hotel drive, the chill pressing at my cheeks, I wondered whether all the secrecy was at least partly intended to feed an aura of exclusivity that the donors craved. Noticing an advisor to major liberal donors waiting for the valets to hail him a cab, I asked him. "Everything that goes on here is confidential," he told me, agreeing to talk only if I didn't identify him publicly. "I didn't come up with the policy, but I think it serves the purposes of allowing people to speak freely and let their hair down."

The secrecy was not unlike that surrounding the Koch brothers' donor conferences, though the Kochs were more aggressive about enforcement. They once commissioned an investigation to see who had leaked a conference invitation to the press. Yet at their core, the Democracy Alliance and the Koch models were strikingly similar. In fact, each was created partly in an effort to copy what the other side was doing effectively. Both saw themselves as shaping their movements around ideological rather than partisan concerns. So they positioned themselves as separate from the Democratic and Republican establishments and intimated they were willing to pressure their own party if they felt it was straying from its ideological moorings.

The Democracy Alliance was the inspiration of a little-known Democratic operative named Rob Stein, who even before the 2004 election had been arguing that wealthy liberals were going about political check writing all wrong, and urging them to give more like their conservative counterparts. Bush's 2004 reelection seemed to prove his point and provide the spark to get the Democracy Alliance off the ground. Soros, Lewis, McKay, and a few dozen other big donors combined to donate the lion's share of the then-unprecedented $200 million raised by a suite of nonprofit groups created to take down Bush through sharp attack ads and robust ground organizing. When that spending spree failed to achieve its goal, the donors were left questioning whether their cash had been squandered. Stein's plan addressed these concerns in two ways: it would create more permanent groups intended to help liberals win the battle of ideas rather than individual elections, and it would give donors more control over the groups they funded.

The blueprint was patterned on the model that a few dozen conservative families, including the Kochs, the Scaifes, and the Coors family, had pursued for decades.[12] Stein laid it all out in a confidential Power-Point presentation under the cryptic auspices of something called the Phoenix Group[13]—so named because he and the other operatives argued it would help the progressive movement rise from the ashes. The PowerPoint slides carefully traced rich conservatives' giving since the 1960s—hundreds of millions of dollars to think tanks, policy groups, and niche media that worked together to influence the terms of the public policy debate, which eventually—and inevitably—also influenced the campaign landscape. It was a hit in the clubby world of ultra-rich Democrats. Stein showed it to hundreds of donors,[14] who were enticed by the prospect of recentering the Democratic Party—and eventually the entire body politic—around their unabashedly liberal vision. As Stein told a reporter not long after unveiling the Democracy Alliance: "In the world of ideas and movement-building and politics, there are short-term needs and long-term needs." Liberals, he said, "have to build for the long term."[15]

Democracy Alliance partners would pay annual dues of $30,000 to fund activities like the twice-a-year conferences, which feature a mix of policy briefings, dinners, and receptions. The money also would fund staff who would vet and recommend groups to which partners might contribute. They could give to whichever recommended groups they wanted as long as they hit a minimum annual donation total of $200,000. (Later, a lower membership tier was added that required only $15,000 in dues and $100,000 in donations. The ever status-conscious DA called these lesser donors "general partners"—not to be confused with the "governing partners" who gave the full amount.) The

Democracy Alliance held its first meeting in 2005. It wasn't long before it helped build out a robust network of think tanks and advocacy groups fronted by operatives who bought into the DA concept, like David Brock (founder of the watchdog group Media Matters) and John Podesta (who founded the activist research group Center for American Progress). Their immediate goal: giving Democrats cover to pursue liberal objectives by providing supportive research, while skewering conservative politicians, rhetoric, and ideas. Then there was the nonprofit America Votes, which organized voter mobilization efforts, and even a private company called Catalist, run by veteran Clinton operative Harold Ickes, that assembled a massive voter database, which it rented to all manner of liberal politicians and groups—even the Democratic Party. The DA-blessed groups teamed up with traditional Democratic allies in the labor, environmental, and abortion rights communities to create a formidable juggernaut.

The dividends seemed evident on Election Day 2006, when Democrats took control of the House of Representatives for the first time since 1994. Rep. Nancy Pelosi, a San Francisco liberal and big-donor favorite who attended Democracy Alliance meetings, was sworn in as the first female Speaker of the House. Of course, a number of overarching trends conspired to make 2006 a horrible year for Republicans, but the Democracy Alliance and its beneficiaries were rightfully given credit for providing critical infrastructure that allowed Democrats to capitalize. The DA was riding high.

But politics, like most other realms of life, lives by certain principles. One is that high tide doesn't last forever. Another is that consensus is hard to reach and harder still to maintain. Not long after the 2006 midterms, dissension began simmering in the DA ranks. Some partners thought the group was straying from its founding principles by aligning too closely with the Democratic Party and its politicians. Even among those who were okay with a more partisan focus, there was a real split between those who wanted Obama to become the Democratic nominee, such as Rob McKay and Steve Phillips, and those who wanted Hillary Clinton, such as Susie Tompkins Buell. Even years later, as Clinton's backers began urging her to run again in 2016, some still harbored ill will, believing that the DA's progressive majority had put its thumb on the scale for Obama, who in 2008 was seen as more of a liberal champion than Clinton.

Buell, who cofounded the Esprit clothing line, left the DA in protest, as did a number of other partners—upset either because they perceived the DA as being too supportive of Obama or because they saw it as too electorally focused in general. In the latter category was Guy Saperstein. The San Francisco lawyer had famously clashed with Bill Clinton at a 2006 DA meeting because he thought the ex-president's remarks there whitewashed his wife's support for the invasion of Iraq, which many DA partners opposed. It was "nothing but a veiled pitch" for her 2008 presidential campaign, he told me.[16] "One of the failures of the Democracy Alliance, I think, is that they're susceptible to that kind of bullshit. They like the access. They want to be in the room. They want to feel important," Saperstein added.[17]

The Democracy Alliance was debating whether to pull back from campaign politics just as Karl Rove and the Koch brothers' allies were quietly wading more aggressively into it. The big-money wings of the two parties, which so often talked about needing to catch up to the other side, were like ships passing in the night in the run-up to the 2008 election, with Republicans headed toward a robust if stealthy big-money campaign apparatus and Democrats backing away.

The Democratic retreat was expedited by an unlikely leader, Barack Obama. The powerful narrative that propelled Obama's meteoric rise from unknown Illinois state lawmaker to US senator to viable presidential candidate in just twelve years was one of an anti-establishment reformer. A central thesis of his politics was that big money corrupted democracy. Even before he ran for office for the first time, he had established himself as a player in an influential circle of intellectuals in his Hyde Park neighborhood of Chicago working to reduce the role of money in politics, earning a seat on the board of a major foundation that gave grants to reform groups. During his first campaign—for the Illinois State Senate in 1996—he told a reporter that he was disturbed by the hefty checks Democrats were raising for their convention that year in Chicago to nominate Bill Clinton for reelection. "You got these $10,000-a-plate dinners and Golden Circles Clubs," Obama said.[18] "I think when the average voter looks at that, they rightly feel they're locked out of the process. They can't attend a $10,000 breakfast and they know that those who can are going to get the kind of access they can't imagine."

As a lawmaker, Obama helped pass campaign reform bills in Springfield and then later in Washington. And when he ran for president, he immediately reached for the reform banner. In his soaring announcement speech to a crowd of thousands outside the historic Old State Capitol in Springfield, Illinois, on February 10, 2007, he derided the "cynics, and the lobbyists, and the special interests who've turned our government into a game only they can afford to play. They write the checks and you get stuck with the bills, they get the access while you get to write a letter, they think they own this government, but we're here today to take it back. The time for that politics is over. It's time to turn the page."[19]

Obama pledged not to accept contributions from political action committees or lobbyists for his presidential campaign. And he promised to participate in the federal public financing program, which would have given him $84 million in taxpayer cash for his general election campaign but also would have forced him to limit his spending to that amount. His reform allies applauded him for putting idealism over political expediency. But Obama didn't stop there. He urged supporters not to give to any big-money groups that might emerge to support his campaign. It was a bold position for a man who could have used the money to battle his primary challengers: Hillary Clinton, with her close ties to big donors, and John Edwards, with his support from deep-pocketed labor unions.

Such public posturing is usually accompanied by a telepathic wink, as if to tell supportive operatives and donors, *You know I have to ask you to stand down, but please don't.* But the Obama of 2008 seemed to mean it. What the Obama campaign knew—and what the rest of us would soon find out—was that Obama then did not need any outside financial help. The campaign was investing heavily in state-of-the-art online fund-raising and organizing platforms, and word from the young digital staffers who built and monitored the systems was that it was starting to pay dividends. The goal was to mobilize an army of grassroots activists whose stream of small donations could challenge and maybe surpass the revenue from Clinton's network of rich backers. Better still, it dove-tailed with Obama's anti-establishment messaging and would free him from the white-tablecloth fund-raising circuit, from which presidential candidates had traditionally raised a large proportion of their cash. Obama's campaign dubbed it "the small donor revolution" and—in a bit of self-referential hyperbole—compared it to the founding of our nation, with Obama confidant Norm Eisen boasting, "Like that other great revolution that resulted in our presence here today—the American Revolution—a revolution can take a long time to institutionalize and to bear fruit."[20] By the end of July 2007, fruit was being borne, and Obama shocked Washington by outraising Clinton's campaign for that month, pulling in $59 million[21] versus Clinton's $53 million.[22]

With that type of cash flow, having outside groups out there acting on your behalf was more risk than it was worth. While the groups were technically independent, any misstep or discordant message from them could trip up the candidate they were trying to help.

So when news broke a few days after Obama's big July fund-raising haul that a group of wealthy backers were writing big checks to an independent pro-Obama nonprofit group called Vote Hope 2008, Obama tried to put the kibosh on it. "We would rather have them . . . involved in our campaign," Obama said at an impromptu August 2007 press conference in East Oakland, California.[23] "My recommendation to people who are interested in supporting me," he went on, "is to support me through our campaign—the way over 250,000 donors have supported us, the way hundreds of thousands of volunteers have supported us. Get involved in the campaign that we've set up, that is above board, that is transparent, that is legal." In other words, Obama was saying, *I'll take limited contributions that I can control over unlimited ones that someone else gets to spend.*

That didn't stop Vote Hope's leader, San Francisco lawyer Steve Phillips, who thought Obama could use the help and plowed ahead, raising big money to boost Obama in key primary states. When word reached Obama's campaign headquarters in Chicago that Phillips wasn't taking the hint, he got a sternly worded letter from Obama's bulldog of a lawyer, Bob Bauer. "We have been made aware of your efforts at Vote Hope, and while we acknowledge and appreciate your strong support of the senator's candidacy, we must ask that you discontinue without further delay any further independent efforts on his behalf," Bauer wrote to Phillips.[24]

But for Phillips, this was about more than just reformist messaging. "I came of age in the Jesse Jackson presidential campaign. And having worked those twenty-plus years and then see the potential to elect an African American president, we weren't going to be easily deterred from doing everything we could to make that happen," Phillips, who is African American, told me later. A Democracy Alliance partner, Phillips donated or loaned at least $1.7 million to Vote Hope and related groups, which ended up spending more than $11 million during the 2008 campaign.[25] The groups registered and mobilized Hispanic and African American voters in key primary states and supplemented Obama's field operations in those states with $890,000 in direct mail, plus newspaper and radio ads, including the first advertising in the pivotal state of South Carolina. Ironically, Obama, the candidate who most ardently opposed big outside money in politics, was benefiting most from it in the Democratic presidential primary.

John Edwards, who had set up a network of big-money groups to help pave the way for his presidential campaign,[26] quickly fell behind Obama and Clinton in fund-raising and delegates, and dropped out of the race. Meanwhile, Clinton backers had been planning their own big-money groups funded by the Hollywood producer Steve Bing and other major donors for an anticipated general election campaign. But they were caught off guard by Obama's insurgent campaign and didn't get their act together before Obama started to pull away. Without much big-money support, Clinton ended up waging a bitter five-month battle against Obama, even as she fell further and further behind in cash and delegates. As Obama's candidacy began to take on the aura of inevitability, a small crew of donors and operatives connected to the Democracy Alliance—including Soros and McKay, along with Clinton backers Brock and Ickes—tried to launch a suite of big-money groups that would have helped Obama in the general election against presumptive GOP nominee John McCain. A couple of them—the Campaign to Defend America and Progressive Media—aired ads attacking McCain toward the tail end of the Obama-Clinton primary. But some of Obama's allies saw them as vestiges of the Clinton operation, while others simply opposed outside spending for the same reasons that prompted the Obama campaign to ask Phillips to cease and desist. So, soon after the Campaign to Defend America and Progressive Media aired their ads, Obama's finance chair, billionaire hotel heiress Penny Pritzker, at a meeting of the campaign's national finance committee in Indianapolis emphatically instructed supporters not to give money to any of the independent groups,[27] and both groups quietly fell off the radar.[28]

By the time Clinton dropped out of the race in June 2008, Obama's campaign had raised $288 million,[29] compared to Clinton's $209 million[30] and McCain's $110 million.[31] The lure of that cash gusher was too much for Obama to resist. He opted out of the public financing system, freeing him from the cap on how much he could spend and sending ripples of disappointment through a reform community that thought it had found a champion. Without outside groups to muddle the message or compete for cash, Obama's campaign dominated the landscape. It dwarfed McCain's in the money race, $750 million to $290 million (with McCain's final tally including the $84 million public financing grant). Obama handily won the presidency and took office pledging to empower regular folks over monied interests. The way his team looked at it, they didn't owe their victory to special interests and wouldn't have to smile and pretend to enjoy the kind of "donor maintenance" that they saw as a relic of the cash-for-access Bill Clinton years.

Lost in the liberal euphoria over the ascendance of Obama's new brand of high-tech, regular-people-powered politics was a development with potentially dire implications for the long-term health of the Democratic Party: the quiet demise of big money. In just two short years, Obama had undone two decades of delicate Democratic cultivation of the business community, annoying Clinton operatives who saw Obama's behavior as a repudiation of the Clinton coalition. The big-donor schmoozing by Bill Clinton and his allies, the presentations by Rob Stein, the Democracy Alliance conferences—all were cast aside in the Obama age.

When Obama became president, his attitude toward business donors—especially those on Wall Street—turned from relative indifference to open antagonism. The country was spiraling into an economic crisis, and the new president loudly blamed Wall Street. Obama's campaign had reaped $26 million from the finance industry, making it one of his top giving sectors,[32] but when Wall Street balked at tougher regulations being pushed by Democrats, Obama lashed back. "I did not run for office to be helping out a bunch of fat cat bankers on Wall Street," he said in late 2009.[33] His populist rhetoric only became more strident after *Citizens United,* which he criticized as an affront to democracy. By the time of the 2010 midterm election, Obama's criticism of the unlimited-money boom had become increasingly shrill. He called some of the groups airing attack ads against Democrats "a threat to our democracy." Democratic operatives urged Obama to concede to the new reality and bless the efforts of big-money operatives. Ickes, the former Clinton aide who played a central role in the 2004 Democratic spending boom and the failed 2008 effort, confronted the Obama team about the damage they were doing to the party by shoving its richest patrons to the sidelines. And he wasn't alone. "Plenty of us have asked them until we're red in the face over the last few years. I've had any number of conversations with fairly high-ranking officials," one operative told me.

In this environment, it was all but impossible for Democratic operatives to raise big money for IEs, or "independent expenditures"—ads by outside groups supporting Democratic candidates or opposing Republicans. The administration "put a wet blanket on IE spending," Rob Stein told me. "They started in 2008 and they haven't really changed that message, so that has a chilling effect."

Even in the wake of the disastrous 2010 midterms, after Obama and his top aides withdrew their opposition to big money, wealthy donors were still waiting for a sign that the Obama team was ready to put on a full-court press for their affections, and they weren't particularly convinced by what they were seeing. Many were further discouraged by the caliber of the operatives who emerged to run the Obama big-money operation. In February 2011, former deputy press secretary Bill Burton, then thirty-three, and White House staffer Sean Sweeney, then thirty-nine, left the Obama administration, and about three months after the Mandarin meeting, they started a pro-Obama spending outfit called Priorities USA. It actually consisted of two groups—a super PAC called Priorities USA Action and a nonprofit counterpart called Priorities USA. The nonprofit was registered under section 501(c)(4) of the IRS code, allowing it to shield the identities of its donors. Not only did Burton and Sweeney have no relationships with the big donors who would be expected to fund the newly formed groups, but they also lacked the high-profile cachet that could help offset their inexperience. Making matters worse, Burton was the one the Obama campaign had dispatched back in 2008 to publicly reinforce the message the campaign's fund-raising operation was privately relaying to big donors: *Do not give to outside groups*. Some of Obama's top political advisors, including campaign manager Jim Messina, had quietly implored Obama to re-cruit someone with deeper ties to Democratic money to start a super PAC.[34] Obama World didn't really have a Karl Rove analogue, but even a Mike Duncan type would be vastly superior to Burton and Sweeney, the thinking went. Names floated internally at various times included the hotel billionaire and Obama 2008 finance chair Pritzker,[35] former White House press secretary Robert Gibbs, and even 2008 campaign manager David Plouffe.[36] But, given the lack of enthusiasm among big Democratic donors, it was seen as kind of a thankless job with a low reward margin, and it ultimately fell to Burton and Sweeney mostly because they were the only ones who expressed interest.

It was quite a contrast to what was happening on the other side of the aisle, where big-money skills were becoming a major status symbol. So much so that after the 2010 election, Duncan—his leadership role at Crossroads a feather in his cap—found some support when he explored the possibility of running for the RNC chairmanship from which he had been unceremoniously ousted two years earlier. The hope was that he could bring back to the cash-strapped party some of the big-money magic that had allowed it to retake the House. After a brief flirtation, Duncan ultimately decided not to pursue the post, a tacit acknowledg-ment that the real action had officially shifted from the party to the soft-money groups. Before bowing out of the race, though, Duncan ap-peared at an RNC chairman's race forum in December 2010—ironically sponsored by the big-money group FreedomWorks. There he hinted that the big-money explosion was just getting started, and he dropped some knowledge about mega-donor fund-raising that Democrats might have been wise to jot down: "I couldn't have done the things that we did without major donors. And you win those major donors by your business practices. You win them by putting a plan forward, by showing them that you're reducing the cost of funds, and that you have a plan to spend the money effectively."[37]

Burton and Sweeney didn't have a track record of any of that, but that didn't stop them from announcing a bold $100 million fund-raising goal when they rolled out Priorities USA in late April 2011. Burton brashly declared, "Karl Rove and the Koch brothers cannot live by one set of rules as our values and our candidates are overrun with their hundreds of millions of dollars. We will follow the rules as the Supreme Court has laid them out, but the days of the double standard are over."[38]

To fill the star-power void, Burton and Sweeney brought on veteran Democratic operative Paul Begala. He had cemented his political reputation twenty years earlier by helping steer Bill Clinton's 1992 presidential campaign and more recently had become a household name as a CNN pundit. He didn't have a lick of fund-raising experience, however. "This is the first time I've ever raised money," he told me. "I know it's your beat, but it's not my beat." Priorities USA also enlisted Harold Ickes, who maintained close ties to the donors of Clinton Land and the Democracy Alliance. It was a depressing measure of the state of Democratic finance that its guiding light in 2011 had last raised serious big money in 2004 and had failed to deliver the next time he tried, back in 2008.

So the motley crew at Priorities—Burton, Sweeney, Begala, and Ickes, along with pollster Geoff Garin and fund-raiser Teddy Johnston—set out on a tricky mission: to create an Obama big-money culture from whole cloth. First stop was a private upstairs dining room at a swanky Italian restaurant in Beverly Hills called Scarpetta. That's where the foursome made their first major pitch, on March 23, 2011[39]—five weeks before they would even register Priorities USA with the Federal Election Commission. They were courting the man they thought could become the George Soros of 2012: movie producer Jeffrey Katzenberg, the CEO of DreamWorks Animation. He had long been a major Democratic whale, and he had a measure of Hollywood flair, often coaxing donations for his causes from other celebrity types. The Obama-backing actor Will Smith once cracked, "Jeffrey has no problem asking for way too much money."[40]

Best of all from the Obama team's perspective, Katzenberg wasn't a part of the Democracy Alliance set. He was seen neither as an ideological purist nor as a prima donna requiring constant stroking. Katzenberg did, however, evoke memories of the Clinton era by occasionally blurring the lines between his business and politics. An old-style Hollywood Democrat, Katzenberg was one of the first to break with the Clintons and support Obama, holding a major fund-raiser only ten days after Obama announced his candidacy. Attended by Jennifer Aniston, Tom Hanks, Denzel Washington, and dozens of other big Hollywood names, the Katzenberg event raised $1.3 million. It marked Obama as a serious candidate by Washington's money-drunk standards and Katzenberg as a serious Obama rainmaker. At Scarpetta, Begala laid out the plan to help reelect Obama by airing blistering ads that turned Romney's strength—his business record—against him. Katzenberg, then worth an estimated $800 million, was sold. Not only did he pledge $2 million on the spot to help launch the effort, he also promised to solicit contributions from his rich Hollywood pals.

A few weeks later, buoyed by the status of Katzenberg as an anchor donor, Sean Sweeney flew out to Laguna Beach, California, to pitch Democracy Alliance donors at a luxury hotel on an oceanfront bluff. Among the attendees were DA chair Rob McKay and Patricia Stryker, whose grandfather founded a leading medical technology company. Sweeney sat on a panel with representatives of other emerging big-money Democratic groups. A pair were intended to boost the party's congressional candidates, while one called American Bridge, which was founded by David Brock, would focus on digging up and publicizing damaging information about Republicans. It was significant that the DA was, for the first time, providing the super PACs a platform for talking to its donors. It was interpreted as a de facto endorsement by one of the pillars of the big-money left—and as a signal that the DA was openly embracing the very sort of big-money election spending that some of its donors eschewed. Days after the Laguna Beach confab, McKay agreed to chair Priorities USA, lending the not-yet-public outfit his name and fund-raising clout. It was a legitimate get for the group, though not a game-changer. McKay was no Soros, but he did give the group a foothold in the DA from which to try to influence other donors. McKay knew it would be a slow grind. "There is a sales cycle, sitting down and explaining to folks the role that these organizations play. And I've been in a lot of these conversations and you don't always close the sale immediately," he recalled in a deep, mellow California cadence that called to mind a cross between the Keanu Reeves character in *Bill and Ted's Excellent Adventure* and the patrician millionaire Thurston Howell III from *Gilligan's Island.*

A couple of weeks after the Laguna Beach confab, I ran into Soros in Washington, D.C. Now that the DA had kicked the tires of the big-money Democratic outside groups, was Soros ready to support them? "Since I don't know what I'm going to do, I can't tell you," he told me. Well, I asked, had anything changed since 2008 or 2010, when he sat on the sidelines? That prompted his hyper-protective Vachon to step in impatiently. "Ken, you got your answer," he said.

I really hadn't, and neither had the Democratic operatives hoping to match Rove and the Koch brothers. By the end of 2011, finance reports showed, Priorities USA and a network of outside groups set up to support Obama's campaign and those of Democratic congressional candidates had raised far less than half the $51 million brought in by Karl Rove's Crossroads groups. Obama needed to do more to court donors, or he was going to get crushed. On the very day the anemic Democratic super PAC finance reports were filed with the Federal Election Commission and made public, Obama's motorcade left the White House at 6:45 p.m. for a four-block drive to the St. Regis Hotel, where in an intimate, dimly lit dining room fifty Democracy Alliance–linked donors were waiting, including McKay and his wife, Anna Hawken McKay.[41] The event was a fund-raiser for Obama's reelection campaign, organized by McKay, along with Democracy Alliance's president, Kelly Craighead, and founding strategist, Rob Stein. But technically it wasn't sponsored by the Alliance, which—because it is structured as a taxable not-for-profit corporation—is barred from spending money to directly boost a federal campaign. Still, most of the DA partners at the St. Regis had donated the maximum $35,800 to Obama's reelection campaign, and most had the capacity to give much more to the outside groups helping Obama. Here was a perfect chance for Obama to make the sale, to demonstrate that he was over his too-cool-for-school approach to high-dollar fund-raising.

After a flattering introduction, McKay turned the mic over to Obama. "As Rob said, I see a lot of friends here, people who supported me since way back when, before people could say my name," Obama told the crowd.[42] "And as I look around the room, folks from all across the country, I am mindful of the fact that not only have you done so much to help me be in a position where I can make a difference in America, but separate and apart from my election, so many of you have supported good causes that are making a difference day in and day out. And so I just want to say thank you for that," he said, before launching into an early version of his standard stump speech. Then he got down to business, telling the donors he needed them to make his vision possible. "I think we're going to get there. But—in fact, I know we're going to get there—but I'm going to need all of your help to get there as well. So thanks for the support in the past and I'm looking forward to you guys being in the foxhole with me this year."

That Sunday, hours before Obama would settle in to watch the Super Bowl, he taped an interview with NBC's Matt Lauer in which he bemoaned the *Citizens United* decision. "One of the worries we have, obviously, in the next campaign, is that there are so many of these so-called super PACs, these independent expenditures that are going to be out there, there's going to be just a lot of money floating around. And I guarantee you a bunch of that's going to be negative," he predicted to Lauer, adding he would "love to take some of the big money out of politics."[43] The interview aired the next morning on NBC's *Today* in what turned out to be very bad timing for the Obama campaign. It came near the end of a long-evolving debate about how to respond to the GOP's super PAC advantage. At some point in the day and a half after Obama taped the NBC interview, he signed off on a political shift that flew in the face of his comments to Lauer—not to mention his twenty years of advocacy on the issue. At ten o'clock that evening, the Obama campaign organized an emergency conference call of its National Finance Committee, consisting of its biggest fund-raisers. It was time, they were told. Obama was finally going to officially bless Priorities USA and even dispatch some of his top administration and campaign aides to raise funds for it.

About an hour later, campaign manager Jim Messina emailed Obama's grassroots supporters—the kind who couldn't afford to fork over the $35,800 to attend the Democracy Alliance's fund-raiser with the president at the St. Regis—to explain the decision. "We decided to do this because we can't afford for the work you're doing in your communities, and the grass-roots donations you give to support it, to be destroyed by hundreds of millions of dollars in negative ads," Messina wrote. He laid out some data to show the power of rich donors: "In 2011, the super PAC supporting Mitt Romney raised $30 million from fewer than two hundred contributors. Ninety-six percent of what they've spent so far, more than $18 million, has been for attack ads. The main engine of Romney's campaign has an average contribution of roughly $150,000." The stakes, he wrote, "are too important to play by two different sets of rules. If we fail to act, we concede this election to a small group of powerful people intent on removing the president at any cost."

So that was it. After a decades-long crusade to rid politics of the corrosive influence of big money, Obama was raising the white flag on one of his signature issues because political reality made it too hard not to. In 2012, big money was going to continue growing in volume and importance whether or not he abandoned his principles. Whatever the calculation, the result was the same: the Hyde Park reformer was no more. In his place was a calculating political pragmatist.

The Republican press releases virtually wrote themselves. "In less than 24 hours, Obama has gone from decrying super PACs in the morning to opening up the door to their money during a conference call with his big-money donors in the middle of the night," read a statement from the Republican National Committee.

Eleven days later, Obama justified the reversal to ultra-rich liberals, including Microsoft billionaires Bill Gates and Steve Ballmer, who had gathered for a fund-raiser in a modernist mansion in Seattle's eastern suburbs.

"I am in the unfortunate position of not being willing to unilaterally disarm," Obama said in previously unreported remarks described to me by a source familiar with the event. The president told his wealthy supporters that he needed his own super PAC to combat the historic conservative fund-raising surge triggered by *Citizens United*. "I mean, the Koch brothers aren't being shy about it. They said, 'We're going to write a $60 million check to support whoever it is that can beat Obama.' And they've been very blunt about it. They had a meeting with two hundred folks and they said, 'Our goal is to raise a couple hundred million' from those people." Neither Gates nor Ballmer donated a dime to Obama's super PAC, or any super PAC, for that matter. And Obama's support for his super PAC wasn't winning over the Democracy Alliance, where super PACs were becoming a source of acrimony. The DA had secretly loaned $25,000 to the Democratic super PACs to help them raise money, despite the fact that it claimed not to spend money on direct partisan activity. Some partners and operatives argued that the DA's embrace of big-money election spending to help Democrats represented a betrayal of its focus on ideas and not candidates. Billionaire insurance magnate Peter Lewis, who had teamed with Soros on the 2004 spending spree and the subsequent founding of the Democracy Alliance, eventually dropped out of the DA in protest. For Lewis, an exceedingly private and eccentric fellow who died in late 2013, the embrace of advertising-focused super PACs was the last straw. Where was the focus on his policy priorities? he wondered. He had spent heavily, for instance, on efforts to legalize marijuana, which he smoked regularly to relieve pain from a leg that had been partially amputated as a result of chronic circulation problems.

A source close to Lewis told me that he was "more focused on building the long-term progressive infrastructure—the ideas, think tanks, policy solutions, media monitoring, and marijuana reform, not electioneering or political candidates." He simply didn't think political ads like those planned by the super PACs were a good use of his cash.

That was ironic, one big-money Democratic fund-raiser pointed out, given that Lewis's insurance behemoth, Progressive, was renowned for its punchy ad campaigns featuring the spunky saleswoman Flo. But it also showed that rich liberals weren't ready to fall into line despite urgent warnings from Burton, Begala, and Messina. Luckily for the Democrats, though, the Republican big-money groups would have to endure a civil war against one another.

CHAPTER 5

The Political Fantasy Camp

O
On December 15, 2011, the battle for the Republican presidential nomination was nearing peak frenzy and the billionaire casino mogul Sheldon Adelson, the single biggest whale in the new big-money politics, was on the line venting about a story I had cowritten with Maggie Haberman. In dispute was our assertion that he had discussed donating $20 million to a super PAC to save Newt Gingrich's sinking campaign.

At the time, Adelson and his family had donated only $7,500—pocket change for him—to Gingrich, and hadn't given a dime to any of the pro-Gingrich super PACs jockeying for his affections. When I reached out to Adelson's spokesman, he denied that his boss had promised anyone he'd give $20 million. But Maggie had heard otherwise through multiple sources in her extensive network, so we stuck with the story, adding the spokesman's denial. That wasn't good enough for Adelson.

"I'm a little frustrated that my head of PR called you, and you said you don't want to accept a message from the horse's mouth. So I figured, I'm the horse's mouth—I'm the horse—and I'm going to call you and I'm going to neigh to you, and tell you that what you printed is wrong," Adelson fumed,[1] mangling his metaphor to the point of near incomprehensibility. Adelson was seventy-eight years old and, in GOP politics, was feared, revered, and regarded as something of a batty old crank—a seemingly contradictory reputation rather common among the biggest mega-donors. President George W. Bush once reportedly described a White House meeting with Adelson as "this crazy Jewish billionaire, yelling at me."[2]

Now Adelson was yelling at me. "I've not made any commitment, whatsoever. To anybody. To super PAC, to not-so-super PAC, to under-super, to ordinary PAC, to anybody," he insisted.

It was about two weeks before the first contest of the primary season, the January 3, 2012, Iowa caucuses, and so far it was other billionaires giving the jaw-dropping sums. The chemical tycoon Jon Huntsman Sr. had donated more than $1.6 million to a super PAC supporting his son, the leveraged-buyout billionaire Harold Simmons had plunked down $1 million to support Rick Perry, and the super PAC–backing front-runner Mitt Romney had already pulled in about a half dozen $1 million checks. Still, $20 million from one donor to support a single candidate would be unprecedented in American political history. Even if it didn't lift Gingrich to the nomination, it certainly had the potential to throw the race into total chaos. And it would decisively signal a major shift in power away from the party elders who had long exerted quiet control over the presidential nominating process. A procession of GOP muckety-mucks—including fellow Jewish mega-donors who supported Romney, like Florida mall developer Mel Sembler and Houston executive Fred Zeidman—were at that moment trying to talk sense into Adelson. Romney was unquestionably going to get the nomination, and any money spent helping rival primary candidates would weaken him in the general election, they argued. Adelson tried to put their minds at ease. "I'm not only not giving $20 million, I haven't given any money at all," he reportedly told Sembler.[3] But that didn't assuage party elders, who kept hearing rumblings that Adelson was poised to go in big for Gingrich, much to their annoyance. Romney gave the Republicans the best chance of winning the White House, but he could ill afford interference from renegade donors in the primaries. He had come close to the nomination in 2008 but been edged out. Now it was his turn, and he needed time to unite the fractious conservative movement before heading into the general election against Obama. Who was this stubborn old billionaire to stand in the way?

Born to poor Jewish immigrants and raised in a working-class Massachusetts town, Adelson made his fortune by aggressively following his gut even—and especially—when others warned him not to. Through sheer hustle, he forged a business convention industry in Las Vegas when it was considered just a gambling town. He exponentially grew his empire by rushing into the uncertain middle-class gambling market in the Macao region of China.

Adelson and Gingrich hit it off the first time they met. Newt was the swashbuckling star of the political world, having just led Republicans to sweeping victories in the 1994 elections that gave them a governing majority in the House for the first time in forty years. Adelson and his wife, an Israeli-born physician named Miriam, were in Washington, D.C., to lobby for the relocation of the US embassy in Israel to Jerusalem—one of the many Israel-related causes that animate much of Adelson's political activity. They were introduced in the Capitol Rotunda to Gingrich,[4] who supported the relocation. A nine-term Georgia congressman, Gingrich had just been sworn in as Speaker of the House, making him perhaps the most important player in a reconfigured Washington. Gingrich welcomed Adelson into his circle of hawkish, pro-Israel advisors and was soon borrowing one of the mogul's Gulfstream jets for cross-country flights.[5] By late 1998, though, Gingrich's high-flying career was rapidly losing altitude. His House GOP caucus had a disastrous showing in that year's midterm elections, and he was facing challenges to his leadership along with a slew of ethics charges. He paid $300,000 to settle them, resigned the Speakership, then left Congress entirely in 1999, his tail between his legs. Out of office, but not out of ambition, Gingrich soon began rebuilding his brand and parlaying it into a living, and found in Adelson a devoted and generous supporter. Adelson wrote nearly $8 million worth of checks to a nonprofit group[6] that formed the hub of a network of companies and groups that Gingrich insiders dubbed "Newt, Inc." It paid for Gingrich to travel the country in chartered jets and town cars and, most crucially, to keep him involved in the political debate.

Now—thirteen years since he had last held elected office, and against all odds—Gingrich was running for president. Washington Republicans wondered whether it might be some kind of cynical ploy on Newt's part to boost his earning power. But Adelson didn't care why his old buddy was running, and he wasn't going to abandon him just because some political hacks thought it was a bad bet. That only seemed to build his resolve.

"I'm just a loyal guy. I'm a guy who practices loyalty," Adelson told me on the phone, his dudgeon starting to fade. Nearly every Republican whose name had been mentioned as a possible 2012 presidential candidate had made a pilgrimage to Adelson's casino on the Las Vegas strip, the Venetian, including Michele Bachmann, Mike Pence, Herman Cain, and even Sarah Palin, who had a long chat with Adelson about her love of Israel. The courting clearly pleased Adelson, but he was sticking with his guy. "I wouldn't step away from Gingrich because I think another candidate is the best. I think that Gingrich is the best candidate and he'll make the best president. That doesn't mean that the other guys would make lousy presidents, okay? But on a scale of one to ten, I got to make a priority of who I think will make the best president. It's my own opinion. Listen, I'm only one out of 308 million people in this country."[7]

But only one of a handful who could write a $20 million check. I asked Adelson why he thought Gingrich would make the best president.

"Why do you want to have a steak for dinner?" he answered.

Me: "Because steak tastes good."

Adelson: "Steak tastes good. Okay, well, who would be good for the country? That's why I want him to be president."

As I wrestled with this latest turn of phrase, I asked Adelson one more time if he was sure he hadn't talked to *anyone* about stroking $20 million to help Newt.

"No, no, no, no," he said, annoyed again. "Political support is my personal life, okay? And to the extent that I have to be high-profile for the benefit of my business, I'm willing to be so. But when it comes to political issues, or my personal issues, or my philanthropic issues, I only allow anything to be done, I never talk about what I'm going to do to anybody. All I just do is do." Then he reached for the rhetorical sledgehammer. "I'm going to say the same thing to you five times, because I've already said it three times and it doesn't sink in," he began. "Okay, I've made no commitment. I've stated no amounts. I've made no commitment. I've stated no amounts. I've made no commitments. I've stated no amounts. I've made no commitments. I've stated no amounts. And for the last time, I've made no commitments, and I've stated no amounts. Do you get the picture?"

I got the picture. Adelson liked talking a big game about his political spending, but didn't like anyone else talking about it. We added his denial to the story.

Gingrich badly needed $20 million at that precise moment. Laughed off as a sideshow as soon as he declared his candidacy, then left for dead when his campaign staff quit en masse in the spring, Gingrich five months later was trying to mount an improbable comeback. Lacking anything approximating a presidential-level campaign operation, he surged on the strength of strong performances in the GOP presidential debates and a logic-defying repositioning of himself as an anti-Washington alternative to Romney. Somehow, to the surprise of even the most seasoned political analysts, Newt entered the three-week home stretch before the January 3 Iowa caucuses with double-digit leads in not only Iowa but also two of the next three states on the primary calendar.

He might have been able to continue his shoestring campaign even without assistance from Adelson, except that his rivals' sugar daddies were in the process of using their fortunes to nuke Newt. Romney and his allies had been laying the groundwork for this moment ever since he dropped his 2008 presidential bid. With his blessing, former Romney aides quietly created a super PAC called Restore Our Future to reap mega-checks from rich supporters. Romney embraced the PAC, appearing at its early fund-raisers in Boston, New York, and Beverly Hills[8] before reporters like me even caught wind that the super PAC existed. By the time Adelson was toying with the idea of writing a check to help Gingrich, Romney and his allies had outraised the Gingrich campaign and its super PAC $87 million to $15 million.

In early December, polls had shown Gingrich leading Romney 33 percent to 20 percent among likely Iowa caucus-goers. Then Restore Our Future went to work. It began a negative TV ad blitz against Gingrich that would saturate the Iowa airwaves. The final tally—$3.4

million—was more than double what all the GOP candidates in 2008 spent on ads in Iowa combined.[9] The ads highlighted past positions Gingrich had taken that were anathema to the staunchly conservative GOP primary electorate: supporting mandatory health insurance for all Americans, so-called amnesty for undocumented immigrants, and efforts to reduce carbon pollution through a cap-and-trade system. "Newt has a ton of baggage," one ad asserted. "More baggage than the airlines," another ad quipped. The none-too-subtle suggestion for Iowa caucus-goers: Obama would crush Gingrich if they made the mistake of nominating him.

With Restore Our Future playing bad cop, Romney's campaign mostly played good cop. It spent hundreds of thousands of its own dollars on sunny ads featuring wholesome portrayals of Romney's family and record. Gingrich's cash-strapped campaign, with no super PAC cavalry behind it, simply lacked the resources to respond in kind to the onslaught. After a week of asymmetric warfare, Gingrich had plunged an astounding twenty points in the Iowa polls, leaving him complaining that he was getting "Romney-boated"[10]—a reference to the 2004 negative ad campaign against John Kerry by the group Swift Boat Veterans for Truth. Gingrich's attackers were, in his words, "a bunch of millionaires getting together to run a negative campaign, and Gov. Romney refusing to call them off."[11]

Romney—whose own campaign had set up the super PAC[12]—disingenuously distanced himself from it when it became controversial. "Super PACs have to be entirely separate from a campaign and a candidate. I'm not allowed to communicate with a super PAC in any way, shape, or form," he said on MSNBC's *Morning Joe* when pressed on why he didn't ask Restore to tone down its Iowa onslaught against Gingrich. "My goodness, if we coordinate in any way whatsoever, we go to the big house," he said, adding that he considered super PACs a "disaster" and that "campaign finance law has made a mockery of our political campaign season. We really ought to let campaigns raise the money they need and just get rid of these super PACs."[13]

Yet with the Romney super PAC gleefully focused on eviscerating Gingrich in Iowa and Adelson on the sidelines, the field was open for the other candidates and their sugar daddies to romp around. A super

PAC backed by energy concerns and rich Texans including the billion-aire Harold Simmons was airing millions of dollars in ads backing Texas governor Rick Perry's much-ballyhooed campaign. At that moment, it was seen as the most serious threat to Romney's nomination. Simmons, who has since passed away, hyperbolically called Obama "the most dangerous American alive" because "he would eliminate free enterprise in this country."[14] It was also notable that Simmons and the energy companies had fared well under the Perry administration in Austin.[15] Were their big checks to the Perry super PAC a token of thanks or a down payment on favorable treatment they expected from a Perry White House? Maybe it was just as simple as a show of support for a guy they liked or an effort to oust one they detested. These patron-politician relationships had always been more complicated than the simple quid pro quo suggested by Obama and other advocates for stricter campaign rules, but in the new big-money world they'd gotten trickier still, as the 2012 GOP presidential primary was about to prove.

The quirky billionaire PayPal cofounder Peter Thiel had never even met the libertarian Texas congressman Ron Paul, but by the time the Iowa caucuses rolled around, Thiel had donated $900,000 to a super PAC that was mounting an untraditional social media effort to boost Paul's insurgent campaign for the GOP presidential nomination. Thiel would triple that investment before Paul ended his long-shot bid. Paul was never going to win, but his continued presence in the race, abetted by the Thiel super PAC, had an impact: his consistent criticism of Romney as a big-government Republican reminded everyone of the tea party's beef with the front-runner, and Paul ended up winning a plurality of delegates in four states, bruising Romney.

Yet Thiel and most of the other large donors supporting Romney's rivals were inconsequential gadflies compared to Foster Friess. Starting with the Iowa caucuses and extending through the long and bitter trail of contests over the next several months, the partnership between Friess, a wealthy retired investor, and Rick Santorum demonstrated the rising power of mega-donors like no other. The two had first met back in the 1990s and quickly found common cause over their zealous Christianity (Friess is a born-again evangelical and Santorum a devout Catholic) and their concerns about Islamic extremism. Back then,

Santorum was a largely unremarkable social conservative congressman from Pennsylvania who had upset an incumbent Democratic senator in the Gingrich-led Republican wave of 1994. Friess and Santorum grew closer over rounds of golf and visits to each other's homes, and Friess became a leading donor to Santorum's political efforts, sticking with him even after his 2006 reelection defeat seemed to spell the end of his political career.

Friess was born in small-town Wisconsin to a cattle-dealer father and a mother who dropped out of school in the eighth grade. He had met his wife at the University of Wisconsin, and after the couple graduated, they started a small investment firm that eventually made them very rich. The firm specialized in managing mutual funds, which experienced explosive increases in the roaring 1980s and 1990s, and grew its assets to $15.7 billion. The hard-earned fortune allowed the Friess family to indulge in a lavish nouveau-frontier lifestyle, including a private jet and exotic animal hunting expeditions around the world (grizzlies in Alaska, cape buffalo and crocodiles in Tanzania), as well as sprawling ranches in Jackson Hole, Wyoming, and on the Shoshone River near Cody, Wyoming. In the winter, they retreated to the warmer climate of Arizona. When the couple sold a majority of their interest in the firm for $250 million in 2001, they became full-time philanthropists, giving tens of millions to water purification projects around the world and to relief efforts after the Asian tsunami, Hurricane Katrina, and the Haitian earthquake.

Friess had been a big GOP giver even before the 2012 presidential election, donating $2.7 million (30 percent of which had gone to help Santorum) during various campaigns. But he had largely stayed in the background. That changed in the weeks before the Iowa caucuses. At the time, Santorum was mired in the low single digits in most Hawkeye State polls,[16] yet he had adopted an all-Iowa-all-the-time campaign strategy. That was partly because the state's brand of social conservatism seemed a good fit for his own, but it was also out of desperate necessity. His campaign was running on fumes and didn't have the cash to mount major operations in multiple early states. Instead, he crisscrossed Iowa's rugged terrain at a punishing pace in a gunmetal Dodge

Ram pickup nicknamed the "Chuck Truck" because it belonged to a local supporter named Chuck Laudner. Santorum made stops in all of the state's ninety-nine counties, sometimes at tiny gatherings of only a handful of people, dozens of which were held at outposts of a midwestern fast-food chain called Pizza Ranch. As the caucuses approached and the state's significant evangelical population began giving him a second look, Santorum's crowds started to swell.

Despite a bum knee that would soon require surgery, Friess joined Santorum on the trail and was having the time of his life, vicariously living his own political fantasy camps of sorts through Santorum. Back in 2007, a secretive group of influential Christian conservative leaders with which Friess was associated actually floated his name as a possible alternative presidential candidate to counter the insufficiently conservative crop of contenders for the 2008 GOP nomination.[17] And during one of his 2012 campaign trail trips with Santorum, Friess told the candidate, presumably with tongue planted in cheek, "Rick, you think I'm out here to encourage you and support you. I'm just kinda sizing things up. I'm gonna make a 2016 run myself."[18] Friess had a politician's gift for creating a sense of intimacy with relative strangers, he reveled in shooting the breeze with reporters—an extreme rarity for mega-donors—and he was energized by the crowds of supporters and television cameras he and Santorum encountered. "Rick, this is the most attention I've ever gotten since I was seventeen years old and held up my local 7-Eleven store," Friess cracked to Santorum,[19] recalling later, "It was like being with a rock star."[20]

Friess, who was seventy-one years old in 2012, was like a grandfather from central casting: he had a full head of white hair (over which he often wore a white Stetson) and a vast repertoire of corny jokes. He loved offering up his own novel political analysis and casting Santorum's run in David-vs.-Goliath terms. "We were in our Chuck Truck, a Dodge Ram, with a four-hour ride from point A to point B, and there was a possibility Mitt Romney was whipping over us in his jet, but that's not going to discourage us," Friess recounted gleefully. "Not that I belittle Romney for having a jet. You know, I've got a jet. I know how important it is to have that. I just think that the energy that Santorum brings to this—the fact that he went to 381 [town halls in Iowa]. He starts every morning out with fifty push-ups. I'll bet you Obama can't do twenty."[21]

By itself, Santorum's energy wouldn't have been enough to power his surge, though. Friess's money was proving pivotal. The day Adelson denied he'd discussed a $20 million donation to save Gingrich, a mysterious super PAC called the Red White and Blue Fund began airing an ad on statewide television in Iowa. It touted Santorum as "the true conservative you can really trust," a "visionary that saw and understands the threat of radical Islam, and a proven reformer who took on Washington and won." The initial buy—a relatively modest $200,000—was just the beginning, but it dwarfed the TV ad spending by Santorum's own cash-strapped campaign. Unbeknownst to all but a small circle of insiders, the ad was funded by Friess through a $250,000 donation the previous month to Red White and Blue, which would not be publicly disclosed until weeks later in a filing with the Federal Election Commission.

It had an immediate impact. Three days after the ads hit the air, Santorum cracked double digits in the polls[22] and seemed to be separating from the second tier of candidates struggling for traction. Santorum was even closing in on Romney, Gingrich, and Paul. Within a week, Santorum got another huge boost when the influential Iowa Christian conservative leader Bob Vander Plaats endorsed him. Vander Plaats needed money "to promote the endorsement," he told Santorum,[23] and three days later, Vander Plaats's right-hand man set up another super PAC called Leaders for Family Values,[24] which in short order received a total of $125,000 from Friess and the Red White and Blue Fund. By the time the caucuses rolled around on January 3, Red White and Blue had spent nearly $1 million on ads boosting Santorum.[25] The lion's share had come from Friess, who would keep a steady stream of six-figure donations flowing to Red White and Blue over the coming months.

Friess had his finger on the pulse of the campaign and the super PAC, and he occasionally seemed to blur the boundaries between them. He was so involved that independent watchdogs alleged that he and Santorum were flouting the federal coordination ban—the one that Romney feared could land him in "the big house" if he communicated with his super PAC. Friess, on the other hand, freely discussed strategy with both the campaign and the super PAC. He told the latter that he didn't want his cash used on negative ads, instead suggesting he'd like to see ads focusing on Santorum's work against Islamic extremism. Nothing came of the watchdog complaints against Santorum and Friess, and the donor even represented the candidate at one of the caucuses. As the Iowa results started rolling in, with Santorum looking good, Friess described his time on the trail in Iowa as "one of the most incredible experiences of America I've ever had."[26] Santorum finished a razor-thin eight votes behind Romney, but no matter. The former senator from Pennsylvania was considered the runaway star of the caucuses and gave a soaring speech, which he started by declaring, "Game on!" On the stage behind him, beaming and clasping a Rick Santorum sign across his chest, was the man who'd done more to make the night happen than any single person except Santorum himself, the man who'd indisputably proven the impact of the new big money: Foster Friess.

Gingrich finished a disappointing fourth in Iowa. That seemed to get Adelson's attention. Three days later, he finally joined the billionaire primary derby. He penned a $5 million check to a pro-Newt super PAC called Winning Our Future, to the annoyance of Romney's team. Not only did they think they had convinced Adelson to sit out the primary, but they also believed they had finished off Gingrich in Iowa, and were preparing to turn their attention to nuking Santorum in the upcoming states. Suddenly, though, a single donor was forcing them to recalculate their entire strategy. Adding insult to injury for Romney, a recount later showed Santorum had in fact won Iowa by thirty-four votes. Game on, indeed.

The Iowa caucuses woke everyone up to the power of big money. After Santorum's breakout performance, his campaign boasted a surge in small donations, but none of it would have been possible without Friess. The liberal website Daily Kos posted a feature on Friess with the headline "Meet Foster Friess, Billionaire Who Bought Iowa for Santorum." When I caught up with Friess on the phone a few days later, he had clearly been reading his own press, even in the liberal blogosphere; he referred unprompted to the Daily Kos headline, which amused him. "I told my wife, 'Wow, I got a bargain,'" he quipped. He attributed Santorum's win to his retail politicking, and dismissed as negligible the

$985,000 spent by the Red White and Blue Fund in Iowa. "Well, I guess if Newt's got $5 million, it makes sense that Rick should have a little bit," he said, making clear that his wealth wasn't in Adelson's league. "If you're going to put me in that crowd, you ought to call me the underdog billionaire," he cracked.

Occasionally Friess's ebullience left him singed by the spotlight. During one of his many live TV interviews following the caucus, talk turned to Santorum's hard-line stance on social issues like contraception. "People seem to be so preoccupied with sex. I think it says something about our culture. We maybe need a massive therapy session so we can concentrate on what the real issues are," Friess said, before getting a bit tongue-tied and stumbling into the danger zone. "And this contraceptive thing, my gosh, it's such inexpensive. Back in my days, they used Bayer Aspirin for contraceptives. The gals put it between their knees and it wasn't that costly." The remark momentarily stunned the host, MSNBC's usually unflappable Andrea Mitchell, into silence. "Excuse me, I'm just trying to catch my breath from that, Mr. Friess, frankly," she said when she recovered. Friess's quip quickly ricocheted through the political media, forcing him to apologize and Santorum to distance himself. Privately, though, Friess was soaking up his buddies' praise for the line. "All my older friends—the people who weren't in D.C. or San Francisco—they gave me high-fives and chuckled and thought it was a great joke," Friess told me later. He wasn't going to let a little liberal media outrage dissuade him from continuing his political fantasy camp.

After Iowa, it was no longer possible for Romney to quickly wrap up the nomination. Some of the GOP establishment began seeing Santorum as a potentially serious threat, while various super-PAC-backed challengers seemed to have openings in the next several states—New Hampshire, South Carolina, and Florida. The super PACs supporting Santorum and Gingrich focused on South Carolina and Florida, leaving the New Hampshire airwaves to tea party favorite Ron Paul and Upper West Side darling Jon Huntsman. A super PAC supporting Huntsman, called Our Destiny, spent more than $2 million on New Hampshire ads touting the centrist former Utah governor as "a conservative who actually has a chance to win" and trashing Romney as a political "chameleon." Our Destiny was almost entirely funded by the candidate's billionaire father, whose son declared himself "mighty thankful" for the "air cover." Did Jon junior and Jon senior ever discuss Our Destiny or campaign strategy? Heavens no, of course not. Otherwise they could wind up in the big house for violating the coordination rules, which looked increasingly unenforceable as the 2012 big-money primary roared on. Not that it helped Huntsman, who finished a disappointing third in New Hampshire and before long bowed out altogether.

Meanwhile, the pro-Gingrich Winning Our Future super PAC was using Adelson's cash to reciprocate the thrashing that Newt had received in Iowa, taking to the South Carolina airwaves with ads that cast Romney as a coldhearted corporate raider who slashed jobs and destroyed companies so he could boost investor profits. The ads were based on a half-hour documentary called *When Mitt Romney Came to Town,* purchased by the Adelson-funded super PAC for $40,000 from an operative with ties to Rick Perry. The film featured video of Romney's lavish homes juxtaposed with interviews of laid-off workers. It accused Romney and the firm he had cofounded, Bain Capital, of "playing the system for a quick buck" and being "more ruthless than Wall Street." Its producer actually had entered talks about selling it to the pro-Huntsman super PAC Our Destiny, which was interested and got so far as bringing in its attorney to talk terms. But Our Destiny was slow to pull the trigger, perhaps leery of opening the senior Huntsman to charges of stoking anti-capitalist sentiments.

Adelson was being lobbied by Romney supporters to at least keep the super PAC ads he was funding positive. A source close to Adelson told me the casino mogul hadn't even seen *When Mitt Romney Came to Town* before Winning Our Future bought it, but that didn't stop the super PAC from posting it in full at the URL www.KingOfBain.com and splicing some of its content into devastating ads.

The attacks generated a swift backlash from Washington's GOP establishment, which was already queasy that Adelson and Friess were making a mess of Romney's coronation. On top of that, though, Republicans grumbled that the ads attacking Romney for his stewardship of Bain betrayed conservatives' faith in free markets. The ads—coinciding as they did with the Occupy Wall Street protests—helped caricature

Romney as the archetype of corporate greed. Former New Hampshire governor John Sununu, a Romney backer, went after Adelson personally: "Does he think that people don't remember when you attack 'em and pay for the attacks in a primary? Especially when one of the parties receiving that attack is the same investment community that he likes to go to to finance his expansions? There is just no common sense in this process, and you kind of feel sorry for people that aren't that bright."[27] Adelson's corporate communications director, Ron Reese, took offense, emailing to point out that his boss had risen "from humble beginnings to become one of the wealthiest people on the planet, so apparently there's still some hope for the 'not so bright.'" But the uproar from the GOP elite bothered Adelson—he told associates that he had nothing to do with the ads or the super PAC's strategy.

Whether Adelson was directly involved or not, the ads had an impact. They were credited with helping suppress the vote for Romney in South Carolina, which gave Gingrich his first primary win. As for the Adelsons, they must not have been too put off by the ads. Three days after South Carolina, Miriam Adelson donated another $5 million to Winning Our Future, which used the cash to fund a $2.2 million advertising campaign in Florida that included more attacks on Romney. The pro-Romney Restore Our Future answered back with $8.5 million of Sunshine State ads, mostly eviscerating Gingrich.

It was tough to turn on a TV in Florida without seeing an ad viciously targeting one of the GOP's wannabe presidents, and the super PACs were responsible for the vast majority. The campaigns were left trying to anticipate what their super PACs—and those of their rivals— would do next, then scrambling to respond accordingly. And many of the super PACs' moves were being salted to the personal tastes of the big donors. That meant that some of the most significant tactical decisions were being dictated not from backrooms at campaign headquarters or in Washington but from whichever corner office, yacht, or vacation home the donors of the moment happened to be occupying.

Usually, those donors—and, therefore, the big-money power—were scattered all over the country. But in the days leading up to the Florida primary, even as their candidates and super PACs were duking it out in the Sunshine State, many of the sugar daddies quietly came together for the winter Koch seminar. It started on January 29 and wrapped up three days later on the morning of the Florida presidential primary, at the Renaissance Esmeralda Resort and Spa in Indian Wells, California. The Koch operation had rented out the entire hotel, successfully preventing any media infiltration. Friess was there. So was Adelson,[28] and so was Oklahoma oil billionaire Harold Hamm, who gave about $1 million to the Romney super PAC. If only the whales could somehow have gotten together and reached a consensus on who should be the nominee, they could have ended the primary contests right then and there, and begun stockpiling cash for the general election. It didn't happen, though Friess tried. He lobbied donors—including, improbably, Adelson—to rally behind Santorum, he told me later.

Though David Koch had opened his Hamptons estate to Romney for a meet-and-greet with some of the deepest pockets in GOP politics back in 2010,[29] the Koch political operation remained mostly on the sidelines during the Republican primary—at least publicly. There was good reason for that, and it's worth stepping off the 2012 campaign trail briefly to explore at least part of their thinking. Much of it boiled down to the fact that the men the Kochs most wanted to run had chosen not to, despite the best efforts of the Kochs and their allies.

Like most brothers, Charles and David don't always agree on things. Charles Koch hasn't always been a big fan of politicians. One of the few he was keen on, Indiana congressman Mike Pence, resisted a sustained draft movement to lure him into the race. It had been organized by a former staffer named Marc Short, who was hired soon after by the Kochs. David Koch liked politics more than his brother did, and he was focused on Chris Christie, even though the New Jersey governor's in-your-face style and hawkish sensibility contrasted sharply with the Kochs' clenched-jaw reserve and non-interventionist foreign policy. Nonetheless, the two men hit it off during an early 2011 meeting in Koch's corner office on Manhattan's Madison Avenue. Koch had invited Christie to chat, and after about two hours of conversation about Christie's approach to governing, Koch was sold. He invited Christie to keynote the brothers' June 2011 seminar near Vail, Colorado, a full year before the primaries. By the time the seminar rolled around, Christie had already publicly ruled out running, but he was under heavy pressure from Koch and other GOP billionaires to reconsider. So, despite a hectic schedule, Christie quietly jetted into Vail for the Koch seminar after a Sunday morning interview on NBC's *Meet the Press,* where the host accepted Christie's previous statements forgoing the race and asked if he might consider being someone's vice presidential pick. Christie said he wouldn't, but the billionaires at the Koch seminar later that day were less willing to take no for an answer.

At the carefully guarded Vail seminar, David Koch introduced Christie as "a true political hero." Then he nudged him a bit more, saying, "Someday we might see him on a larger stage where, God knows, he is desperately needed." During Christie's speech, Minnesota media mogul Stan Hubbard thought, "This guy can connect,"[30] and he used the post-speech question-and-answer session to pick up where Koch had left off. "You're the first guy that I've seen who I know could beat Barack Obama," Hubbard said to loud cheers and whistles, "and if you love your country as I think you do then you'll rethink what you've said."[31] Christie shut Hubbard down—demanding, "Next question!"—but the billionaire wasn't satisfied. After the last of the questions, Hubbard hustled over to intercept Christie as he was headed for the door, and pressed him further on a 2012 bid. "You know, I made a commitment to New Jersey, and I'm a man of my word," the governor responded,[32] then left the hotel and was whisked off to the airport.

But some of the billionaires still weren't willing to give it up. Three weeks after the Koch seminar, venture capitalist Ken Langone summoned Christie to a private Manhattan club where about fifty major Republican donors and power brokers were waiting. Others, including David Koch and Hubbard, were participating via conference call. It had the feel of an intervention, and it lasted more than an hour.[33] "We wanted to convince this guy to run for president and show him that we could really give some good backing for him," Hubbard told me later.[34] Langone told Christie, "Everyone in this room will raise every dollar you need."[35] Finally the conservative icon Henry Kissinger, then 88, rose and ambled to the front of the room with the help of a cane and said to Christie, "Being a successful president is about two things, courage and character. . . . You have both and your country needs you."[36]

Christie professed humility, but he didn't budge. Still, he left the distinct impression that a 2016 run was in the cards. Some donors came away thinking 2012 might still be in the offing.

Exactly one week after the meeting, a mysterious Koch-linked 501(c)(4) nonprofit group launched an effort to draft Christie into the race. Puzzlingly, Koch spokesman Rob Tappan told me he was not familiar with the group, Americans for Responsible Leadership, despite the fact that it received a majority of its $1.8 million 2011 budget from another mysterious nonprofit, the Center to Protect Patient Rights, which was run by the Kochs' top political operative Sean Noble and was used as a conduit to steer cash from Koch seminar participants to Koch-backed groups. On October 2, Americans for Responsible Leadership released a slick advertisement urging Christie to "get the hell in the race."

Despite, or maybe because of, the coordinated pressure, Christie called a press conference two days after the ad release to publicly reaffirm his original position. "Now is not my time. I have a commitment to the people of New Jersey that I simply will not abandon," he said.[37]

When the Kochs' January 2012 seminar rolled around, it found the mega-donors still in their respective camps, with no Chris Christie–like white knight to bring them together. On the night the conference wrapped, on the other side of the country, Romney clinched the Florida primary on the strength of a superior ground game and a costly super PAC assault on Gingrich and Santorum. Even then, though, Santorum and Gingrich wouldn't go away. Nor did they have to, as long as Friess kept the spigots open for Santorum, and Adelson did the same for Gingrich.

A day before the next contest, in Nevada, Romney paid a visit to Adelson's office at the Venetian to make the case himself.[38] At this point, the message that had been coming from Adelson's allies was simple but not comforting: if and when Romney won the nomination, he'd get Sheldon's support, but as long as Newt was in the race, that was where the billionaire's loyalties lay. As if to drive home the point, Gingrich also had stopped by the Venetian to see Adelson earlier the same day.[39] Apparently he was more successful than Romney. Even though Gingrich came in a distant second to Romney in Adelson's home state, two weeks later Adelson and his wife wrote matching $2.5 million checks to the Gingrich super PAC. Romney's Jewish donors urged Adelson to stop, and at various junctures, news outlets including the *New York Times* and Bloomberg reported that Adelson was signaling he would stand down.[40] But those who had worked with the headstrong casino mogul suspected that pressuring him would backfire, and it did. Adelson continued dispensing the big checks, impervious to—or maybe fueled by—the criticism. Establishment Republicans cringed. They were concerned, and for good reason: while Obama sat unopposed, Romney was getting beaten up by his own party. He was absorbing hits and tacking right to fend off Gingrich and Santorum, and he was growing progressively weaker for the general election as a result.

The thinking was that if Romney could muster a strong showing in the next contests—a February 7 trio in Colorado, Minnesota, and Missouri—he could force Gingrich and Santorum to quit, or at least compel their mega-donors to stand down. But the Red White and Blue Fund was advertising heavily for Santorum, and the candidate was making sure his sugar daddy felt the love back. At one point on the trail, Santorum called Friess "someone who I enjoy the company of," someone "who I talk to, who gives me plenty of advice on how I say it and what I say, someone who's been involved in a lot of public policy issues that I've been involved in for years." Pressed by reporters on the propriety of such a major super PAC donor being so involved in the campaign, Santorum added, "We never ever begin to broach the topic of what the super PAC is or does or what he does or is with it. That to me is a completely walled-off area." When Santorum scored a resounding sweep of the February 7 contests, he took the stage in St. Charles, Missouri—with Friess standing behind him—and declared "a victory for the voices of our party, conservatives and Tea Party people." The sweep guaranteed at least another three weeks of damaging battles with Romney before the next contests in Arizona and Michigan.

Santorum was starting to attract interest from other rich Republicans, and he was demonstrating that he knew a thing or two about the art of donor maintenance, mimicking Romney and Gingrich by making time in his hectic campaign schedule to court rich supporters. Annette Simmons, the wife of Dallas leveraged-buyout billionaire Harold

Simmons, had never been a huge political giver in her own right, but as the primaries wore on, she started thinking Santorum was "the kind of man I would want to be president."[41] So after his February 7 sweep, her husband, who had already donated $1 million each to the super PACs supporting Rick Perry and Newt Gingrich, called Karl Rove and asked whether it was "worth investing" in the pro-Santorum Red White and Blue Fund. "Does he have a chance?" Simmons reportedly asked Rove, who responded, "I wouldn't count him out."[42] So on February 15, Annette Simmons donated $1 million to Red White and Blue. A couple of days later, Santorum, accompanied by his wife, Karen Santorum, and three of his children, visited the Simmonses in Dallas to express their appreciation. "We had about an hour and a half visit," Annette Simmons said. "I liked him even more after that."[43] Around the same time, Santorum was the featured guest at a fund-raiser for the super PAC at a Dallas country club, and gave about twenty-five donors a behind-the-scenes glimpse of the campaign.[44]

Romney won the Arizona and Michigan primaries on February 28. In any other year, that probably would have been enough to end it. But not in the year of the billionaires' primary—not with Adelson and Friess still reaching for their checkbooks. On and on it went, with Santorum winning just enough states to claim a credible rationale for continuing his campaign and Gingrich floundering but refusing to quit. By the time Santorum finally suspended his campaign on April 10 amid mounting debt, Friess had donated $2.1 million to supportive super PACs, helping Santorum win eleven contests and 202 delegates to the national convention. Gingrich kept going for another three weeks before mercifully declaring an end to a campaign he called a "truly wild ride." He singled out Adelson and his family for a special thank-you, as well he might. The family's final tally? More than the $20 million that Sheldon Adelson had ardently denied months earlier.* Once it was

_____

*In fairness, the final $5 million came from Miriam Adelson on March 21—so late as to be completely useless—and was ultimately returned, putting the family's final tally to the pro-Gingrich Winning Our Future super PAC at roughly $15 million.

finally over, both Adelson and Friess quickly pledged their support to Romney, which they backed up with contributions to the pro-Romney super PAC. But their most lasting—if unintentional—contribution to the 2012 election may have already occurred by that point: the damage they inflicted on their party's nominee, Mitt Romney.

CHAPTER 6

The Big-Money
Prototype Candidate

Mitt Romney may have come across as an awkward stiff before crowds at VFW halls or county fairs, but put him in a hotel banquet room full of rich Republicans and he blossomed. And why wouldn't he? He was an idealized version of what his audience aspired to be—tall, fit, and handsome, with abundant dark hair, a prestigious pedigree, a large and photogenic family, and a $250 million fortune[1] that stacked up pretty well against those of many of his wealthiest backers. He'd made his millions in management consulting and private equity, and his startlingly effective approach to political fund-raising borrowed heavily from those worlds. Just like in management consulting, he knew the precise words needed to break through to his audience. And, just like in private equity, he started with the biggest whales, knowing that they made the best early investors, both because they could single-handedly write the largest checks and because their reputations would compel others to follow suit.

"He knows what he's doing when it comes to getting people to come out and raise money," Frank VanderSloot, a wealthy Idaho businessman, told me early in the general election, after he'd held a high-dollar Romney event and been named a national finance cochair for the campaign. "The big donors are the places to go to get money quickly."[2]

Once Romney was in the room, he also knew how to close a deal. The billionaire Home Depot investor Ken Langone was among the leaders of the movement to lure New Jersey governor Chris Christie into the race, but when Christie begged off, Langone agreed to meet in his Park Avenue office with Romney. "I didn't look or talk to him any differently than a guy coming in here pitching me on a start-up company," Langone said of his hour-long sit-down with Romney. "They are exactly the same. I am investing in a person."[3]

When it comes to big-time politics, there have always been two campaigns running side by side, yet totally separate from each other. One is a public campaign for voters, the people who ultimately decide the election. The other is a private campaign for donors, the people who fund it. If ever there was a candidate lacking in one race but exceptional in the other, it was Mitt Romney. His campaign was the grand experiment of the *Citizens United* era, testing a key proposition in this new world: could a campaign geared toward the donor track achieve success without generating a backlash from the voter track?

It wasn't just that Romney clicked easily with wealthy donors. The primary focus of some of Romney's closest aides—the ones that he'd brought along from his first forays into public life—was honing the sophisticated, cutting-edge methodology that he and his confidants applied to high-dollar fund-raising. They were constantly pushing the frontiers of election rules, and taking donor-stroking to new levels. The Romney finance operation was so aggressive and solicitous that it might even have elicited blushes from the masters of the craft, folks like Presidents George W. Bush and Bill Clinton. For most politicians, fund-raising and donor maintenance were unenviable but necessary chores. For Team Romney, they often seemed more like a raison d'être.

The fixation on big donors—targeting them, coddling them, telling them what they wanted to hear—would eventually backfire in a major way for Romney, colliding head-on with a populist strain coursing through the electorate. But it had also helped get Romney further than many political observers thought an awkward, rich Mormon candidate could ever go—all the way to the Republican nomination. Headed into the general election, it appeared that Team Romney might just be able to harness the rising power of these big donors and ride right into the White House. Romney was, in many ways, the prototype candidate for the big-money era—but also, in some ways, a victim of it.

Willard Mitt Romney was born into money, but he had a complicated relationship with it. His father, George Romney, had deep connections to wealthy players in Republican circles and the Mormon Church.
He was no pauper himself, having served as CEO of Detroit's American
Motors Corporation for eight years. He led the cluster of Mormon
congregations in and around Detroit, and the family's circle of Mormon friends included the Marriotts of hotel-chain fame, after whose
patriarch—the late John Willard Marriott—Mitt Romney was named
(his full name is Willard Mitt Romney). The Romneys moved to the
affluent Detroit suburb of Bloomfield Hills when Mitt, the youngest of
four siblings, was a tyke. In seventh grade, Romney's parents enrolled
him in Bloomfield Hills's prestigious Cranbrook prep school, where
the wealthiest families in the area sent their children.[4] When George
Romney was elected Michigan governor in 1962, young Mitt went off
to board at Cranbrook, becoming engaged to Ann Lois Davies, a student at Cranbrook's sister school, around the time he graduated. He
enrolled in Stanford but left after one year for a two-and-a-half-year
Mormon mission in France, then returned to the States, enrolled at
Brigham Young University, married Ann, and started a family. From
Utah, he and his young family were off to Boston, where he earned
business and law degrees from Harvard and transitioned immediately
after graduation into a lucrative career as a management consultant,
helping companies devise and implement new ways around old problems and beginning to compile his own fortune.

His contacts from private equity and the Mormon Church would
become critical pieces of the political finance operation he soon started
building. It anticipated—years before *Citizens United* appeared on
court dockets—the importance of maintaining multiple networks of
rich supporters. Its roots began taking hold during Romney's first
foray into public life, at the helm of the 2002 Winter Olympics in Salt
Lake City. He had become wildly successful in the cloistered board-
rooms where private equity deals get done, and was looking to try his
hand at something higher-profile and more civic-minded, so he leapt
when in 1999 he was recruited to help save the US Olympic Organizing Committee, which had been rocked by a bribery scandal and was
running a deficit of nearly $400 million.[5] Like a consultant brought

in to restructure a failing business, Romney slashed costs, streamlined processes, and shuffled the leadership. Perhaps most important, he won new Olympic sponsors and boosted commitments from existing ones. In the process, he made a name for himself and also forged connections with deep-pocketed benefactors who would form the foundation of the national fund-raising network that would propel Romney's future in politics.

He also met Spencer Zwick, a Brigham Young University student who would come to personify—almost as much as Romney himself—his sophisticated approach to fund-raising. Zwick, the son of a wealthy businessman who held a high-ranking post within the Mormon Church, was fluent in Portuguese, Spanish, and Thai,[6] and he had volunteered to translate documents for the Olympic organizing committee. He impressed Romney, and soon Romney recruited Zwick to be his personal assistant. Zwick became so close to the Romney family that he was sometimes referred to as the Romneys' "sixth son"—a characterization that seemed to fit not only because of the sheer amount of time he spent with the Romneys but also because he looked and acted just like the rest, with his dark, slickly parted hair, crisply tailored suits, aw-shucks demeanor, and tendency to speak like a management consultant. Of course, he dismissed the sixth-son references with bashful grace.

Less than a month after the closing ceremonies of the 2002 winter games, which were an unquestioned success and for which Romney won much of the credit, Romney declared his candidacy for the governorship of Massachusetts, and Zwick went along for the ride. Romney parlayed his Olympic network into a vehicle for raising campaign funds, but he also spent $6 million of his own cash. When the votes were counted, he was governor of Massachusetts—his first and only general electoral victory—whereupon he installed Zwick, still only twenty-three, as chief operating officer in the governor's office. Romney had bigger plans for his political operation, though, and for Zwick. It wasn't long before the new governor pulled aside Zwick, who had no high-dollar political fund-raising experience, and made clear the scope and urgency of his ambition. "I'm thinking about running for president. Would you leave the state offices and go figure out what we need to do to begin a process, an exploratory process, to run for president?"[7] In the summer of 2004, scarcely eighteen months after taking the oath of office as governor and well before there was any buzz about him as potential presidential timber, Romney quietly launched the Commonwealth PAC, a complex multistate political fund-raising apparatus. The ostensible purpose was to raise money to support like-minded candidates, which it did rather effectively. But the unstated mission of Zwick, then twenty-four, and the Commonwealth PAC was to build the foundation of a 2008 presidential campaign.

Zwick set up his own fund-raising company, SJZ, to hire fund-raising subcontractors and pay commissions. Enlisting the help of the envelope-pushing election lawyer Ben Ginsberg, Zwick and his team registered versions of the Commonwealth PAC in six states—half of which didn't have any contribution limits. Together, the Commonwealth PACs constituted a sort of ad hoc super PAC that allowed a handful of rich backers to finance a below-the-radar political operation even before there was an actual campaign.

It was during this period that I first caught wind of what Romney and Zwick were quietly building, and quickly realized it had the makings of a campaign cash juggernaut. Taken together, the PACs created an under-the-radar architecture with an explicit purpose: to support a political staff and travel schedule for Romney, and allow him to build alliances with additional donors and other politicians—all in preparation for an expected presidential campaign and all free from federal limits on fund-raising. It was impressive. They were masterfully set up to operate in the vacuum between state and federal law. They complied with the letter of both, but advocates of reducing the role of money in politics—the tribe of so-called goo-goos from which Obama hailed—were outraged. To them it seemed that Romney was raising cash beyond the federal contribution limits in order to prepare for a presidential campaign that would be bound by the limits.

When I put that criticism to Ben Ginsberg, he rejected it with characteristic bluntness. "That's a real Washington view of things," he told me at the time. "Anybody who says that ought to get their head out of their Washington ass." Ginsberg is a swashbuckling lawyer who gained prominence as one of the key strategists during Florida's contentious 2000 presidential recount. Through his work with the Commonwealth

PACs, Ginsberg became a key Romney insider, charting a bold path that cast a searchlight on all potential paths to campaign cash. Romney jockeyed his way into the leadership of the Republican Governors Association (RGA) just as the Commonwealth PACs were ramping up operations. The RGA paid for him to travel the nation campaigning for the party's gubernatorial candidates, gaining him exposure to key politicians and donors across the country. Romney made the most of it. In 2005, when he was vice chairman of the RGA, he and Zwick paid a visit to the Houston home builder Bob Perry (now deceased), who was at the time a top donor to the George W. Bush–era GOP establishment. Perry wasn't easily impressed by politicians and mostly shunned the inaugural balls and closed-door retreats offered to mega-donors.

Whatever it was Romney said, Perry clearly sensed that the man he was meeting had ambitions beyond the liberal bastion of Massachusetts. Perry asked Romney flat out: "Mitt, are you going to run for president?"[8] Romney's answer must have been impressive, because Perry wrote six checks totaling more than $2 million to the RGA over the course of 2006, when Romney chaired the governors association. Then, four days before the election, Perry wrote three checks totaling nearly $90,000 to the Commonwealth PACs in Alabama, Michigan, and South Carolina. In all, the state-based Commonwealth PACs, combined with a federal political action committee by the same name, raised more than $8.75 million while Romney was governor. The PACs used the cash to hire political staff and make contributions to down-ballot candidates who might make strong allies in a presidential campaign—all while helping Mitt raise his political profile. Almost always, Zwick was by his side.

On January 3, 2007—a day before his term as governor expired—Romney registered a presidential exploratory committee with the Federal Election Commission. Zwick was made national finance director. He was twenty-seven, the youngest person to hold that position for a presidential campaign. Though he was technically a contractor being paid through the SJZ limited partnership he had set up, Zwick was responsible for creating and managing a team of a hundred senior executives and seventy-five staff, imploring them to focus on numerical goals, just like a business would. "If we can't measure it, we can't manage it," he told them. "The numbers don't lie."[9]

Five days after the announcement, Romney and Zwick put on a shock-and-awe fund-raising display that showed off the potency of what they had created, staging an all-day call-a-thon that raised $6.5 million for the nascent campaign. The exploratory committee had rented out the brand-new Boston Convention and Exhibition Center for the event and invited wealthy and well-connected supporters to make calls—including Jon Huntsman Sr., Meg Whitman (then CEO of eBay), and Missouri governor Matt Blunt. Each caller brought his or her own list of associates or supporters and was provided with a phone line and a laptop equipped with Romney and Zwick's secret weapon— a patented software system called ComMITT that used telemarketing technology to build and track contribution bundling networks. Developed by campaign techies under Zwick's oversight, ComMITT enabled donors to easily solicit donations from their friends and associates using information contained in their email contacts or online social networks—all of which fed automatically back to the campaign, allowing it to keep a real-time running tally of the pledges and to build out its growing donor database. The impressive final tally led Romney to declare to his prestigious telemarketing corps, "This is the most advanced technology ever employed as a fund-raising effort,"[10] which it may well have been. Either way, it marked Romney as a force in the race, despite higher-profile rivals like John McCain and Rudy Giuliani. In big-money circles, credit went to Zwick.

Yet even as Zwick was planning how to use ComMITT to vacuum up as many $2,300 contributions (the maximum one individual could give) as possible, he was also plotting how Romney could benefit from much bigger money. Unbeknownst to anyone beyond Romney's inner circle until now, a few top Romney aides quietly dispatched a thirty-something operative named Phil Musser to set up a big-money outside spending outfit to boost Romney. Musser, who had been executive director of the RGA under Romney, retained a lawyer and drew up filings to create a group called Turnaround America, to be registered under section 527 of the tax code. The idea was to raise huge sums from Romney's richest backers to spend on television ads boosting Romney or, more likely, ripping his GOP primary opponents—all done completely independently of the campaign. It was a bold plan for which there was no real precedent or clear legal authority. Think of it as a pre–*Citizens United* super PAC. Musser laid it all out in a PowerPoint presentation, and he spent a few months crisscrossing the country on his own dime, delivering it to Romney's richest backers. Several liked the plan and made tentative commitments. But most got cold feet after they checked with their lawyers, who explained that it could expose them to legal risk. The plan was too far ahead of its time, and Musser scrapped it before he ever filed the paperwork, leaving no trace that more than two years before the *Citizens United* decision Romney's allies had foreseen the power of what would become super PACs. Romney's official campaign operation was a model of fund-raising efficiency, pulling in $60 million, to which the candidate added another $45 million from his own pocket. Even without his own contribution, he brought in more cash than anyone in the field other than the man who would become the party's nominee, John McCain. While McCain's campaign looked like chaos compared to Romney's smooth-running operation, the Arizona senator connected with voters in a way Romney did not. Mitt dropped out of the race and endorsed McCain after the February 5, 2008, Super Tuesday contests left McCain with a commanding lead in the delegate race.

The campaign left Romney insiders wondering whether they could have won if only they'd been able to apply their organizational and fund-raising prowess to the big-money world. They vowed that if Romney ran again, a prospect he seemed to be leaning toward, they wouldn't be left asking the same question. Even as Zwick helped pack up the campaign, he and his team worked to maintain and improve the fund-raising technology and network from which Romney drew his strength. By the time all the invoices were settled, Zwick's company, SJZ, had been paid more than $1 million by Romney's campaign and the Commonwealth PACs, essentially to run a privatized fund-raising shop that handled everything from planning fund-raising events to subcontracting with regional fund-raisers. Arrangements like Zwick's would become more common in the emerging big-money political economy, but Romney cut the first path.

Just as Bain Capital might when it identified a business that had failed, Romney's aides quickly and quietly moved to salvage the campaign's valuable assets—its large donor network and ComMITT fund-raising system. Zwick helped launch a private Boston-based company called BlueSwarm to take the new fund-raising model private. By the 2010 campaign, BlueSwarm's executives were boasting that it had helped candidates raise more than $150 million. BlueSwarm was being used by a third of all gubernatorial candidates and half of all US Senate candidates, including the campaigns of emerging Republican stars Marco Rubio of Florida[11] and Rob Portman of Ohio.[12]

Zwick didn't invest in the company, but he found an innovative way to make a living while staying connected to the wealthy donors who powered Romney's 2008 bid and would be key to any future political endeavors. About two weeks after Romney ended his 2008 presidential campaign, Zwick joined with Romney's son Tagg and a third partner to launch a private equity fund called Solamere Capital. It was named for a private community in Deer Valley, Utah, where the Romneys owned a ski chalet. Solamere's partners began hitting up some of Romney's biggest campaign supporters to invest in the fund, quickly raising tens of millions in private equity, including $10 million from Mitt Romney himself, who advised the fund. Zwick, who by this point had young children, upgraded from his $1.5 million Boston condo, moving into a $2.7 million five-bedroom house in the affluent Boston suburb of Wellesley.

Within two years, Solamere had accumulated $244 million from sixty-four investors. Zwick and his partners were in position to reap at least $16.8 million in fees over the first six years of the fund, according to a Securities and Exchange Commission disclosure. Solamere invested in other funds, including many run by major Romney donors.

Solamere was sort of a privatized version of the Romney fund-raising network, and Zwick kept the motor idling during the wait for a possible 2012 encore performance. In truth, there was very little intermission. Less than three months after Romney ended his 2008 campaign—and more than six months before John McCain would lose to Obama—Zwick's team had relaunched the public fund-raising side, resurrecting the old Commonwealth PAC network and rebranding it Free and Strong America. The funds it raised paid for Romney to continue to fly around the country meeting with prospective donors one-on-one, while paying SJZ hundreds of thousands of dollars for Zwick's help.

But the biggest boost to Romney was one that his operation had nothing to do with—the 2010 federal court decisions in the *Citizens United* and *SpeechNow* cases. They wiped away the legal uncertainties that had prevented Musser from fully tapping the resources of all those big donors Romney and Zwick had so assiduously courted. And so in the months after the decisions, some of Romney's closest aides began discussions about how to create a big-money outfit to capitalize on the new landscape. The consensus was that they should form a super PAC exclusively dedicated to Romney—one that would have his blessing and be operated by his people, with the sole purpose of soliciting huge checks from his donors, unrestricted by the campaign contribution limits, to boost his presidential campaign, starting in the primaries. It would be the first such super PAC. Those that emerged as players in the 2010 midterms were broadly focused on electing Democrats or Republicans to congress, not on any specific candidate.

The goo-goos might argue—as they eventually did—that the idea Romney's aides were discussing violated the spirit of campaign rules, allowing candidates to "massively evade and circumvent candidate contribution restrictions," as one goo-goo group put it.[13] After all, the goo-goos reasoned, contributions given to a super PAC devoted exclusively to a single candidate are functionally indistinguishable from contributions given directly to that candidate and, as such, should be capped at $5,000 per candidate in 2012. But Romney's aggressive legal advisors considered such reasoning whining by sanctimonious scolds whose efforts to clamp down on campaign spending had been dismissed by the courts as unconstitutional infringements on free speech. Complaining about super PACs now that the courts had cleared them was "a real Washington view of things," as Romney campaign lawyer Ginsberg might have said. Besides, Ginsberg and another lawyer who had worked on Romney's 2008 campaign, Charlie Spies, had gamed out the law and felt their efforts were protected by the federal court rulings.

The super PAC, by law, wouldn't be able to coordinate with Romney's campaign aides within four months of its first planned ads on Romney's behalf. So the super PAC team needed to be able to sense where the campaign might be headed, and vice versa—the better to ensure complementary efforts. The trio that was chosen was well-suited to such telepathy, having worked together on Romney's 2008 campaign. There was the lawyer Spies, who was also a savvy fund-raiser; the strategist Carl Forti, a Karl Rove protégé who had worked with Crossroads; and attack ad master Larry McCarthy, who was known for what was arguably the most devastating negative advertisement in political history—the Willie Horton ad that helped sink Michael Dukakis's 1988 presidential campaign.

Unlike in Obama's orbit, where the super PAC was an afterthought and the task of running it fell, thanklessly, to the poor schlubs who volunteered, in Romney's operation it was considered vitally important to the overall plan. Running it was a plum gig, Spies, Forti, and McCarthy were told. They had been tapped because they were considered part of the Romney family and would be able to convey to donors the sense that their super PAC was the official unofficial super PAC of Romney World. And so on October 8, 2010—more than six months before Romney officially declared his 2012 presidential campaign—Spies quietly filed papers with the Federal Election Commission to create a new super PAC called Restore Our Future. Spies drew up a memo to prospective donors explaining the new legal landscape and how donations to Restore Our Future posed no legal risk, and started rehearsing his pitch.

Just as Zwick became Romney's consigliore to big donors for the campaign, Spies became Romney's consigliore to big donors for the super PAC. Zwick's focus was getting as many donors as possible to write the maximum permissible check under the federal limits—so-called hard money. Spies's focus was a subset of those donors who had the capacity to write much, much larger checks to the super PAC, unbound by the federal limits—so-called soft money.

Spies was perfect for the task. A thick pillar of a man with a shiny bald head and a penchant for accessorizing his elegant suits with pricey Turnbull & Asser shirts and flashy pocket squares, Spies had grown up in an upper-middle-class Republican household in East Grand Rapids, Michigan, and graduated from the University of Michigan. (He still returns for Wolverines football games,[14] and for a time his cell phone ringtone was the school's fight song).[15] He met Romney when he became the top in-house lawyer to the Republican Governors Association during Romney's chairmanship. The two developed a good working rapport:

Romney admired Spies's diligent attention to the legal intricacies of the patchwork quilt of election rules in the different states, but also his willingness to push right up to the letter of the rules.[16] In 2008, Spies went all in with Romney, moving to Boston to become chief financial officer and counsel to the Romney-for-president effort. He remained part of Romney's small but loyal inner circle after Romney dropped out of the race, and he once hosted an ice cream social in the downtown Washington penthouse condo that he shared with his wife, Lisa Spies. Dubbed "Sundaes with Mitt," the get-together was officially a fund-raiser for a former Romney staffer who was running for a northern Virginia state House seat.[17] But Romney was the main attraction, donning a Häagen-Dazs apron and scooping sundaes himself.

Spies had been rising through the ranks of Republican election law and fund-raising circles. He probably would have been in line for a top spot on Romney's 2012 presidential campaign—and maybe in his White House counsel's office, if all had gone well. But there was no way he was going to displace Ben Ginsberg as Romney's top lawyer. So, sensing the possibilities *Citizens United* was creating outside the party hierarchy, Spies made his break for the bold new big-money world. He brought with him valuable connections in the mega-donor world—a rarity among lawyers. Spies's fund-raising network was an influential one, consisting mostly of wealthy Jewish Republican donors who could seriously boost a candidate's chances. Spies had converted to Judaism before marrying his wife, Lisa. She grew up in a kosher home in Milwaukee and got Charlie to attend weekly services at Washington's Orthodox Chabad synagogue.[18] Lisa was the charismatic charmer. She was even approached about appearing on the 2010 Bravo reality series *The Real Housewives of D.C.*,[19] though she turned it down—it would have flown in the face of the discretion required in the Spieses' shared line of work. (Also, more than one of the "housewives" ended up as ex-wives.)

Lisa Spies was regarded as perhaps the leading Republican fund-raiser in that niche, having long been retained by candidates and groups with a hawkish foreign policy to vacuum up cash from American Jews for whom Israel was a top voting issue. She did work for a nonprofit group called the Republican Jewish Coalition, which was freed by *Citizens United* to be more aggressive in its political activity. It was generously supported by none other than Sheldon Adelson. The signature line in Lisa Spies's emails included Mark Hanna's infamous quote about the two important things in politics: "The first is money, and I can't remember what the second one is."

Not long after Charlie Spies registered Restore Our Future in October 2010, Romney brought on Lisa to cultivate relationships with Jewish donors and leaders. She was one of Romney's first staff hires and the first staffer on any 2012 Republican presidential campaign focused exclusively on the Jewish community. Her official title was director of Jewish outreach, but the Jewish media outlet JNS.org dubbed her Romney's political *shadchan*—the Hebrew word for "matchmaker." Lisa Spies did everything from helping Romney recruit top Jewish donors like St. Louis investor Sam Fox and New York real estate lawyer Phil Rosen to arranging for kosher catering at donor events. Many of her big donors became Charlie's big donors for Restore Our Future. The Spieses had become *the* power couple of Republican Jewish money in politics. They were careful to stay within the letter of the Federal Election Commission's rules barring coordination between super PACs and campaigns or party committees, of course, but their overlapping roles were among the many arrangements in the new big-money politics that seemed to wink at the irrelevance of the rules. (One of the more revealing examples was that of Ali Lapp and her husband, John Lapp. She ran the top super PAC supporting Democratic House candidates, while he ran a Democratic Party effort doing the same, though she explained to me they abided by "a very simple rule—we don't talk about House campaigns that John is working on.")[20]

Spies and Ginsberg had determined that the red line for ending cooperation between the campaign and the super PAC was 120 days before Restore Our Future planned to air its first ads. Until that point, they decided, based on their reading of the coordination rules, Restore and the Romney campaign could remain in contact. And that's what they did, talking generally about how things might go and also agreeing that Romney wouldn't bash Restore even if it came under fire from his opponents.[21] Cementing the bond between the soft-money and hard-money operations—and demonstrating the importance that Team Romney placed on having a robust super PAC—one of the Romney campaign's lead fund-raisers, Steve Roche, during the summer of 2011 departed the campaign and joined the super PAC. And more than a month before the 120-day blackout began, federal regulators gave Spies and Ginsberg a very helpful gift. The Federal Election Commission, in trying to draw a clearer line between the campaign and outside groups, issued a ruling allowing candidates to appear at super PAC fund-raisers as long as they didn't explicitly ask for donations larger than $5,000 per year.

That was all the space Spies and Ginsberg needed. Within a few weeks, Romney had appeared at multiple Restore Our Future fund-raisers, including a July 2011 dinner party in Manhattan with hedge fund billionaire John Paulson, who had already donated $1 million to Restore Our Future, and about two dozen other Wall Street executives. Pursuant to the FEC ruling, Romney didn't directly ask for any cash for the super PAC; his boosters waited until after Romney left to reach their hand out. But Romney's presence was significant confirmation of the importance of Restore Our Future, giving it an edge over competing outside groups, including Rove's.

Just before the FEC-enforced coordination blackout began in August 2011—chosen because it was 120 days before Restore would start airing ads in the Iowa caucuses—Spies, McCarthy, and Forti met secretly in Ben Ginsberg's Washington offices with representatives from the official campaign team, including top advisors Beth Myers[22] and Peter Flaherty. They agreed that the delegate-rich Florida primary would be a firewall. If Romney hadn't secured the nomination by then, the super PAC would use its financial superiority to saturate the state's expensive airwaves with ads eviscerating any remaining rivals. Then they said their goodbyes—they wouldn't be able to gather like this until after November 7, 2012, if everything went according to plan. From that meeting on, the only time they'd run into one another would be when Spies showed up on the sidelines of Romney campaign donor events to pitch big donors on Restore.

The plan worked. Romney's campaign entered 2012 having raised $57 million, more than twice as much as the next-best fund-raising Republican candidate, Ron Paul.[23] Only 9 percent of Romney's cash came from small donors, compared to almost half for Paul.[24] Still, Obama was well ahead, having raised $132 million, half from small donors.[25] But of the groups orbiting just outside the campaigns, Spies's Restore Our Future was by far the class of the field, having pulled in $30 million, about twice the combined total of the super PACs supporting Obama and all the Republican candidates combined.[26]

Were it not for those donations to Restore Our Future—which spent the cash carpet-bombing Gingrich and Santorum in the primaries, especially in Florida—there was a good chance one of these other two candidates would have claimed the nomination. As Bill Burton, the cofounder of Obama's super PAC, put it, Romney "wouldn't be the nominee today if weren't for Charlie [Spies]" and Restore Our Future.[27] Romney, perhaps more than any presidential candidate in the post-Watergate era, was almost completely dependent on the rich—people who made roughly as much money as he did, and in many cases more. The efficiency with which the Romney/Restore inside/outside, hard-money /soft-money model vacuumed up cash was shaping up as a blueprint for presidential candidates from both parties in 2016 and beyond.

Romney needed every penny of that money as he headed into the general election. He had almost no cash left because of the extended primary struggle. In fact, Romney's campaign had to take out a $20 million loan over the summer to get through to the general election, partly because half of each large donation it had accepted could only be spent in the general election. Once the primary season was over, Romney's campaign turned its attention back to what it did best—soliciting big checks. And it was no longer just Restore that could accept them. Starting back in April when Santorum and Gingrich were on their way out, Romney's campaign had turned to a mechanism extended to presidential nominees of both parties that allowed them to accept exponentially larger donations than they could accept during the primaries—so-called joint committees that presidential nominees could form with their respective national parties. The joint committee formed by Romney for President and the RNC was called Romney Victory. During the primaries, the campaign could only accept checks as large as $2,500 per person, while Romney Victory was now able to accept contributions as large as $75,800 per person—same as the Obama campaign's joint fund-raising committee.

Romney wasted no time taking advantage of this flexibility, rewarding donors with all manner of perks and access. The more you gave, the higher you ranked and the more you got. Couples who contributed $100,000 or more were known as "Founding Partners," while those who gave $50,000 were "Founding Members." Supporters who collected from others, or "bundled," $500,000 worth of checks were known as "Stripes," while those who bundled $250,000 were "Stars." All qualifying donors would be invited to participate in weekly briefing calls with the campaign, lavish retreats the campaign was planning at tony hotels, and special guest packages at the convention. They'd get all manner of Romney-branded accessories indicating their status, as well as a dedicated campaign staffer they could call with questions—something akin to a personal broker at an investment firm. Founding Partners, according to a brochure circulated among big donors,[28] were promised recognition at the convention and on Election Night, as well as "Green Room Level" access to debates, an array of convention parties, and an election-night celebration. The most elite levels of Romney's big-donor offensive made George W. Bush's famed Ranger program look like a public radio pledge drive.

Where Romney ran into trouble was when his courtship of big donors ran afoul of the voters. Five days after Santorum dropped out, Romney was speaking to donors in the backyard of a Palm Beach, Florida, estate, and was overheard by a pair of reporters standing on a public sidewalk. He was at once more relaxed and forthright than the candidate that voters saw on TV, telling the donors that he supported the idea of scaling back or eliminating a pair of massive federal agencies that cater to the poor—the Department of Education and the Department of Housing and Urban Development—as well as a trio of tax breaks.[29] The discussion went much further than anything he'd said to voters, to whom he'd offered scant details on how he'd pay for his plans to cut income taxes and reduce federal spending. So when the reporters published Romney's remarks to the donors, Democrats sought to cast Romney as secretly plotting with wealthy backers to undercut the middle class. Romney's aides said their candidate was simply kicking around ideas, not making concrete proposals.[30]

The incident was revelatory but not particularly damaging. While it provided a look into the donor-track side of the campaign, it was soon forgotten. But a month later Romney made a return trip to South Florida for another fund-raiser—this one at the Boca Raton mansion of private equity investor Marc Leder. This time, Romney's unscripted private remarks would not only send his campaign lurching but also grimly define him to middle-class voters. The event was secretly recorded by a bartender working the fund-raiser. One exchange in particular was interpreted as proving that Romney regarded his base—the 1 percent—as fundamentally superior to the 99 percent. When the liberal magazine *Mother Jones* published the video months later,[31] it turned what was among Romney's greatest strengths— his instinctive connection with the ultra-rich—into one of his greatest weakness.

One of the donors in attendance was lamenting that Americans had been seduced into thinking that government would take care of them, and asked whether Romney thought he could convince people to take care of themselves. "There are 47 percent of the people who will vote for the president no matter what," Romney began. The 47 percent, in Romney's telling, were those "who are dependent upon government, who believe that they are victims, who believe that government has a responsibility to care for them, who believe that they are entitled to health care, to food, to housing, to you name it." They "are people who pay no income tax. Forty-seven percent of Americans pay no income tax. So our message of low taxes doesn't connect." And then he added a line that did more to sink his presidential hopes than any other he uttered in his entire political career: "So my job is not to worry about those people—I'll never convince them that they should take personal responsibility and care for their lives."[32]

Democrats pounced, seizing on the comments as smoking-gun proof that Romney didn't care about average Americans struggling to get by. Both the Obama campaign and the supportive Priorities USA super PAC quickly produced ads incorporating a clip of the offending words. A particularly biting Priorities radio ad, produced with the government employee union AFSCME, declared that Romney had attacked "150 million Americans—seniors, veterans, the disabled . . . when he thought no one else was listening."[33]

In a press conference the night the video was posted, Romney tried to sand the edges off his comments, but he didn't entirely back away from them. "It's not elegantly stated, let me put it that way. I'm speaking off the cuff in response to a question and I'm sure I can state it more clearly and in a more effective way than I did in a setting like that."[34]

The chattering classes spent countless cable hours and online inches dissecting the 47 percent remark, puzzling over how Romney could say something so insensitive. But as I watched the clip and read the transcript, it dawned on me that this was just another example of the candidate performing in that other campaign—the donor campaign, which targets an audience that has a relationship to money similar to his own. The 47 percent remark felt like the kind of assessment a fund manager would make to his investors as he sold them a new product, and when viewed through that prism, the whole recording made much more sense.

One audience member, whom on the tape Romney called George (he seemed to be on a first-name basis with most of the folks in the room), noted that Romney had traveled the country talking to all kinds of people, "perhaps people with different backgrounds [than] people in this room," and wondered, "To what extent do people understand the severity of the fiscal situation we're in? Do people get it?" Without missing a beat, Romney told George, "They don't," then, surveying the splendor of his host's home, added, "It's like, I mean, there won't be any houses like this if we stay on the road we're on."[35]

Another donor demanded to know why Romney didn't stick up for himself: "To me, you should be so proud of your wealth. That's what we all aspire to be—we kill ourselves, we don't work a nine-to-five. We're away from our families five days a week. I'm away from my four girls five days a week and my wife. Why not stick up for yourself and say, 'Why is it bad to be, to aspire to be wealthy and successful?' You know, 'Why is it bad to kill yourself?'" Romney protested that he did defend "success in America and dreamers and so forth" in every stump speech. "And the Republican audience that I typically speak to applauds," he

said. "But in terms of what gets through to the American consciousness, that's—I have very little influence on that in this stage." Romney
and his assembled donors were at odds with the American consciousness, by his own admission.

The donors were impatient: what, one asked, could they do to convince women, Hispanics, and college students to support Romney? Sen-
sibly, the candidate demurred, urging them to simply raise millions of
dollars. Someone else asked why they couldn't go out and actually make
the case themselves. Romney deflected again, telling them to stay put,
that it was his job to make the case. Then a donor asked how Romney
might "duplicate" a scenario like the Iranian hostage crisis, which was
seen as working in Ronald Reagan's favor during his 1980 campaign
against President Jimmy Carter. And so on—veering ever further into
the realm of the absurd. It was no wonder why Romney tried to keep
the two worlds separate.

The Obama campaign, sensing that it could use Romney's big-
money supporters against him, extended its attacks beyond Romney
to the donors themselves. It posted an item on its campaign website
singling out eight major Romney donors as having "less-than-reputable
records." This prompted howls and accusations of McCarthyism from
the right, where the picked-on donors became something of a cause
célèbre.

"This idea of giving public beatings has been around for a long
time," one of the donors, Frank VanderSloot, told me. A wealthy Idaho
businessman who donated $1.1 million in corporate cash to Restore
Our Future, he also raised between $2 million and $5 million for the
Romney campaign, qualifying him as a national finance cochairman.
The Obama website touted an article in the liberal magazine *Mother
Jones* suggesting that VanderSloot was anti-gay and citing his support
for an "ultimately unsuccessful effort to force Idaho Public Television
to cancel a program that showed gays and lesbians in a favorable light
to school children."[36] VanderSloot objected strenuously, siccing his lawyer on *Mother Jones,* which issued multiple corrections. But that wasn't
good enough. He also sued for defamation and launched a major public relations campaign to push back against the allegations—and the
Obama campaign.

In a series of appearances on Fox News, VanderSloot said his health and home products company, Melaleuca, had lost hundreds of customers, and suggested Obama might be using the power of the government to target Romney donors. Behind the scenes, VanderSloot quietly embarked on a less confrontational form of damage control. He arranged conference calls with customers to explain his stance on gay rights issues, and he had one of his openly gay business associates set up a meeting for him to try to make peace with executives from the Human Rights Campaign (HRC), a leading gay rights group. That group had blasted out a press release calling on Romney "to fire his National Finance Chair Frank VanderSloot who has a long history of anti-LGBT extremism." The release included a link to a petition urging Romney to dismiss VanderSloot and return any cash raised by him, as well as a scathing quote from an HRC executive named Fred Sainz, who called VanderSloot "a bully who uses his vast resources to vilify and demonize lesbian, gay, bisexual and transgender people."[37]

The meeting was off the record, VanderSloot told me, "so I can't tell you what happened there." Generally, though, he said Sainz and the other HRC officials in the meeting "were cordial, very accommodating. I think I came away with some better understandings of them and they came away with some better understandings of me and my position." VanderSloot found himself thinking, "We want solutions to the same problems. We may not be in total agreement. We're almost in agreement with what those solutions would be."[38] Hardly, said Sainz, who told me VanderSloot's "public conduct can and should rightly be perceived as homophobic and inconsistent with the American values of equality for all. That's why we were a bit surprised when Mr. VanderSloot approached us about a meeting. He believed that he has been misunderstood. It turns out that Mr. VanderSloot wasn't misunderstood at all. As is his prerogative, he was able to rationalize all of his various actions over the years and still contend that he's not anti-gay. We didn't buy it—any of it."

VanderSloot was a bit taken aback by Sainz's characterization. "Fortunately, none of my gay friends have ever categorized me as a homophobe," he told me later, though he conceded that he could see why someone who read the *Mother Jones* story might. "Inaccurate or untruthful stories by politically motivated media can unjustly destroy lives and reputations," he said, to explain why he sued the magazine. The attention also emboldened VanderSloot to get more involved in Romney's campaign, a representative of which talked to him about how he was holding up.

Romney's finance operation had a way of making donors feel valued, like they were part of the team, their ideas were being taken seriously, and their cash was being well spent. A perfect example of the Romney style of donor maintenance—as well as the symbiosis between Restore Our Future and the campaign—was a late June 2012 donor retreat, organized by Romney for President. This bit of donor coddling was a remarkable production. The campaign invited its Founding Partners, Members, Stripes, and Stars—a group that reached into the hundreds—to a three-day weekend at Deer Valley. Upon arrival, the donors received tote bags from the preppy outfitter Vineyard Vines, branded with Romney's "Believe in America" campaign slogan and containing a Romney baseball cap and pins designating donation levels. Each of the hundreds of donors received a handwritten note from Zwick welcoming them to the event.

Call it Romney-palooza. The weekend kicked off with an evening cookout at Utah Olympic Park, which sits atop a mountain overlooking Park City, and featured a welcoming talk in which Romney spoke emotionally about his family under a tent adorned with chandeliers as the sun set against the mountains. The remarks were "very moving" and "gave you a really good glimpse at the personal Mitt Romney," one donor who was there told Bloomberg News.[39] Romney was on his game, greeting donors by name at the cookout, schmoozing with them after a morning speech by John McCain, and fielding their questions after panels on finance and health care.[40] Donors got face time with several party luminaries—senators and governors as well as RNC chairman Reince Priebus, former Florida governor Jeb Bush, Karl Rove, and former secretaries of state Condoleezza Rice and James Baker. The level of access made even seasoned donors giddy. One called a lunchtime speech by Rice "one of the best speeches I've ever heard,"[41] while another gushed about Baker's speech, comparing him to U2 frontman Bono.[42]

It was a faux political war room for very rich activists. On Saturday, they were invited to listen in on the campaign's normal weekly briefing session, including top Romney strategists Katie Packer Gage, Eric Feh-rnstrom, Beth Myers, Rich Beeson, and Neil Newhouse.[43] And such access was what these donors now expected. "We need one-on-one time with the people who make decisions," is how a Florida doctor named David Wish put it to the *New York Times* just before buttonholing Feh-rnstrom to chat.[44]

Along the sidelines, Spies was working the donors on behalf of Re-store Our Future. Rove, meanwhile, put in an appearance, too, raising the hackles of goo-goos who suggested improper coordination between Crossroads and the campaign. A group of bankers gushed about having had the chance to talk electoral math with Rove one night on a hotel balcony. "That's the price of admission right there," one of the banker types said, according to a *New York Times* reporter who overheard the conversation. "Your six minutes with Rove."[45] Everyone seemed happy and confident of success.

Some 750 miles away there was another big-money force that wasn't as gaga for Romney. On the same weekend as Park City, the Koch brothers were holding their annual summer donor seminar in San Di-ego. Some of the donors—as well as Virginia governor Bob McDon-nell[46]—stopped by both. (Passage between Park City and San Diego is a lot easier when you have access to a private jet.) Koch guests were greeted by heavy security and slickly produced signs and packets dub-bing the seminar "Path to Freedom."[47]

The Koch operation had remained publicly neutral in the primaries, and while it had certainly spent heavily attacking Obama and his Dem-ocratic congressional allies, its plans for the general election weren't completely clear. It was a sign of the times that the Koch network—a collection of donors and operatives with plenty of cash but no official role in the political process—could compete on the same weekend for mega-donor attention with the campaign of a man who could become the next president. Romney loyalists considered it a show of disrespect that the brothers didn't reschedule.[48] *We appreciate their support,* the thinking went, *but we're the main attraction now.*

CHAPTER 7

The Brothers Behind
the Tea Party

In August 2012, Americans for Prosperity, the most muscular arm in the billionaire Koch brothers' sprawling political network, called a special meeting of its board of directors to vote on what it considered a major course change. Since its inception in 2004, the group had steadfastly refused to either support or oppose any specific candidate or party. Now, three months before the election, it was considering a move that would upend that doctrine. Effective immediately, pursuant to a unanimous vote by its directors,[1] Americans for Prosperity would officially oppose the reelection of Barack Obama for a second term as president of the United States. They stopped short of endorsing Mitt Romney, mind you. The decision was purely oppositional: Americans for Prosperity was against Barack Obama.

The vote went largely unnoticed. After all, for months AFP had been airing ads that sharply attacked Obama over Obamacare, the $800 billion stimulus package, and the failure of the government-subsidized solar company Solyndra. To the casual observer, the Kochs already seemed to be operating as opponents of the Obama administration. But Koch World didn't see it that way at all. Its operatives constantly pointed out that those AFP ads, tough as they might seem, were actually "issue advocacy," an election law term meaning messages that only critiqued candidates on specific issues and didn't explicitly urge a vote against them. Ads that crossed that line would be considered "express advocacy," which would have been illegal for groups like AFP to fund prior to *Citizens United.* Even after the decision, AFP had continued voluntarily adhering to its nonpartisan policy, which was central to its identity. But with the Supreme Court's decision and the board's vote, Americans for Prosperity could cross that line and use its millions to blanket swing states across the country with TV ads calling for Obama's ouster in no uncertain terms.

The vote to do so was a pivotal inflection point in the evolution of money in politics on a number of fronts. First, it made AFP among the deepest-pocketed groups to take advantage of the spending avenues afforded by *Citizens United.* Second, there were immediate repercussions for Romney and the Republican establishment, which had been eyeing the Koch network as a potential wild card. The Koch network was poised to spend as much as $400 million before Election Day[2]—a greater sum than any private political effort ever—and that cash could either make it a major booster of Republicans or a major thorn in their side. AFP's board vote pointed to the former.

Third, the vote was a victory of sorts for a faction within Koch World that for years had been pushing for more direct forays into partisan politics. By playing directly in campaigns, the argument went, the Kochs stood a better chance of ensuring that the candidates who won were those who would govern according to the libertarian-infused free market philosophies the Kochs held dear. There was an equally compelling argument on the other side, though, which held that by throwing in with a candidate or party, the Kochs would give opponents fodder to dismiss their small-government ideology as merely a thin veneer for plain old Republican boosterism. And the Kochs, their allies had long stressed, saw both parties as culpable for the country's dire fiscal state, and prided themselves on fighting reckless policy no matter which party was pushing it. Yet over the last four years, their operation had been increasingly wading into partisan politics squarely on the Republican side, at first cautiously. Koch political operatives had started coming to the table with establishment Republican shadow party operatives and groups, including Karl Rove's Crossroads network, to lend their groups' muscle to boost Republican candidates—still mostly by attacking their

Democratic rivals. The quiet coordination began tentatively in the 2008 election, blossomed in 2010, and had reached a new level at the time of the Americans for Prosperity board vote. It seemed as if parts of Koch World had concluded that sometimes the biggest impact can be had by playing within the system, not bucking it. The AFP vote to expressly oppose Obama appeared to be a conspicuous step out of the closet.

That was not the way some of the leading players in Koch World saw things.

"It was a very difficult decision for this organization," AFP president Tim Phillips said at the time,[3] calling it "unprecedented"[4] and explaining, "We don't want to do this, and I don't suspect next year you'll see us, or the next year, doing this again, or in a very limited fashion."

So why break with tradition at all? AFP's hand had been forced by Obama's agenda, the group's chairman, Art Pope, explained to me soon after the vote. "President Barack Obama is on the opposite side, I think, of every issue that Americans for Prosperity is involved with, cares about—that our grass roots care about—and we do think it is absolutely vitally important on those issues for the overall future prosperity of America, as the words used in our name, to expressly oppose the reelection of President Obama, to urge his defeat for a second term." To Pope, though, opposing Obama did not imply a broader merger with the GOP: "We really, truly are nonpartisan. And there are Republicans who have been criticized by Americans for Prosperity because of their voting records on specific issues. But I will fully acknowledge that, more often than not, it is obviously the Democrats who are on the other side of the issues."

Pope was a bona fide Koch insider, a regular at the Kochs' conferences, a major contributor to their network, and a close confidant of the brothers. He had his finger on the pulse of Koch World, and, unlike the brothers themselves, he wasn't shy about sharing his views on politics, policy, and especially campaign finance rules. Though he would often stress that he wasn't speaking for the Kochs, he offered a crucial window into the Kremlinology of their world, even if Pope's rapid-fire speaking style and marble-mouthed drawl sometimes made it difficult to follow all of his words.

Pope, in his mid-fifties, was a short, bald, energetic North Carolinian who owed his multimillion-dollar fortune to a regional chain of discount stores he had inherited from his father. He expanded the chain and used the cash to become a formidable political player in North Carolina and nationally. He wrote large checks to Americans for Prosperity and in North Carolina built his own network of conservative nonprofit groups, which eventually was credited with helping turn the state government deep red, attracting some small measure of the scorn that liberals heaped on the Koch brothers. "North Carolina's third, lesser known, Koch brother," one prominent liberal columnist dubbed him.[5] When the GOP governor Pope helped elect, Pat McCrory, tapped him as state budget director in 2013, Pope resigned from the AFP board.

Before he left the board, Pope loved to talk about the lengths to which AFP and other groups went to adhere to campaign finance rules, despite his obvious disdain for them. A lawyer by training, he generally saw the rules as infringements on the First Amendment, once telling me, "Free speech, I'm glad to say, in a positive sense, is like a balloon— you squeeze it to one side and it will balloon out on another side, and voices will be heard." To Pope, liberal critics of AFP and other groups were hypocrites trying to intimidate conservative donors like him. He was a big fan of the *Citizens United* decision, but he also took glee in noting AFP's diligence in navigating the complicated rules without ever running afoul of them. "Americans for Prosperity, like a lot of issue advocacy groups, are often under attack for walking up to the line between express advocacy and issue advocacy. So, when it comes to President Barack Obama's reelection and all the issues that we were doing, we said, 'Listen, let's go ahead and cross the line and acknowledge it and report it,'" he told me after the vote.

Pope made clear that the shift didn't apply to any of the Senate races in which the group was airing ads. And while he told me he didn't envision AFP going after other candidates as sharply as Obama, he wouldn't close the door when I pressed him. "I will never say never. But there are no present plans during this election cycle or in future election cycles to engage in express advocacy again. If you endorse a candidate, you in essence endorse everything that candidate stands for. There are some congressmen, some senators, some state legislators who we strongly support their positions on one of our issues such as health care or cap and trade, but we may actually differ with them on other issues such as earmarks or pork barrel, or that we just simply don't take positions on those issues, such as the social issues."

Immediately following the vote, AFP began a month-long $27 million advertising campaign urging viewers to defeat Obama. None of the ads mentioned Mitt Romney. Most expressed unhappiness but not anger over Obama—a tone that dovetailed with focus group results showing that voters still liked Obama personally.

Soon after the ads went up, I traveled to one key battleground where Americans for Prosperity had a particularly pronounced presence: Pope's home state of North Carolina. I wanted to see for myself how the Koch political operation was spending its stockpile of cash and to what extent it was taking advantage of the new freedom allowed by *Citizens United* and the AFP board vote.

So on a sunny Friday afternoon in the heart of the general election, I found myself among a few dozen folks waiting on the sidewalk in front of the First Baptist Church in the declining tobacco town of Smithfield, North Carolina. We were there for an Americans for Prosperity rally that the group billed as intended to educate people about "Obama's failing agenda." The crowd included two elderly women clutching small American flags, a young reporter from the Raleigh newspaper, and various curious onlookers, including a scraggly, glassy-eyed gentleman who kept asking where he could get a free T-shirt. Before long, a maroon tour bus emblazoned with the words "Obama's Failing Agenda Tour" pulled up. In smaller letters was a list of the president's purported failures—$1.7 trillion health care takeover, $16 trillion national debt, billions wasted on Solyndra and green energy scams, et cetera. There was also a giant photo of Obama's head in profile. The bus was one of three crisscrossing the country at that moment as part of an expansive—and, I imagined, expensive—tour. Together, according to AFP, they would travel a combined fifty-five thousand miles through thirty-one states, making stops at nearly four hundred events.[6]

At the Smithfield stop, a trio of officials from AFP's North Carolina office called for the repeal of Obama's health care overhaul and urged the crowd to get involved with AFP. "We need to turn this country around and that's what we're trying to do," implored a young AFP field organizer, who asked for volunteers to "go door-to-door to tell your neighbors that this isn't the right direction." During the canvassing, no one would be told whom to vote for, the organizer stressed. The disclaimer, a nod to AFP's nonpartisan branding, seemed slightly disingenuous, given that inside the doors on which canvassers knocked, televisions were carrying the group's ads urging votes against Obama. Walking a tightrope between GOP politics and free market advocacy required some artful finesse, and I was impressed by the dexterity demonstrated by even relatively junior ground troops.

I didn't hear Mitt Romney's name come up a single time at the Smithfield rally. Speakers made clear that AFP's long-term vision wasn't linked to the GOP or even the tea party. "We've been around longer than the tea party, but when the tea party started, it was like the cavalry had arrived," Chris Farr, a top AFP official in North Carolina, told the crowd. "We need more people to grow this army, so we can fight these issues," she said. A mother of three in her fifties, dressed in green yoga pants, running shoes, and a technical hoodie, Farr had been a teacher and real estate agent before going to work full-time for AFP in 2007. Since then, she'd climbed the ranks from grassroots coordinator to deputy director of the group's North Carolina chapter, one of the most robust of the thirty-two permanently staffed state operations.

All told, Americans for Prosperity employed several hundred people at the peak of the 2012 campaign—by far its highest staffing level since its inception—including field staff who mobilized voters through phone calls and knocking on doors. AFP, which claimed more than two million activists, saw itself as the conservative movement's ground troops—the right's answer to the pavement-pounding labor unions. Democrats had reason to worry about AFP. It had helped Wisconsin governor Scott Walker keep his seat in a recall election initiated by unions angry with his efforts to clamp down on their power. At the time, AFP claimed that its campaign was about "just educating folks on the importance of the [union] reforms"—not advocating for Walker or other Republicans in the recall election.[7] But, like the issue ads the group aired in the presidential race before its board vote, there was little doubt what result AFP wanted, and the recall victory emboldened AFP and Koch World. It was seen as a validation of both AFP's ground game and the power of a massive voter database, called Themis, which Pope had helped organize and into which the Koch network had sunk at least $24 million.[8] If the Koch network ever decided to challenge the Republican establishment, it certainly had the trappings of a political party that might give the GOP a good run for its money.

In fact, the Koch operation was far more sophisticated than the actual Republican Party. It was also more secretive, though, and tracing its ever-shifting contours was an ongoing challenge for me and my colleagues in the press corps, not to mention Democratic operatives, and even rival Republican ones. Each time I thought I had solved the puzzle by piecing together tax filings and other public documents, I'd discover a new nonprofit group or for-profit company that played a pivotal role of which I had been totally unaware. The basic model of the Koch operation starting in 2008 was that cash flowed from the donors who attended the twice-a-year summits to mysterious nonprofit clearinghouses with anodyne names like the Wellspring Committee or Freedom Partners Chamber of Commerce or the Center to Protect Patient Rights. From these groups, the money traveled to an array of Koch-backed organizations with equally oblique names that would target Democrats and their policies in different spaces. The leading member of the family was, of course, Americans for Prosperity, but there was the pro-fossil-fuel American Energy Alliance, the youth-engagement nonprofit Generation Opportunity, and the Latino-voter-targeting Libre Initiative, among others. Then there were nonprofits and companies that provided back-end services or support to the various groups, including the nonprofit voter-data vendor Themis and its for-profit arm i360. There was even a nonprofit called the Center for Shared Services that helped the other groups in the network with administrative functions like human resources and outfitting office space. The sprawling network spent plenty on legal fees and prided itself on complying with all relevant tax and election laws. A California Republican operative named Anthony Russo who in 2012 worked with groups in the network described them as "well-lawyered—they sort of, I assume, do things, you know, the right way." Yet the "Kochtopus"—as the many arms of the Koch network were inevitably known—was so vast and so complicated that it could cause confusion even for the operatives who worked with it. As Russo put it, "I mean, my knowledge of the Koch network is there's all kinds of groups all over the country that I wouldn't even know."[9]

One thing was for sure: the Kochtopus's ability to tap into donors emboldened by *Citizens United* and infuriated by Obama left it with plenty of money and eager for effective ways to spend it. For the first time, in 2012, AFP began paying activists to knock on doors and make phone calls to get out the vote, a traditional tactic of the labor unions, but not one widely utilized on the right. "Will work for limited government . . . and $15.00 an hour!" read an AFP email trying to recruit ground troops in Sarasota, Florida, one of many such emails forwarded to me by conservative sources who regarded the development as a distasteful professionalization of a passion-driven enterprise.

As the country headed into the general election, Koch-backed groups were active in competitive districts and states all over the country—airing ads, sending mailers, making calls, knocking on doors. It was the very picture of what I imagined a privatized political party would look like, and while it was in most ways working in support of the official Republican Party, I couldn't help but picture the battle royal that would ensue if the Kochtopus ever squared off in a campaign against the GOP establishment.

Such a battle wasn't inconceivable, judging by the anti-GOP sentiments I'd been hearing from all levels of Koch World. The day after the Smithfield rally, for instance, Farr, the AFP North Carolina official, told me, "We do not want to become a branch of the Republican Party." Farr, who would leave AFP after the election, admitted she was "shocked" by the AFP board vote to expressly oppose Obama's reelection, which she suggested brought her group uncomfortably close to the GOP.

We were walking between houses during an afternoon of door-knocking in a blue-collar suburb of Wilmington, North Carolina. Farr and her team split into two crews, each armed with a tablet equipped with an app called AFP Knocks that mapped out walk routes covering households that had been pinpointed as having at least one undecided voter. The list of addresses had been automatically generated from the Koch-backed Themis database, which contained a hundred data points for each voter culled from magazine subscription lists and other commercial data sets, as well as voter files from the state government and information AFP employees had gleaned from direct contact with targeted voters. Each target household received a phone call from an AFP phone banker. The results of that call were entered into Themis and automatically integrated into the app. The goal was both to collect more data on these households for use in this and future elections and to make in-person contact with every voter who could be identified as undecided. Once the canvasser knocked, he or she was to ask a single simple question: "Do you believe President Obama's policies have helped or hurt the economy?" The canvasser entered the answer into the tablet. If the voter thought Obama was doing a great job, that household was removed from the pool of persuadables and wouldn't be encouraged to vote. But if the voter thought Obama was leading the country down the road to ruin, he or she would be urged to get out and vote, receiving a reminder mailer or phone call closer to Election Day.

Such a system might seem pretty basic, but this type of voter mobilization—mixing cutting-edge technology with on-the-ground organizing—was key to winning elections in which only a tiny fraction of the electorate is actually in play. And it was an area in which Democrats and their allies enjoyed a huge advantage over conservatives, thanks in large part to the extensive work done by unions and their members. Themis and the Koch-backed groups had invested more in closing that gap— and were further along toward that goal—than any other operation on the right, including the RNC, so the Kochtopus's voter mobilization, while sometimes tough to track, was worth watching. Hopscotching between low-slung ranch homes in the working-class Monkey Junction neighborhood of Wilmington, Farr and a young field organizer elicited a range of reactions. "You're preaching to the choir," one man told the field organizer. "You keep going, sister."

At the next house, a woman curtly told Farr that Obama "ain't failed no worse than Reagan or Bush."

At another house, a seventy-five-year-old retiree named Fred Tedesco was napping in a rocking chair on his front porch and barely opened his eyes when Farr gingerly approach and asked the prescribed question about Obama's impact on the economy. "Are you out of your mind, asking a question like that?" Tedesco, a registered independent, asked back. "If that guy wins again, we're down the tube."

Cordelia Lewis, a sixty-eight-year-old who had just retired to Monkey Junction to be closer to her family, said she was neutral on Obama's policies. Farr, careful not to push too hard, said, "There is no doubt that he took office during a difficult time and his job isn't easy." Still, Farr left Lewis with an AFP door hanger, which she said had "some information about Obama's agenda and how it is hurting the economy."

I split off from Farr's crew and returned to Lewis's stoop alone a few minutes later. She told me—unprompted—that she planned to throw out the pamphlet because she didn't trust any group funded by the Koch brothers. I was surprised she knew who the Koch brothers were, let alone that they had helped fund AFP, but she had her information—and her opinions. She was sick of all the ads bombarding her television from big-money groups on both sides, she said. "There is an iota of truth and a whole lot of untruth," she said. "The Kochs and—what's his name, Soros?—they're giving that money because they want something."

It had come to this for the Koch brothers: the group they'd formed in an effort to keep the spotlight on free market policies and away from the brothers themselves was being rejected on a doorstep in Monkey Junction, North Carolina, by Cordelia Lewis, a retiree who knew who they were and wasn't willing to listen to AFP's free market gospel because of its links to them. The Kochs had officially become bogeymen.

It hadn't always been this way. In fact, despite having steered tens of millions of dollars to free market causes for decades, until very recently the Koch brothers were almost completely unknown outside a small but adoring band of libertarians, and an even smaller group of business analysts. On Election Day 2012, Charles was seventy-seven and David seventy-two, and their net worth was an estimated $31 billion each, tying them for the sixth spot on the *Forbes* list of the world's richest billionaires.[10] They owed their fortunes to the Wichita, Kansas–based oil and natural gas refining and transportation company that they and their two other brothers—William (David's twin) and Freddie—had inherited when their father, Fred Koch, died. Charles and David bought out their brothers' stakes in Koch Industries for $1 billion in 1983, and under Charles's stewardship, the company grew exponentially[11] through acquisitions and diversification into a wide array of businesses including chemicals, electronics, paper, and household products. At the time this book was published, Koch Industries was the second-biggest privately owned corporation in the United States and employed seventy thousand people around the world.

Charles and David embraced Austrian free market economic theories about the power of unadulterated capitalism. Not long after inheriting the company, they started donating to think tanks and advocacy groups with the goal of spreading the Austrian gospel and stripping away regulations and taxes that inhibit free enterprise, including that practiced by Koch Industries. They provided the funds to launch the nation's first libertarian think tank, the Cato Institute, in 1977, and what became the Mercatus Center at George Mason University in 1980. To start Cato they teamed with Ed Crane, who was then the national chairman of the Libertarian Party, while Mercatus was started by an academic named Rich Fink. Both men would become key players in the Kochs' political evolution, although Crane would later fall out of favor—a not uncommon occurrence in the famously temperamental Koch World.

In 1980, David Koch used his fortune to try to advance libertarian ideas by taking the Libertarian Party mainstream, getting himself tapped to be its vice presidential nominee. Koch spent $1,675,300 of his own cash on the race.[12] The campaign, with lawyer Ed Clark as the presidential nominee and Crane as communications director, adopted a classic libertarian platform. It was neutral or even left-leaning on many social issues—David Koch, for instance, expressed support for gay rights and legalizing pot[13]—and strident about slashing government spending. The ticket pledged to dismantle social security, welfare, the Federal Reserve Board, the Environmental Protection Agency, and the Securities and Exchange Commission, not to mention the Federal Election Commission and its campaign contribution limits.[14] Their ticket garnered only 1 percent of the vote, and gradually the Kochs turned their backs on the Libertarian Party and electoral politics as a whole. They considered Republicans and Democrats alike to be enablers of big government and beholden to special interests.[15] They largely floated above party politics, using their cash to fund groups and research that would show politicians of both parties the error of their ways and convince them to adopt policies grounded in the teachings of Ludwig von Mises and Friedrich Hayek.

"The Kochs only played on the Libertarian side for a long, long time," the disgraced former lobbyist Jack Abramoff[16] recalled. Abramoff had solicited big donors for an array of Republican-focused groups he started in the 1980s and 1990s, and had tried to make inroads with the Kochs. "They wouldn't come near the Republican side," he said.

Instead, they continued pouring cash into Cato, Mercatus, and other wonky think tanks and activist groups like the Institute for Justice and Citizens for a Sound Economy. Sometimes the groups' efforts to slash taxes and regulations jibed with the bottom-line interests of Koch Industries, including their fight against environmental regulations that could seriously crimp the company's fossil fuel business. Koch supporters are quick to cite their opposition to federal subsidies that their company collects as an example of a policy position that runs counter to their bottom line. Mostly, though, the brothers stayed clear of elections and rejected entreaties to come more fully into the GOP fold.

By the time George W. Bush and Karl Rove took over the Republican Party, the Kochs' libertarian-style conservatism was losing out. Republicans decided Bush's compassionate conservatism was their future after Bush and Rove helped lift the party to 2002 midterm election gains that bucked historical trends. Their focus on social issues like opposing abortion rights and gay marriage and Bush's aggressive—and expensive—foreign policy were contrary to much of the belief system the Kochs held dear. The capstone came when Bush invaded Iraq, a decision the Kochs deemed reckless and costly.

It had become clear that if they wanted to reverse what they saw as an accelerating rush toward big government, the Kochs would need to expand their political footprint, even if they stopped short of expressly supporting or opposing candidates. In 2003, Charles Koch and Richard Fink organized the first of what became the semiannual seminars. The following year, the Koch brothers provided the funding to start Americans for Prosperity.[17] Then, toward the end of the Bush presidency, the Koch operation began to wade into GOP politics, though no one knew it at the time. In Bush's last year in office, Koch operatives started a nonprofit group called the Wellspring Committee that would set the stage for all their political activity going forward. Registered out of an untraceable UPS Store mailbox in rural Manassas, Virginia, Wellspring's actual offices were in a downtown Washington office described by a visitor as "a windowless bunker." The group was structured as a 501(c)(4) nonprofit group, so it could shield its donors' identities. Without so much as issuing a press release or even attracting a single media mention, Wellspring raised $10 million, according to its tax filings. The money came from participants in the Koch donor seminars, I was told.

While Wellspring eventually attracted some attention in 2013 as reporters began delving into the big-money economy, no public account prior to this book has connected Wellspring to the Kochs or explained its significance in their political evolution. In fact, when I asked Koch PR about Wellspring, Rob Tappan told me, "I am not familiar with this group." But several people who worked with the group back then characterized it to me as the Kochs' primary political money clearinghouse in 2008—a precursor to the Center to Protect Patient Rights and the Freedom Partners Chamber of Commerce, and the Kochs' first foray into the nonprofit-based political model that they went on to employ so aggressively in 2010 and beyond. The fact that it did not formally list any Koch officials among its board or staff created the kind of plausible deniability that also has become a hallmark of the Koch political operation.

When I asked an operative who worked with the group how it flew so far under the radar, I was told, "That was by design. Wellspring would never have put their name on anything. At that time, we probably wouldn't have commented on anything like that" if asked by the media. "It just wasn't in the model. And that's how a lot of the donors wanted it."

To run the operation, Wellspring contracted with Rick Wiley, a former RNC official, whose firm was paid $210,000 in 2008 by Wellspring. He assembled an experienced team. Three staffers were hired to do what's known in politics as opposition research—essentially digging up dirt on your opponent to use in ads or leak to the media. Wellspring also spent what at the time was considered big money, $1.3 million, to build a voter database. They assembled "the premier data for a number of states in 2008," including microtargeted lists and information on voter preferences, according to an IRS filing. Those data were shared with other Koch-backed groups for which Wellspring served as something of a funding conduit in 2008, donating $7.3 million, according to its tax return. Americans for Prosperity got $1.7 million, Americans for Job Security got $2.6 million, and American Future Fund got $367,000. In another first for the Koch operation, Wiley closely coordinated 2008 strategy with big-money groups aligned with the very Republican establishment from which Koch World had long kept its distance. Wiley met with representatives from the US Chamber of Commerce and even attended regular coordination meetings at the sprawling downtown offices of Freedom's Watch, the group run by Karl Rove's allies and funded largely by Sheldon Adelson. Groups supported by Wellspring funded radio ads and direct mail campaigns attacking Democratic congressional candidates on issues of concern to the Koch network. But they mostly shied away from the presidential campaign.

After Obama and the Democrats won sweeping victories on Election Day 2008, the Kochs severed most ties to Wellspring. But as I pieced together the secretive group's activities from documents and interviews, I realized that Wellspring had served as an important beta test for everything that the Kochtopus would do on a grander scale in the coming years. It marked their first organized foray into nonprofit-based advertising and organizing in congressional races, nominally focused on issues but in a way that left little doubt that the Republicans were the candidates of choice. It also marked the first clandestine alliance with more establishment GOP groups from which Koch operatives claimed to keep their distance. And it was the first example I could find of the Koch network using the innovative nonprofit banking technique that others would copy in future elections. Its investment in voter data even presaged the massive Themis project. Perhaps most interesting was the timing. The Wellspring experiment showed that the Kochs had laid the groundwork for their rapid political expansion well before President Barack Obama became their target. That chronology seems to buttress the Kochs' claim that they are motivated by ideology and undermines liberal characterizations that the Kochs increased their political activity exclusively because of enmity for Obama.

Once Obama took office, however, the Kochs not only ramped up their activity but also tiptoed out of the shadows. They made their debut in the national spotlight with their opposition to Obamacare, and their network pushed the attack by steering huge sums to Americans for Prosperity, 60 Plus, Americans for Limited Government, and other groups that unsuccessfully sought to block the bill from becoming law. As the Kochtopus charged into battle with the Obama administration, Fink warned the brothers that they would become political targets and that it could get nasty.[18] Charles braced for the harsh glare of the spotlight, telling himself that any attacks would be an indication that he and his brother were considered effective.[19] David, on the other hand, seemed to take the criticism personally[20] and was shocked when he saw distortions of their positions.[21]

Their divergent reactions weren't surprising. Lumped into one by the liberal imagination, the Kochs were in reality quite different people. Charles lives in Wichita, where he's an exceptionally involved executive given the size of Koch Industries. He seldom takes much time to schmooze politicians. He probably doesn't *have* time. For someone of his wealth and his history of vast donations, Charles Koch's name graces very few institutions that aren't related to public policy. One visible exception is Wichita State University's 10,500-seat basketball arena. Charles donated $25 million to build it in 2003, but someone who knows Charles described that to me as a notable anomaly: "That's just not his thing. The whole premise of the seminars is to get people to stop giving money to schools and museums and to start giving money to things that will save the country."

David, by contrast, took a less intensive approach to Koch Industries. He runs a division of the company from New York City, where he lives. But he's better known for spending his time and his billions establishing himself as a fixture of New York's society scene, moving into a vast eighteen-room apartment occupying two floors of one of the most prestigious buildings on the Upper East Side and buying an $18 million spread in the Hamptons, where he hosts lavish parties and political fund-raisers. The pillars of New York culture pay testament to his generosity—including a number of institutions you might not associate with a man whom many liberals consider the personification of right-wing extremism. There's the David H. Koch Dinosaur Wing at the American Museum of Natural History, as well as a plaza and fountain renovated with more than $10 million of his money at the Metropolitan Museum of Art. He donated $23 million to public broadcasting, a favorite target of congressional conservatives, even serving stints on the boards of Boston's WGBH and New York's WNET. He gave $100 million alone to modernize the Lincoln Center theater—now named the David H. Koch Theater—that houses the city's ballet and opera, both of which have benefited from his largesse. American Ballet Theatre, to which he'd donated millions, appointed him to its board of directors in the 1980s.[22] He was feted by the ballet company at a 2010 gala kicking off its seventieth-anniversary season. It was a snapshot of the New York society scene, and the honorary cochairs included Caroline Kennedy and, ironically, Michelle Obama, though the First Lady did not attend.[23]

David Koch's rarified version of New York seemed a long way from the mysterious and fast-changing world of conservative big-money politics into which he and his brother were increasingly being drawn. Just as the brothers were expanding their network, a new force was coming on the scene: the tea party movement. Its activists, just like the Kochs, claimed to be disgusted by both major parties and alarmed by what they saw as reckless spending by a government by, of, and for the special interests. It was an organic movement at heart, despite liberal efforts to brand it as a corporate front concocted in a Koch laboratory in Wichita. But the Kochtopus and other fiscal conservative groups quickly seized on it as a chance to move beyond the small world of libertarian activists and superrich donors. Suddenly there were actual grassroots activists angry about big government and ready to do something. Hundreds of small shoestring local groups sprang up across the country, and tens of thousands of activists flocked to congressional town halls and marches in their communities to protest.

The Kochtopus had found its volunteer army—but other big-donor-backed groups wanted in, too. Americans for Prosperity, Freedom-Works, and a host of others scrambled to help the fledging movement and to win its activists' allegiance. They arranged buses to take tea partiers to rallies and town halls, staged protests under their own banners, and provided training, online war rooms, and canvassing literature.

The courtship had to be delicate. Many local activists felt like the big-money groups were trying to co-opt them. "There are some high-powered lobbying groups that are using the tea parties movement to try to build their lists," a Hot Springs, Arkansas, tea party activist named Glenn Gallas told me in 2009. The local tea party group he had helped organize was being courted by Americans for Prosperity. "A big organization like that will never affect people at the local level," he said. "You just become another name on their email list to ask for money from." Steven F. Hayward, a political scientist who has served as a fellow at Koch-backed think tanks, told me that the tea party "is a genuine grassroots phenomenon that a couple of larger groups—Americans for Prosperity and FreedomWorks—have tried to take over. Essentially, they've seen a big parade going down the street and they've tried to get in front of it."[24]

After Obamacare was signed into law in March 2010, tea party anger boiled over into the public consciousness, with noisy protests against—and calls to defeat—members who supported the new legislation. Though an overwhelming majority of the tea party's activists were civil, a tiny minority adopted violent or extreme rhetoric that made the movement suddenly a toxic object of derision in some of the elite New York circles in which David Koch traveled.

The reaction from Koch World to the tea party's sudden impact was schizophrenic at best and dishonest at worst. Publicly, the Kochs offered cautious praise of the tea party but bristled at the suggestion they had anything to do with the movement. "I see these people on TV, and they're interviewed, and it's obvious no one's pulling their strings," Charles said.[25] "There are some extremists there, but the rank and file are just normal people like us. And I admire them," David said.[26] But he also told a reporter for *New York Magazine*, "I've never been to a tea-party event. No one representing the tea party has ever even approached me."[27] And when he was asked directly by the Daily Beast whether he was funding the tea party, his response was, "Oh, please."[28] In an effort to officially distance the brothers from the rowdy tea partiers, Koch Industries, on the night before a Washington, D.C., tea party rally organized by FreedomWorks, emailed reporters who had covered the tea party to stress that "Koch companies, the Koch foundations, Charles Koch and David Koch have no ties to and have never given money to FreedomWorks. In addition, no funding has been provided by Koch companies, the Koch foundations, Charles Koch or David Koch specifically to support the tea parties."

Privately, though, Koch World was reveling in the impact of the tea party and working to make sure that Koch-backed groups got credit for it. The race for tea party supremacy was especially heated between AFP and FreedomWorks. Both groups traced their roots to a group started by the Koch brothers in 1984 called Citizens for a Sound Economy. It split in 2004 amid a bitter internal dispute, with the Kochs creating AFP and a dissenting faction led by former House Republican leader Dick Armey creating FreedomWorks. The rise of the tea party seemed to present ample opportunity for both groups to take their game to the next level, and maybe even to bury the hatchet. But old habits die hard. When FreedomWorks was organizing a September 2009 march in Washington that became a seminal moment in the tea party's rise, one of the Kochs' top political operatives at the time, Sean Noble, quietly offered to steer $100,000 to Freedom Works, provided it featured speeches from Americans for Prosperity president Tim Phillips and other officials from Koch-backed political groups. FreedomWorks declined and grumbled that Americans for Prosperity did little to advance the movement beyond slapping its name on a few rallies.

Even as the tea party was highlighting the fiscal issues the Kochs cared about, they were quietly expanding and diversifying their political operation beyond AFP, steering tens of millions of dollars to a range of efforts that were neither focused primarily on free enterprise nor generally regarded as parts of the Koch operation. Recipients— including the conservative seniors group 60 Plus, a Hispanic outreach outfit called the Libre Initiative, and the social conservative nonprofit CitizenLink—aren't technically controlled by the Kochs or their operatives. Rather, Koch World exerts major sway through contributions steered from its donor network, as well as by featuring the leaders of these outfits at its donor seminars. The groups, in turn, sometimes gave lucrative political-advertising contracts to firms of Koch-allied operatives, including Sean Noble. As was the case with many of the consultants riding the big-money wave, Noble vastly upgraded his life-style as his firms landed big contracts. He had left a $160,000-a-year job as a congressional chief of staff in July 2008 owing thousands of dollars in student loans.[29] He personally earned an estimated $5.3 million in the 2012 election cycle.[30] And by 2014 he owned at least five properties—including a pair of homes in gated communities in the Phoenix area, and an eight-bedroom Utah house with four fireplaces. While his sudden wealth caused some Koch allies to grumble about profiteering, Noble's work with an array of groups that weren't core parts of Koch World was seen as highly beneficial for Republicans and the conservative movement. Still, there were inherent tensions as the Kochtopus's expansion increasingly encroached on the turf of both the RNC and the Rove operation. The dynamic was particularly notable in their creation of rival voter databases, since control of data goes a long way toward determining political supremacy.

"With a broad-based conservative movement—or any political movement—it's obvious that there's often going to be competition, rivalries, egos involved," explained Art Pope, who had helped launch the Koch voter database Themis, which was regarded as the dominant player in the field. "But overall, that competition results in a better work product and better results than a single authoritarian decision that there should be only one product—whether it's a voter database or whatever—that everyone must use."

The various rival camps put their differences aside in the run-up to the 2010 midterms, when Noble and others participated in regular Weaver Terrace Group strategy meetings convened by Karl Rove. But the unprecedented coordination wasn't universally embraced by Koch World. Tim Phillips, president of Americans for Prosperity, attended only a couple of the Weaver Terrace meetings, telling me he bowed out because he believed they were too partisan for his group. "We're very much about the issues, and not trying to help anybody win the major-ity or anything like that," Phillips insisted.[31] "It's just not what we do. There are times when we absolutely go after Republicans who are doing stupid things," he said, though he added of AFP's relationship with the groups in the Rove coalition, "We talk and there are moments where we absolutely work together and cooperate. But it's on a project-by-project basis and on an issue-by-issue basis."

AFP's spending and that of the Kochtopus writ large played a significant role in channeling the tea party wave that lifted Republicans to landslide wins in the 2010 midterm elections. But with electoral success came the intense scrutiny and attacks that the Koch brothers' lieutenant Richard Fink had predicted when they started ramping up their political activity.

A month after the election, David Koch faced a smattering of boos at the Brooklyn Academy of Music when he appeared onstage at the holiday debut of American Ballet Theatre's production of *The Nutcracker* to talk about his $2.5 million sponsorship of the production.[32] A debate broke out in the balcony, with one of the booers declaring, "He's an evil man," and a nearby couple imploring her to "shut up" and leave the theater, according to *Financial Times* editor John Gapper, who witnessed the spectacle. "Once Mr. Koch had left the stage, the booing stopped and the ballet started," Gapper recounted for his readers the next day.

The following month, David Koch traveled to Washington to celebrate the Republican majority his political network helped elect. He attended the swearing-in ceremony for John Boehner as Speaker of the House, and afterward was to have hosted a party for newly elected Republican lawmakers. But between the two events, he was buttonholed on the street outside the Capitol by Lee Fang, a liberal reporter then with the Obama-allied blog ThinkProgress, who pelted Koch with a rapid-fire series of questions about the tea party (which Koch called "probably the best grassroots uprising since 1776 in my opinion"), *Citizens United,* and climate change. A ThinkProgress videographer captured the whole interview, including repeated failed efforts by AFP president Phillips to end it by stepping between Fang and Koch. The video ricocheted around the liberal blogosphere—incontrovertible proof in the eyes of increasingly Koch-obsessed liberals that Koch was now, in fact, pulling the strings in the new Republican Congress!

Three weeks later, when the Kochs convened their winter donor seminar outside Palm Springs, California, they were greeted by hundreds of protestors chanting, "David and Charles Koch: your corporate greed is making us broke," and waving signs reading "Koch Kills" and "Uncloak the Kochs." The Riverside County sheriff's department pegged the protest at between eight hundred and a thousand people (though organizers claimed it was twice that) and made twenty-five arrests. David Koch watched the protest from a resort balcony,[33] thinking the protestors were extreme and dangerous.[34]

Despite the Kochs' willingness to steer unprecedented resources toward efforts that led to a Republican majority, it quickly became evident that their network wasn't going to abandon its libertarian principles. As fault lines emerged between the Republican congressional leadership and their new tea party wing, Koch-backed groups leaned toward the tea party. In a high-profile skirmish in the summer of 2011, Americans for Prosperity pressured conservatives to oppose House Speaker Boehner's bill to increase the debt ceiling, which was supported by not only the GOP establishment but also the biggest groups in Karl Rove's network. Why were the Kochs beating up the very majority they had helped elect? The question vexed establishment Republicans.

David Koch seemed to both personify and embrace the contradiction during the 2012 general election, when he willingly emerged more into the spotlight. He hosted a fund-raiser for Romney in the Hamptons, over which protestors had paid to have a plane pull an aerial banner reading "Mitt Romney has a Koch problem." Romney cracked to the donors, "I don't look at it as a problem; I look at it as an asset."[35] David's associates told me he became rather friendly with Romney, and he even became an alternate delegate to the Republican National Convention in Tampa, Florida. On the convention sidelines, AFP hosted a reception honoring Koch and Art Pope. The affair captured a snapshot of the political clout accrued by the Kochs and the tensions they faced between the libertarian and GOP strains of conservatism, and it also highlighted David Koch's own evolution along that continuum.

The event, dubbed "A Salute to Entrepreneurs Building America," was held at a sleek event space a few blocks from the convention arena. Reporters for various out-of-favor media outlets—including *Mother Jones,* NBC News, the Sunlight Foundation, and Al Jazeera—were turned away at the door.[36] Those who were on the list—including me— were ushered upstairs to a sunny glass-enclosed room overlooking the convention center. Around the bountiful spread of sushi and a variety of proteins on skewers, a host of activists from AFP and other Koch-backed groups, along with the politicians who'd benefited from AFP's political organizing, jockeyed with each other to get a word in with Koch and Pope. The two men were the Abbott and Costello of conservative mega-donors. Koch, lanky and regal, with a well-coiffed head of silver-blond hair and a sophisticated international conglomerate bearing his name, was a towering presence, while Pope, pudgy and argumentative, with a bald head and a regional discount store chain, stood a good foot shorter. They positioned themselves next to each other awkwardly, off to the side of a podium in front of a floor-to-ceiling Americans for Prosperity blue backdrop that obscured the view of the convention center, and be prepared to be exalted.

Congressman Mike Pompeo, who represents Koch Industries' home base in Wichita, Kansas, called the Kochs "the most charitable, wonderful people" who "grow their business not because of good government, but in spite of it. They then turn around and do the most remarkable things in our community." He praised AFP in a manner that showed he implicitly understood Koch World's self-image, crediting the group's Kansas chapter for turning the state "from being a predominantly Republican state to being a predominantly free market conservative state," and added, "I hope very much that we can re-create that all across the world." Not the country. The world.

North Carolina state House Speaker Thom Tillis gave a shout-out to Pope's wife, Kathy Pope, and praised Pope for standing up to his liberal attackers. "Because I know—and you all know—that when you're fighting for freedom, the press goes after you, everybody wants to attack you," said Tillis, who was eyeing a run for the state's US Senate seat in 2014. "They want to make you think like you're somebody who wants to destroy this country, but what they're really trying to do is to continue to make this country the great country that it's always been." Tillis, who was less well acquainted with Koch, drew some uncomfortable chuckles when, while trying to thank him, he mispronounced David Koch's surname in an unfortunate way. "Mr. Cock, I thank—uh, Mr. Koch, I thank you for your support," he stammered, clearly embarrassed, perhaps realizing that if you're a politician with national ambitions, it's probably not a great idea to mispronounce the name of one of your side's biggest donors. Especially not like that.

Virginia governor Bob McDonnell—who had attended at least eight of the Koch donor summits and had once retained AFP president Tim Phillips as a political consultant—was smoother, praising David Koch "for his tremendous leadership over the years in bringing this organization from a seed and an idea to perhaps the most effective grassroots organization in America."

Sens. Jon Kyl of Arizona, John Boozman of Arkansas, and Ron Johnson of Wisconsin—all of whom had benefited to some extent from AFP efforts in their states—paid tribute to Koch and AFP as well. "It's one thing to have a vision. It's another thing to actually take that vision and make it a reality," Boozman effused, praising AFP's efforts in his state, which accelerated its progression from blue to red in 2010. "With your efforts, you turned the state around," he said, adding for good measure, "Thank you for sending—" He paused and corrected his choice of words. "*Helping* to get Ron Johnson to the Senate."

Boozman could have been excused for the slip. Johnson has emerged as a Koch World favorite since entering politics with a 2010 Senate run. He had made a multimillion-dollar fortune in plastics, allowing him to largely self-finance his Senate campaign. But his second-largest bloc of contributions came from Koch Industries employees and the company's political action committee. The bond hardened once Johnson arrived in the Senate, where he maintained a perfect rating on AFP's voting scorecard.

Three days before attending the salute, Johnson was spotted by a group of journalists dining with David Koch in a private backroom of a Zagat-rated Mediterranean- and French-influenced restaurant in Tampa. When one of the journalists snapped a blurry photo of Koch glaring at the camera, an aide emerged from the room, huddled with a waitress, then approached the reporters, asking them not to give away the location of the Koch-Johnson sit-down to "your 'Occupy' friends."[37]

The photo taker posted his pixelated trophy to Instagram and Twitter—without identifying the restaurant—prompting a stream of social media pettiness toward Koch ("Did Instagram blur him or is it his evil aura?" wondered University of Pennsylvania associate professor Anthea Butler)[38] as well as a spurt of mainstream media attention. Slate's Dave Weigel, one of the journalists warned not to reveal Koch's restaurant choice to the grimy liberal masses, wrote, "Going into the convention, I'd wondered if Koch's decision to serve as a delegate from New York would expose him to attention that he doesn't usually court. The answer is now on Instagram."[39] At the tribute, Johnson addressed the hubbub created by the photo. "I had the honor and privilege of sitting down and having dinner with David Koch a couple nights ago," he told the crowd. "It got out in the press. And so we responded to an inquiry from the *Milwaukee Journal Sentinel*. They said, 'Well, what did you talk about?' Pretty simple statement: we talked about saving America," he said to applause.

Johnson had met each of the brothers only once before dining with David Koch, but he found them to be men of conviction who were "unfairly demonized" for their activism.[40] In fact, he credited AFP and the Kochs with motivating him to run for the Senate. "I'm standing here before you today because of the activities of Americans for Prosperity," he told David Koch and his admirers. Recalling a protest against Obamacare he attended in Wisconsin Dells as he was deciding whether to run, he said, "It was an Americans for Prosperity event, and I went there and there were thousands of people and there were speakers and they inspired me to run."

Johnson had come to the salute, he said, to offer his appreciation to AFP, its donors, and its leaders. "I'm here to thank Tim. I'm here to thank David. I'm here to thank Art. By the way, your brother Charles as well," he said, adding for good measure, "God bless America."

Afterward, Koch posed for photos and introduced himself to former Wisconsin governor and 2012 Senate candidate Tommy Thompson, who was standing alone near the heaping buffet, liberally helping himself and licking his fingers between bites. How did things look on the ground in Wisconsin? Koch asked Thompson, who was benefiting from Koch-backed groups' attack ads against his opponent, Rep. Tammy Baldwin.[41] Thompson told Koch that Romney's choice of Paul Ryan—a

popular Wisconsin congressman—as the GOP vice presidential nominee "has added a great degree of enthusiasm and I think we've got a
chance to carry Wisconsin." But, Thompson added suggestively, "a lot
depends on how well we do"—as in how well Thompson's own Senate
campaign fared. Thompson later clarified to me that he didn't talk to
Koch or anyone associated with AFP about ads in his race, which, of
course, could be a violation of the much-discussed but seldom-enforced
coordination rules. As for AFP's assistance, Thompson told me, his
mouth full of food he continued to pull from the buffet, "I understand
that they're running some ads, but I don't know anything about it." Ah,
okay then.

Talking about Mitt Romney's battleground-state prospects, being
showered with gratitude by Republican politicians, serving as an alternate delegate to the party's convention—David Koch had come a
long way from his 1980 Libertarian Party vice presidential run, when he
declared, "We're the enemy of big business, more than the Democrats
or the Republican could ever imagine." What had happened since that
campaign? I asked him at the reception honoring him in Tampa.

"Well, we got a million votes, but lost by forty-five million, so someone else became vice president," he deadpanned.[42] He added more
earnestly, "I think the Republican Party has a great chance of being
successful and that's why I support it. The Libertarian Party is a great
concept. I love the ideals, but it got too far off the deep end, and so I
dropped out." He now considered himself a loyal Republican, he explained, "but I believe in the libertarian principles." He still likes to brag
about running in 1980 against Ronald Reagan, who was no favorite of
the Koch brothers, say folks who've spent time with him.

Koch in some ways remained an uncomfortable fit for the Republican Party. In our chat, he expressed views spanning the partisan
spectrum from Libertarian ("I believe in gay marriage" and "I think
we should gradually withdraw from the Middle East, you know, from
Afghanistan and Iraq") to Republican (if the Federal Reserve keeps
"flooding the market with new money, eventually inflation is going to
take off," potentially leading to "what happened in Germany in the
early twenties" when hyperinflation paved the way for Adolf Hitler's rise

to power) to Democratic (in order to balance the budget "it's essential to be able to achieve spending reduction and maybe it's going to require some tax increases").

When I wrote an item based on our conversation about his stances that were anathema to Mitt Romney's Republican Party,[43] his support for gay marriage caused the bigger stir. "Shocker: David Koch Supports Marriage Equality," blared a headline at the gay news outlet Advocate .com[44] posted forty-five minutes after my story. But the one that really raised eyebrows in Koch World—where David's stance on gay marriage was already well known—was his support for the idea of tax increases, which is completely antithetical not only to the Republican and Libertarian platforms but also to the stances taken by Americans for Prosperity and other political groups backed by the Kochs. After my story was posted, Koch's aides huddled to figure out what to do. About a week later—Koch World PR moves slowly at times, requiring multiple levels of approval for even the most basic statement—Koch Industries responded with a statement bearing David Koch's name that sought to reframe his comment as support for repealing corporate tax breaks. Corporate subsidies and tax preferences "not applied equally should be eliminated, or simplified in a revenue-neutral way, which I alluded to last week," read Koch's statement.[45] "Broad-based tax increases make no sense; they would only slow an economy in tremendous need of growth."

The discordance between David Koch's stances and those of the GOP orthodoxy—and even Koch-backed groups—left me wondering if David Koch had a clue about the types of political activity his network was funding. It also made the Kochs an even greater subject of fascination in Washington as the country headed into Election Day. That was compounded by Koch's response when I asked whether he planned to continue his big-money political activism even if Romney lost the 2012 election: "Yeah, we're in this for the long haul, you know?"

CHAPTER 8

The Turnaround

No one inside Obama's sprawling Chicago high-rise campaign offices seized on the need to play the big-money game as devotedly as Jim Messina, the campaign manager.

Raised by a single mother on a tight budget in Boise, Idaho, Messina did not have a particularly deft instinctive touch with the party's longtime mega-donors, some of whom found his trademark profanity and bluntness off-putting. But he was obsessed with them—and their counterparts on the right, according to campaign insiders, who detailed Messina's assiduous efforts to track and court big money. Since the 2010 midterms, Messina, then a top White House aide, was quietly waging a multiple-front offensive that directly contradicted his boss's official line. He pleaded with Obama and other aides to dial back their opposition to big money and consider forming their own super PAC. At the same time, he tried making inroads with rich liberals in preparation for Obama's reelection. It was not an easy task, given the president's populist rhetoric, and it was made harder by the reality that Messina rubbed many elite Democratic donors the wrong way. They had grown accustomed to a more solicitous touch from those seeking their cash.

It said something about the Obama team's approach to big donors that Messina was their point man. Before leaving the West Wing for Chicago to assume his new role on the 2012 campaign, Messina quietly represented the president at a handful of secret conferences of the liberal donor club Democracy Alliance. For one meeting the club had requested Joe Biden, and, when Messina showed up instead, some attendees regarded it as a middle finger from the White House. The purpose of Messina's visits was both to try to befriend the donors and to lend his imprimatur to the fund-raising efforts of a little-known group called the Common Purpose Project. It organized weekly meetings at a hotel near the White House between deep-pocketed outside groups and administration officials to coordinate messaging. Once he transferred to campaign headquarters in Chicago, Messina spent countless hours cajoling major donors, and Democratic money types noticed that he was warming to the task. If nothing else, he was diligent about it, responding quickly to their emails and calls at all hours. When Obama stumbled badly in his first debate with Romney, Messina fielded a flood of panicked phone calls from donors. Messina calmed as many as he could, sharing internal campaign data, including polling and voter mobilization strategy, that he said showed Obama with more of a cushion than public polling or media analyses let on. "Deep breath," he told them.[1] "We're okay, and this is why we were okay."

It was as if Messina was overcompensating for his boss's indifference to the moneyed class. And without much public notice, Messina's money-obsessed cohort within the campaign won converts in their effort to ratchet up the big-donor courtship efforts. An early victory came in March 2012, when Obama's campaign quietly restructured its joint fund-raising committee with the Democratic National Committee—the Obama Victory Fund—in a way that allowed it to double the maximum size of the donation it could accept. By adding state parties to the committee, it was able to increase its contribution limit from $35,800 to $75,800, dwarfing the $5,000 maximum donation that Romney's campaign committee could accept before he became the Republican Party nominee.

Obama exploited this advantage to build a huge financial cushion while Romney was struggling to dispatch Santorum and Gingrich in the protracted GOP primary. Through the end of April, Obama and the DNC raised $416 million versus Romney and the RNC's $234 million.[2] That wasn't going to last, Messina knew. First of all, Obama's fund-raising was showing signs of slipping. More important, Messina expected Romney's cash flow to soar once he secured the nomination, since then he, too, would have the ability to accept much bigger checks with his national party committee. Romney already had a huge advantage in the super PAC race: Crossroads and Restore Our Future had pulled in more than $86 million by the end of April, versus less than $11 million for the pro-Obama Priorities USA super PAC. Messina anticipated a yawning gap, but he wanted to pinpoint as accurately as possible just how bad things could get before he went to Obama to make his best pitch for a full-on Democratic big-money effort.

Alone in his office overlooking Chicago's Millennium Park one night during the final stages of the GOP primary, Messina began jotting on a giant wall-mounted whiteboard how much each of the major players was projected to spend, relying mostly on public news reports. When he added up all the groups on the other side—the Crossroads groups, Americans for Prosperity, the Romney campaign, the RNC, the Chamber of Commerce, and more—the total reached more than $1 billion. If Obama's campaign equaled the $750 million it raised in 2008 and the pro-Obama Priorities USA Action super PAC continued to struggle, Democrats would be significantly outspent. This was the wake-up call the campaign and its allies needed, Messina thought.

Back at work early the next morning, as was his wont, Messina called his chief of staff, Peter Newell, into the office just before the senior staff's 9:00 a.m. meeting, had him shut the door, and motioned to the whiteboard. "This," Messina said, "is what we're going to be up against. This shit is real." Messina walked Newell through the groups on the board—explaining his abbreviations and sometimes difficult-to-decipher handwriting—then asked him to enter the projections into a spreadsheet. "We're going to want to talk about this to show what we're up against." The spreadsheet formed the basis for a chart they called "Storm of Spending," which Messina showed to Obama and to key donors. "It was intended to scare," someone familiar with Messina's presentation told me, "to get people to donate more than they had come to that meeting hoping to spend."

Team Obama was obsessed with data, and Messina was no different. He leaned on shock charts when trying to close the sale with donors, and he also used the raw data to find and develop fund-raising leads. He had his staff query the campaign's massive secretive database, named Narwhal, to identify the most persuadable donors who had maxed out in 2008 but hadn't yet in 2012. "It allowed us to spend less time bugging the shit out of you and more time just getting your money, which I appreciate," he recalled later to members of the campaign's National Finance Committee.[3] And on the twentieth of each month—Federal Election Commission filing day—Messina had several members of the Chicago research staff work late into the night at headquarters analyzing the monthly reports filed before the midnight deadline by all the various campaign and party committees and super PACs. The team in Chicago used the data to compose a chart known around headquarters as "Money Wars," which was included in the daily briefing binder top staff was provided the next morning.

On the morning of June 21, the fresh-off-the-presses version of "Money Wars" laid bare an alarming development for Obama's high command. Mitt Romney in May had outraised Obama by $17 million. It was the first month that Romney's campaign had beaten Obama's in the money race. The result sent shock waves through the political world, but it wasn't a surprise in Chicago. After all, it was the first month that Romney had been able to raise money jointly with the RNC, allowing him to accept $75,800 checks through a joint committee, and he had taken full advantage.

Touting the May figures in his *Wall Street Journal* column, Rove argued that Obama "was hoping for a repeat of 2008, when financial muscle made it possible to spread out the battlefield and make a (successful) play for more states. That won't happen this time." The combination of Crossroads and other groups with Romney's own stellar fund-raising left Obama "in a precarious position as the campaign enters the summer," Rove crowed.

But the Obama campaign and the DNC still had more cash in the bank overall, and Messina hatched a plan to blitz Romney over the summer with a barrage of negative ads stigmatizing him as an out-of-touch elitist divorced from the middle class. The plan dovetailed closely with the one being pursued by the pro-Obama Priorities USA Action super PAC, which concluded that branding Romney as a bad guy was the best way to spend its limited resources. The thinking from Team

Obama was that Romney would still be scrambling to replenish his reserves after the brutal primary season and wouldn't be able to vigorously defend himself.

The main target, starting early in the summer, was Romney's tenure at the helm of Bain Capital, his private equity firm. A series of harsh and factually loose ads from the Obama campaign and Priorities USA cast the firm, and the private equity industry more generally, as one in which the rich got richer on the backs of the poor. An early Obama campaign ad told the story of a Kansas City steel plant bought and subsequently closed by Bain. "It was like a vampire. They came in and sucked the life out of us," one of the laid-off workers said in the ad. Only it failed to mention that Romney had left Bain by the time the steel company was placed in bankruptcy. The ad was faulted as misleading by fact-checkers, and soon after it aired, some Democrats with ties to Wall Street—up to and including Bill Clinton—criticized the Obama team's attacks on private equity. "I don't think that we ought to get into the position where we say this is bad work," Clinton told CNN in the days after the vampire ad debuted. "This is good work." That infuriated Obama's team, but the feeling was mutual. One fund-raiser who specialized in raising money from Wall Street told me, "It breaks your heart that all the work that Bill Clinton did to make the business community comfortable with Democrats is slowly but surely being destroyed."

If the Obama campaign's ad didn't fatally poison the Democrats' relationship with Wall Street, Priorities USA may have. The super PAC's ads were even tougher than the campaign's. One went so far as to suggest that Romney was to blame for the death from cancer of the wife of one of the laid-off Kansas City steel plant workers, who had lost his health insurance. In the ad, the worker, Joe Soptic, says, "I do not think Mitt Romney realizes what he's done to anyone, and furthermore I do not think Mitt Romney is concerned." Except the cancer came several years after the plant closed, and his wife's lack of health coverage was not solely related to his loss of coverage, according to fact-checkers, who rated the ad false. Various media outlets called it the most vicious ad of the entire 2012 campaign. At the same time his campaign and super PAC were demonizing wealthy elites, Obama was trying to raise money from them. The conflict was difficult to navigate.

Obama set out on a brisk fund-raising schedule that often took him into Manhattan's finance community. By the time the May fund-raising reports were released, he had attended more than 160 fund-raisers for his reelection campaign and the Democratic Party—more than any president in history and about double the total number of fund-raisers George W. Bush attended in his first term. But the big money was still slow in coming. A few days after the May reports showed Romney surging past Obama, his campaign arranged a phone call between a group of donors and the president, who was flying back aboard Air Force One from a trip to survey wildfire damage in Colorado. "The majority on this call maxed out to my campaign last time. I really need you to do the same this time,"[4] Obama told the donors, using a special phone on the government plane installed for political calls and paid for by the campaign and not taxpayers. The call, which was followed by an urgent email from Messina requesting that participants make a contribution as soon as possible, became public after a donor provided a recording of it to the Daily Beast. In the recording, a tired-sounding Obama warned that not only had his campaign fallen behind Romney's "on a month-to-month basis," but also "we're going to have to deal with these super PACs in a serious way. And if we don't, frankly I think the political [scene] is going to be changed permanently." Warning of a scenario in which the campaign might be caught flat-footed in the closing weeks because "a couple of billionaires wrote $20 million checks and have bought all the TV time," Obama told the donors, "The landscape's changed because of the Supreme Court ruling *Citizens United.* We are going to see more money spent on negative ads through these super PACs and anonymous outside groups than ever before. And if things continue as they have so far, I'll be the first sitting president in modern history to be outspent in his reelection campaign."

He added, "We don't have to match these guys dollar for dollar because we've got a better grassroots operation and we've got a better message," but everyone knew the president could not afford to be outspent by ten to one. "A few billionaires can't drown out millions of voices," he concluded. "I still believe in you guys, and I hope you still believe in me and the possibilities of this campaign."

In fact, a number of major Democratic donors told me that the sentiments Obama expressed during the call, which were similar to what they'd heard from him and his lieutenants in other private settings, were actually discouraging many rich activists from writing checks. "Those kinds of attacks on wealth and success are inflammatory," said real estate developer Don Peebles. He had raised more than $1 million for Obama's reelection campaign, including a 2011 fund-raiser at his Washington home. But he was becoming increasingly frustrated with what he described as the Obama team's "class divisiveness."[5]

The Obama team's attacks infuriated Wall Street donors in particular. They had been among the biggest sources of cash for Obama's 2008 campaign, but by the time his reelection rolled around, Obama seemed to be following public sentiment reflected in polls showing that Wall Street had replaced the Iraq War as the bête noire of the left.

Some Obama donors from 2008 were provoked enough to switch sides. "It's not helping the economy to pit the people who are the engine of the economy against the people who rely on that engine," Michael Zambrelli, a Manhattan advertising executive, told a reporter[6] as he and his wife, Sharon Zambrelli, waited to valet-park their SUV outside a $25,000-a-head Romney fund-raiser in the Hamptons on the weekend after the Fourth of July. The fund-raiser was one of three for Romney that weekend in the Hamptons, including one at David Koch's estate (which the Democratic National Committee highlighted with an ad branding Romney as "great for oil billionaires, bad for the middle class"). The Zambrellis had attended an Obama fund-raiser in 2008 in Manhattan that was packed with Wall Street types, and they had maxed out to Obama's general election campaign that year. But Michael Zambrelli explained that he felt the president had "basically been biting the hand that fed him in '08," and, referring to the Hamptons crowd, he speculated ominously that "25 percent of the people here were supporters of Obama in '08. And they're here now."

A number of wealthy Democrats had warned Obama's political team about the chilling impact of what they saw as class warfare against the very types of folks who had long underwritten Democratic campaigns. But Obama's political advisors had made up their minds.

"It appears that the calculus is that it will resonate with voters in places like Ohio because they're suffering," said the real estate developer Peebles resignedly. "But just because we are down, that doesn't mean that we as a country are going to all of sudden begrudge those Americans who are successful because we want that for our children and our grandchildren," he added. Peebles's father had worked as a hotel doorman in Washington, where Peebles now counts a hotel among his tens of millions of dollars in real estate holdings. On the day we talked, Peebles was particularly upset about a Democratic email he'd recently received about Romney's Fourth of July vacation that called sarcastic attention to his twelve-person speedboat as evidence that the Republican nominee was out of touch. Peebles happened to read the email while he was out on his own boat. Peebles pointed out that the money he paid to operate the boat allowed its captain to support a wife and two children, not to mention all the people at the marina whose livelihoods depended on boat owners like him.

Priorities USA was among the foremost purveyor of anti–Wall Street attacks against Romney, and while it found the theme a winner with focus groups, it complicated the super PAC's fund-raising. Priorities USA's triumvirate of Bill Burton, Paul Begala, and Sean Sweeney worked traditional Democratic fund-raising avenues, knocking on doors on Wall Street and in the broader finance community asking for big checks, but many of those doors didn't open, and sometimes when they did, the fund-raisers ended up wishing they hadn't knocked in the first place. In one pitch meeting, Tony James, the billionaire president and CEO of the private equity firm Blackstone and a major fund-raiser for Obama's campaign, flatly rejected Priorities USA—a rarity in high-level fund-raising, where disinterested prospects usually equivocate and tell suitors they'll get back to them.

The Priorities crew even had the temerity to hit up two top Bain Capital executives who happened to be Democrats, Jonathan Lavine and Joshua Bekenstein. In a move that was brazen even by the standards of political fund-raising, Burton, Begala, and a Priorities official named Jim Dinneen paid a visit to the Boston headquarters of the company whose vilification was critical to their electoral strategy. After getting their Bain visitors' badges, they headed up to Bekenstein's office to talk about how important it was to match the Republicans' outside spending. Instead of a check, they got an earful about Obama's first-term performance.

Burton kept the Bain visitors' badge as sort of an ironic campaign souvenir, but in some ways, the cold shoulder from many Clinton-cultivated Wall Street Democrats turned out to be a blessing for Democrats and their super PACs in the long term. It forced them to switch their attention back to the Democrats' traditional sources of big checks, labor unions, trial lawyers, and Hollywood, with handsome rewards. They also cultivated a new breed of mega-donors—folks who were rich, sure, but whose progressive sensibilities made them more amenable to populist themes.

Steve and Amber Mostyn are both Houston trial lawyers and relative newcomers to the national stage. They had quietly joined the Democracy Alliance a couple of years earlier, but they were kind of an uneasy fit. At one of their first meetings, they gave a presentation on their leading roles in groups intended to return Texas to the Democratic column. This prompted some sniping whispers in the audience about the newcomers, who boasted in their strong Texas accents about how much they had invested. Among the eyebrows raised were those of Lee and Amy Fikes of Dallas, who had made a fortune in oil exploration and were considered the reigning major Democratic donors in Texas before the Mostyns came along. The Fikes had been writing enormous checks for years, but they considered it gauche to talk openly about dollar figures.

I had a hard time imagining the boisterous Mostyns sitting through a DA panel, much less presenting one. They were self-made and still in their early forties, unlike many of the other donors. They had left quite an impression in Texas since they first dove into big-money politics in 2008 using the fortune they collected in legal fees from the class action suits they had filed on behalf of homeowners whose properties were damaged in hurricanes including Ike, Rita, and Dolly. Their original motivating issue was guarding against efforts to make it harder to sue in Texas—which could threaten their bottom line. But they had since emerged as the biggest Democratic donors in Texas, backing all manner of traditional Democratic candidates and causes, and even some

Republican ones. Not only had they donated more than $10 million to various candidates across the state, they'd also financed a web of political groups, prompting a conservative tort reform group to launch a 2010 attack campaign called "The Invisible Hand of Steve Mostyn." It included a video featuring a spiderweb entangling Mostyn-backed groups and candidates. It had a little flavor of the scrutiny liberals had directed at the Kochs. But the Mostyns seemed to find it—and lots of other criticisms—perfectly amusing. Steve Mostyn is a big guy, with a shaved head, a silver goatee, and a booming laugh, who freely voices his opinions. Amber is a stylish social media addict.

Begala and Burton met the Mostyns on their yacht in Fort Lauderdale in the spring and showed them two of the Priorities ads. One of the ads imagined a dark version of "Mitt Romney's America" in which Wall Street banks run amok while the middle class suffers. Jobs are being relocated. Student aid is being slashed. Benefits under social security, Medicare, and Obamacare are being dismantled. In the other ad, a paper mill worker recalled being asked to build a thirty-foot stage at the Indiana plant where he worked, which had recently been sold to Romney's Bain Capital. "A group of people walked out on that stage and told us that the plant is now closed, and all of you are fired," the worker says emotionally, asserting that shutting the plant made Romney more than $100 million. "Turns out that when we built that stage, it was like building my own coffin. And it just made me sick," the worker concludes as the screen fades to black, with white lettering reading, "If Mitt Romney wins, the middle class loses." The "Stage" ad was powerful stuff, testing through the roof among the working-class voters Obama needed if he was to win in swing states.

Over several hours and several cold Michelob Ultras, the Mostyns, who like to take a hands-on approach to the groups to which they give, quizzed Begala and Burton on all aspects of the Priorities campaign. Then they gave the first of three $1 million checks.

Amy Goldman had previously written big checks mostly to support abortion rights, but she consented to a meeting in her apartment on Manhattan's Fifth Avenue with Bill Burton, who talked for about twenty minutes about Priorities USA's goals as Goldman sat stoically. Burton finished his pitch, wondering whether he'd connected. "I want to help you," Goldman said flatly, glancing around her home office in search of her purse, then fishing around in it and pulling out her checkbook. She started to write a check, and Burton's eyes grew wider with each successive zero, until it read $1 million. Often Burton and Begala had to come back five or six times just to get a check one-quarter that size from a new donor, but Goldman was an easy sell and seemed to quickly take to high-dollar politics.

"I felt like super PACs are a reality that I wish would go away, but I had to fight on their terms," said Goldman, a real estate heiress who left a career in psychology and subsequently became a leading heirloom plant conservationist. "I'm new to politics. I have never felt mobilized before to this extent," she explained, adding that she wanted to give early, even while other rich Democrats remained on the sidelines, "to get the ball rolling and encourage other donors to give."[7] She volunteered to host a fund-raiser for Priorities USA in August that drew Democratic donor heartthrob Bill Clinton and top Obama White House advisor David Plouffe. She served up a vegan menu of steamed edamame, potato dumplings, and okra[8] for the forty or so very wealthy Democrats. Some of the attendees were Clinton loyalists, while others had already donated to Priorities USA by the time of the event—Philadelphia lawyer Daniel Berger had given $175,000 a couple of months prior. The third and most important group were fence-sitters like George Soros, who was represented at Goldman's apartment by Michael Vachon. Clinton talked for about half an hour, bemoaning the explosion of big money in politics,[9] but he also "really roused the troops," according to Goldman, by talking about Democratic positions on the economy and health care, and then stuck around chatting for an hour.[10]

It was vintage Clinton donor maintenance, and not surprisingly, the donors ate it up. Many donors gave for the first time, either at the event or in the days that followed. Clinton also had begun lending his big-donor fund-raising touch to Obama's campaign, appearing with the president at three flashy New York fund-raising events over the summer that raised millions. Among them was a private $40,000-a-head reception at the Manhattan home of hedge fund manager Marc Lasry and a five-hundred-person gala at the Waldorf Astoria featuring a performance by Jon Bon Jovi, who flew in on Air Force One with Obama for the evening. That felt like old-school donor schmoozing for once. To me, Clinton's participation and the glamour and access that came with it seemed symbolic. It was as if a switch had been flipped to turn on the sort of high-dollar-driven access campaign that Obama had long eschewed. Afterward there was no turning back.

The new approach started paying dividends in August. Democrats were turning it around through a combination of new donors and a donor-maintenance regime that looked a whole lot like everything Obama despised about Romney. By the time of the Democratic convention in Charlotte, North Carolina, It wasn't hard to find Democratic operatives and politicians sucking up to big money.

On the convention's opening afternoon, Priorities USA said that it had just closed the books on its best fund-raising month to date, pulling in $10 million in August. Later that day Priorities cofounder Bill Burton boasted to me that he had just "picked up $500,000" in a hotel-room meeting with a donor that ran long, making him late for a fund-raiser at a hip nouveau southern restaurant called Roosters. I stood outside the restaurant's floor-to-ceiling windows as the fund-raiser got under way, peering in as Paul Begala climbed atop a table to get the attention of the assembled donors. Begala delivered a pep talk that unintentionally demonstrated why Democrats were having trouble raising super PAC cash. "They will have more money," Begala said of Republican super PACs. "We can survive if we are outspent one and a half to one, two to one, maybe even three to one," he told the onlookers. But, Begala warned, Romney had outspent his opponents sixteen to one in the primaries, and "we can't have that" in the general election.[11] He interrupted his urgent plea with a quick and somewhat discordant public service announcement: "I want to live in an America without super PACs." Until then, though, Democrats couldn't unilaterally disarm while Republicans stockpiled, which is why he implored, "We need your help."[12] Then again, there was some good news, he said: "For the first time in my lifetime, we have our shit together. It's always been the case that the Democrats always bump into each other and they're their own worst enemies and it's the Republicans who are orderly and organized."

Democrats did, in fact, have a superior super PAC hierarchy. Though it was usually said that Democrats were the ones who were less inclined to take direction, they had managed to set up a small group of PACs that each had a defined role and weren't bumping into one another. It was a sharp contrast to the Republican side, where the various groups in the Rove network were competing with one another, and also with the groups in the Koch network. Even House Republican leaders John Boehner and Eric Cantor had started their own separate, competing super PACs. Maybe it was the Republicans' entrepreneurial spirit that fostered competition on the big-money right. Maybe it was the fact that there simply wasn't that much big Democratic money for which to compete that fostered cooperation on the left. Whatever the reason, the Democratic big-money groups were playing a lot better together in the sandbox.

The three that were hosting the Roosters fund-raiser—Priorities USA (formed to help reelect President Obama), House Majority PAC (to elect Democrats to the House of Representatives), and Majority PAC (to support Senate Democrats)—had raised between $60 million and $75 million at that point, Begala told the donors from atop the table, cracking that Sheldon Adelson probably spent that much on his brunch bill.[13] But Democrats had managed to break old competitive habits to forge a close working relationship between super PACs that allowed them to be more efficient than the Republicans. Partly as a result, bragged Begala, who was paid a healthy $480,000 by Priorities USA in 2012, the group had "done more with $20 million to move the race than Rove has with $200 million."

Priorities USA "had one mission for the first half of this race, and that mission was take Romney's greatest strength, his business record, and make it a weakness. And it is. He can't talk about his business record anymore," Begala declared. "Now, we want to close the deal, which is putting their agenda on trial."[14]

It was up to the donors at Roosters, and their friends and associates, to prevent Republicans from taking over Washington, Begala preached. "The old line about give till [it] hurts—that doesn't count here. You need to give till it feels good. Because if you don't give, it is really gonna hurt."[15] Plus, he hinted, there might be something in it for them down the road. "I want you to know this: we will always remember the people who were there for us, the people who were there for this president, the people who were there for Nancy Pelosi, the people who were there for Harry Reid."[16]

I pieced together Begala's pep talk from the accounts of a couple of bloggers who were among the crowd, apparently unbeknownst to the super PAC staff. I had been escorted from the restaurant before the fund-raiser began by Andy Stone, an aide to House Majority PAC. Though I'd never met Stone, he apparently recognized me, because after I walked right past the guy at the door checking names on an iPad, Stone made a beeline through the crowd and extended his right hand to introduce himself while nudging me toward the door with his left. "This is a private party," he explained in a quiet, self-conscious tone that suggested he didn't want to make a scene. I obliged. But as I headed to the door, I found myself contrasting Stone's approach to kicking me out, which was almost apologetic, with the swaggering way Koch security had tossed me from their 2011 seminar in the California desert. I wondered if Democrats might have been a little embarrassed by their big-money hypocrisy. After months of complaining about secretive Republican high-dollar fund-raisers, here they were, engaged in exactly the same pursuit—only they lacked the bravado of their Republican big-money rivals. I encountered a similar sheepishness when another staffer barred me from entering a gala thrown by David Brock's Media Matters and American Bridge nonprofits at a Charlotte art museum, which was catered by the pioneering locavore chef Alice Waters. A dollop of embarrassed hypocrisy with your organic black Beluga lentil salad?

There was one notable exception to this embarrassed approach to vacuuming up big money: a corporate fund-raiser hosted by the Democratic Governors Association (DGA) at an opulent mansion in a tree-lined suburb south of downtown Charlotte. A procession of black town cars and SUVs pulled up to the security checkpoint at the gate, rolled down their tinted windows just enough to produce identification or offer the name of an invited dignitary or donor, then proceeded up a long, winding driveway. As buses sponsored by an energy trade association pulled up, representatives from the human resources company Maximus (which gave $235,000 to the DGA in 2012) and General Motors ($10,000) entered the mansion. I made my way through a kitchen entrance into the mansion's ornate marble foyer, where a string trio was playing soothing classical music. It took less than five minutes for a massive private security guard to zero in on me, approach, and sternly demand I leave the premises immediately. "If you come back in here, you will be arrested for trespassing," said the guard, who identified himself to me by name but whom I'm calling J.B. here to avoid embarrassment. Later I Googled the guard's real name and learned that he had some experience with shadowy rendezvouses involving cash-bearing suitors seeking personal contacts. A decade earlier, when he was a uniformed patrol officer with the Lexington, North Carolina, police department, he had been arrested for running a prostitution ring from his squad car while on duty. He would charge $150 to $175 a pop to arrange meetings at nearby hotels between prostitutes and johns. He resigned from the force, pleaded guilty to one count of aiding and abetting prostitution, was sentenced to one year of unsupervised probation, and eventually transitioned to a career in private security. It was telling, I thought, that it took a roughneck ex-cop to boldly enforce the secrecy of a Democratic big-money fund-raiser.*

Beyond the tone, it was telling that big-money Democratic outside groups like the governors association and Priorities USA—rather than the party committees or the Obama campaign—were behind some of the most exclusive, hottest, and most closely guarded soirees in Charlotte. The super PACs that had organized the Roosters fund-raiser held what was billed as an "intimate" brunch at the suburban Charlotte home of billionaire hedge fund manager Jim Simons, who ended up donating $9.5 million to the three PACs, making him one of the party's biggest super PAC whales. Making the schlep to Simons's place were Jim Messina, congressional leaders Harry Reid, Nancy Pelosi, Dick Durbin, Chuck Schumer, Steny Hoyer, and Steve Israel, and Chicago mayor Rahm Emanuel. During the convention, Emanuel, revered by

---

*When I tracked the guard down by phone months later, he lectured me on the importance of tight security for dignitaries ("Ever since 9/11, the world's changed") and the risks of crashing fund-raisers ("That puts people's lives in jeopardy"). He also threatened to sue me for defamation if I published his name, explaining, "I mean, I'm just telling you up front. If that's what you want to do, I'm fine with that."

donors for his bare-knuckle persona, officially left his honorary post as cochair of the Obama campaign to lead a fund-raising push for Priorities USA in the run-up to the general election. On the final night of the convention, the group and its congressional partners also threw a gala emceed by the actress Jessica Alba, with performances by the New York pop band Scissor Sisters and the Miami rapper Pitbull. According to a sponsorship brochure, donors who gave a combined $100,000 to the three super PACs got six tickets to the brunch at Simons's home, twenty tickets to the Roosters event featuring Begala, and fifty tickets to the party. The convention fund-raising extravaganza, cheesily coined "Super-O-Rama" in the sponsorship brochure, made some Democrats I talked to nervous. A showy super PAC presence created tricky optics for Obama and congressional Democrats, many of whom had long track records of opposing big money. Also, the notoriously control-obsessed Obama campaign, even after embracing super PACs, was still leery of having outside groups, no matter how closely aligned, assuming such a presence at its convention.

In Charlotte, Obama's campaign finally rolled out a comprehensive donor fulfillment program that would have made Romney's team proud. The biggest donors got to choose from a veritable buffet of perks of the sort Obama's top aides privately sneered at, with the most generous getting the best stuff. It was all laid out in a glossy pocket-sized booklet, the "Obama Victory Fund Finance Guests Passport to the 2012 Democratic National Convention," which was emblazoned with a holographic stamp of the Obama campaign's rising sun logo on the cover. The booklet was distributed to designated guests as part of welcome packets containing "SEIU for Obama" thundersticks and various other trinkets as they checked in at a handful of fine downtown Charlotte hotels that had been reserved for donors—the "OVF Finance hotel block," according to the passport. The passport began with an introduction signed by the campaign's national finance chairman, Matthew Barzun, who had been Obama's ambassador to Sweden from 2009 until 2011, and the DNC's national finance chair, Jane Stetson. It promised that "OVF Finance Guests will be treated to a week of exciting and informative events."

Donors got the chance to pose for professional photos behind the podium at the Time Warner Arena, where Obama would later accept his party's nomination for reelection, followed by a dessert reception in the arena's self-described "fine dining" restaurant. That podium sneak peak was available to donors who qualified for the OBX Package (a designation given to those who pledged to raise $1 million or more by Election Day) or the Kitty Hawk Package (between $500,000 and $1 million). Even lower-tier bundlers and donors were entitled to attend "an exclusive campaign briefing" on Tuesday morning with Messina, as well as a Wednesday "toast to the South with President Bill Clinton" and a Thursday rally with Vice President Joe Biden at the NASCAR Hall of Fame. A morning National Finance Committee breakfast meeting with Michelle Obama was open to members of the committee and "Presidential Partners"—those who gave the maximum $75,800 donation to the Obama Victory Fund.

Making sure donors felt like players at the convention—or, more important, did not feel overshadowed by other players—was a major preoccupation for politicians, super PACs, and other groups. Handled right, the donors would only be nominally aware of the transactional cottage industry that existed to keep them giving, consuming hundreds of staffers and volunteers full-time. Democracy Alliance staffers had been dispatched to the convention to serve as concierges for the group's donors, getting them tickets to parties and access to exclusive briefings. The Obama campaign, the Victory Fund, and the convention host committee each stationed a team of staff and volunteers in conference rooms at the donors' hotels to handle all manner of needs and complaints, and senior "fixers" wandered the lobbies, asking donors if they had had a good time at whatever shindig they had attended the preceding evening, and dispensing coveted party tickets or VIP party suite passes to the next night's fun to top donors or to panicked lieutenants who couldn't placate irate donors on their own.

"My advice to donors: throw a fit," one such fixer was overheard confiding in the lobby of the Westin on the first morning of the convention. "You'll get whatever you want."[17]

Complaints from donors unhappy with their level of access were common and, depending on the importance of the donor, were sometimes leveraged to get them to cough up more cash. Donors could "write a check to get a higher package," according to a handbook distributed to Obama campaign staffers and volunteers. "Have the donor call the [Obama Victory Fund] hotline," the handbook instructed, listing an organizational chart with phone numbers for the donor fulfillment staff at each hotel. Volunteers could expect to "interact with industry moguls, diplomats, and ambassadors," advised the handbook. "Keep the relationship formal. Use titles or last names. When addressing dignitaries use titles (i.e. Madame Secretary, Mr. Ambassador, Doctor, Professor)." And no matter what happened, donor handlers were to "keep a positive attitude, especially when met with a negative attitude. DO NOT take someone's frustration personally. Try to keep the conversation focused on accomplishing the task at hand. Whenever possible, please present guests with an alternative," according to the handout. "ALL Finance guests are VIPs," it instructed.

Democrats, it seemed, had come to the conclusion that Jim Messina was right. There comes a time when populist rhetoric needs to take a backseat to big-money reality, and that time is two months before Election Day.

CHAPTER 9

The Biggest Bet Yet

Gusts of warm, damp wind swayed the palm trees outside the waterfront Marriott in Tampa, Florida, on August 27, 2012—what was to have been the first night of the Republican National Convention. A damaging storm named Isaac was pummeling the Gulf Coast hundreds of miles to the west. But at the Marriott, two by two, the Republican Party's wealthiest decamped from black town cars or, for those in nearby hotels, covered golf carts. Through the massive revolving doors they went, into the glimmering, air-conditioned marble sanctuary of the hotel's soaring lobby, then up a long escalator and into a massive ballroom.

They were there for an exclusive party dubbed the Freedom and Opportunity Reception,[1] reserved for major donors to Mitt Romney's presidential campaign. You were required to show a lapel pin signifying your status as a Romney "Founding Partner" (meaning you'd donated at least $50,000 to the campaign) or as a Romney "Star" (meaning you'd raised $250,000 or more from other people). I had no such pin, but the security wasn't particularly thorough.

Inside the ballroom, hundreds of donors and bundlers mingled with Republican dignitaries like Republican Party chairman Reince Priebus, pollster Frank Luntz (who wore his trademark red sneakers), and Newt and Callista Gingrich, the bitter primary of just a few months ago now forgotten as Newt posed for pictures with some of the very donors who'd funded the super PAC attack ads that crushed his White House dreams.[2]

Donors grazed from a buffet featuring house-smoked shredded BBQ pork sliders with coleslaw and all manner of other hors d'œuvres. Jamming at the front of the room were the Oakridge Boys, a patriotic southern gospel and country band with at least one member whose long white beard and dark sunglasses would have fit in nicely with ZZ Top. Tropical Storm Isaac, which had already been blamed for nearly thirty deaths in the Caribbean, was expected to reach hurricane strength and make landfall in Louisiana and Mississippi at any moment, but under the glistening chandeliers of the ballroom the only thing wet was the sprawling open bar. On that bar, in front of the bottles of wine, beer, and top-shelf booze, were samples of the evening's featured cocktail—a red concoction served with a lemon wedge and a maraschino cherry impaled on a toothpick, called the Hurricane.

It was precisely the kind of visual Republican officials had hoped to avoid when they decided to delay the convention a day. Romney's advisors feared a political backlash if it appeared his supporters were partying while storm victims suffered. Imagine the specter of split-screen news reports showing rich (mostly white) Republicans celebrating on the convention floor while poor (mostly black) residents scrambled to flee the storm's path and save their possessions. It could look like George W. Bush's clumsy response to Hurricane Katrina all over again.

So, a few hours before he made his way over to the party, RNC chair Priebus had taken to the podium to announce that the convention would be in recess until the following afternoon. It was the safe thing to do—literally and politically—and it was consistent with Priebus's own memo, sent a couple of days earlier, declaring the safety of delegates and Tampa citizens "our first priority."[3] That may have been the official priority. But behind closed doors, the top priority at the convention was the same as ever: making donors feel loved.

In the past, the donor stroking had had more of a celebratory, retrospective feel. By the convention, the donors had already propelled their candidate through often tough primaries to their party's nomination. Back then, they had been able to sit back and reap the spoils, being rewarded for their generosity with all manner of perks and access. Best of all, since the fund-raising push was over, they'd been able to leave their checkbooks at home. In the general election, the big donors ceased being pivotal, because the presidential nominees accepted public money in return for their agreeing to stop fund-raising. But now things were different. In 2008, the system essentially met its demise with Obama's decision to become the first candidate since the dawn of the public financing system to reject its funds in the general election. John McCain had participated in the system and lost both the fund-raising war and the election. No candidate would ever make that mistake again.

The need for more and bigger checks had only increased since then, thanks to *Citizens United* and the rise of super PACs. So in 2012 it was imperative for candidates to keep their big donors fired up all the way through Election Day. It was one of the fundamental changes to presidential politics in the big-money era, influencing everything from advertising strategy to campaign schedules to the tenor and tone of fund-raising appeals. To be successful in this world, candidates and their allies had to strike a delicate balance between urgency and confidence. They had to create the sense that the donors' cash was absolutely and immediately necessary to prevent a catastrophic loss, but they also had to convey that with that one last big check, a triumphant victory was at hand. It was critical, in other words, to project the feeling that more money could swing the election.

The Freedom and Opportunity Reception was all about projecting that feeling. It was the kick-off for a sort of parallel convention—exclusive, reverential, and lush—with the goal of rewarding donors while also energizing them for the stretch run. While the ordinary delegates, activists, and volunteers endured long lines at the convention gates waiting to get into their nosebleed seats, the mega-donors rubbed shoulders with the Republican glitterati at cocktail parties and in luxury boxes where waiters passed champagne. Romney's "Stars" could attend personalized briefings and pep talks from some of the party's biggest names—Mississippi governor Haley Barbour, Jeb Bush, Nikki Haley, and Condoleezza Rice—and a special performance by former Eagles lead guitarist Don Felder, according to a "VIP Convention" agenda.[4] While the regular delegates were waiting in line for a $12 beer, the big donors were hitting the open bar in a sequestered VIP lounge. It would be the same at the Democratic convention.

At the Freedom and Opportunity Reception, I recognized Andy Puzder, the CEO of the company that owns fast-food giants Carl's Jr. and Hardee's. A rumored cabinet pick in a Romney administration, Puzder, along with his wife, donated more than $165,000 to committees supporting Romney, and he had become something of a surrogate for Romney, going on cable television to convince folks they'd really like Romney if only they had the chance to hang out with him. Just a few hours before the reception, he'd told host Neil Cavuto on Fox News, "Mitt's a very, very decent man. He's a man of incredible integrity, and he's somebody that people need to get to know." And people could get to know him at a host of receptions in Tampa that week like the one at the Marriott—if they raised $250,000 for his campaign. Once Michigan governor Rick Snyder had finished up a brief speech to the donors at the Marriott, the ballroom's podium was turned over to the ever-youthful Spencer Zwick, Romney's finance director.

"This is the kick-off to the convention," Zwick told the Marriott crowd from a three-foot-high stage set up at the front of the room. "We hope you enjoy yourselves this evening." The gathering might even be graced by some Romneys that night, Zwick hinted, right before announcing, "One of those family members is actually on his way here right now, Josh Romney, the governor's son. He actually just walked in, so please welcome Josh Romney."

Onto the stage bounded the middle of the five Romney boys. Then thirty-seven years old, Josh was teased about his matinee looks by his brothers, who called him "the dreamy one." A polished public speaker who was rumored to be eyeing his own political career, Josh had made a full-time job of campaigning for his dad. In Iowa alone, he hit ninety-nine counties in the run-up to the state's caucuses. The donors, of course, would rather have heard from Mitt Romney, who was staying in the Marriott along with the rest of the clan and would eventually make appearances at several big donor gatherings. But Josh quickly created the intimate connection that was a hallmark of Romney donor maintenance, telling the crowd, "I actually just talked to my mom and dad a minute ago, or to my mom, who's got her speech ready. She's excited. She's going to give a great speech tomorrow night." There was even going to be a video capturing a slice of Romney family life, Josh confided. Then he eased into a speech that perfectly struck the balance between convincing donors a win was at hand and making it clear that they were still needed.

"This election is momentous," he told them. "If President Obama is allowed to spend four more years the way he's spent these four years, then this country's future is in jeopardy." Of course, Romney's most generous supporters already knew how dire things were, Josh said. "It's why you guys are in this room." But now, he asserted, that reality was finally starting to sink in with people across the country—by which he presumably meant those who hadn't taken days off work to travel to the RNC, attend fancy parties, and drink Hurricanes.

"I don't know if you remember four years ago—you probably recall the energy that President Obama had on his campaign. He'd do these rallies and thousands of people would come, they had tons of energy, tons of enthusiasm and you could just feel it at his events. And there were a lot of people who got caught up in that and voted for him. This time, that energy is gone," Josh said dramatically. "The good news is, if you've seen my dad's rallies, you know that he's got it." The bundlers and donors cheered lustily, though most looked like they'd much prefer the backstage VIP lounge to the high-energy rally crowds Josh was describing.

"You guys have done so much for us. It's impossible to ever repay everything you've done, except to say that I know my dad will work as hard as he can when he's president to get this country back on track and restore our greatness. I will also just say one last thing, and that is that I feel very good about our chances in November. My dad will be the next president of the United States of America and you are all invited to the inauguration," he proclaimed to rousing cheers before backtracking sheepishly, as if wondering whether the complicated campaign and ethics rules forbade inviting big donors to the inauguration. "I don't think I'm really allowed to do that," he said, looking offstage to his right, perhaps for guidance from a campaign official familiar with the rules, before letting his exuberance and sense of kinship with the campaign's rich supporters take over. "But it's a big place, so you all can come."

Any analysis or polling that countered the narrative that the Republicans were on track to take back the White House and maybe even the Senate was immediately assailed both in private conversations with donors and in the political blabbersphere, since if it went unchallenged, it could chill donor enthusiasm. Who—other than maybe Sheldon Adelson—would want to throw good money at a losing cause?

Denying bad news wasn't just a Republican fund-raising trick. Democrats did it at times, too, though more often they took the opposite tack, highlighting ominous signs as a means to scare donors into giving. Perhaps it said something about the divergent psychologies of the dueling donor pools. Rich Democrats, whose political philosophy was all about government helping the have-nots, wanted to see their candidates as scrappy underdogs fighting the system, even when they clearly were not, as was the case with Obama. Rich Republicans, whose political philosophy was about getting the government out of the way of the haves so that they could help the have-nots, wanted to see their candidates as good investments.

The GOP approach left Republican operatives trying hard to avert the eyes of their donors from any ominous signs. Campaign pollster Neil Newhouse delivered a detailed presentation to top donors over the summer debunking a Bloomberg News poll that gave Obama a thirteen-point lead,[5] instead directing their attention to other polls showing a much tighter race.[6]

Romney's big-money conservative allies were engaged in the same funhouse-mirror-style distortion. As usual, Karl Rove led the way. Since the conclusion of the bitter primary season, Rove had firmly cemented his status as the top big-money operative of the *Citizens United* era. That made him arguably the top operative in all of politics, given the migration of money and power from the candidates and parties to the outside groups, and the Republican big-money dominance. His Crossroads groups were well on their way to raising an astounding $325 million—more than the Romney campaign or the RNC would raise on their own without the assistance of their joint fund-raising committee.[7]

While the Koch network may have raised more than Crossroads overall, it was a sprawling, multipronged operation that lacked a single lead operative who had Rove's combination of fund-raising clout and strategic know-how.

Rove had succeeded in becoming the de facto boss of the shadow party, and he had little choice but to relentlessly argue that things were going his way. To maintain his status, he needed more checks, which meant he needed to keep forecasting success. It became a self-perpetuating loop. Through the summer, Rove was utilizing his close personal connections to donors and his high-profile media platforms at Fox News and the *Wall Street Journal* to project that supreme self-confidence.

In the weeks before the convention, Rove took to Fox News to question some of the polls that showed Obama ahead, telling host Greta Van Susteren that the generally well-respected Quinnipiac poll is "run in combination with CBS, *New York Times,* whose methodology makes them more Democrat."[8] It was a dubious assertion, since Quinnipiac rigorously protected its methodology from any corrupting influences. Around the same time, Rove wrote in his *Wall Street Journal* column that the Obama/Priorities USA summer-long ad blitz had done little to improve Obama's polling numbers on the economy.[9] The reason? A coalition of GOP-allied big-money groups had answered back to the tune of $107 million in ads, "with Crossroads GPS, a group I helped found, providing over half,"[10] Rove wrote.

It's hard to tell whether Rove was drinking his own Kool-Aid or just selling it, but in the end the difference was moot. In the shadow party world which he ruled, Rove had a giant target on his back. It wasn't enough to simply convince donors to keep the checks coming. In the new big-money economy, it was also imperative to make the case that in giving to a particular group, donors were spending cash more effectively than if they'd given it to a rival group competing for the same donor dollars. The result was a vigorous, and sometimes contentious, competition among ostensibly allied groups to see who could corral the most cash and, with it, the most influence.

Koch-linked operatives, for instance, bragged to donors that their Themis voter database was vastly superior to rival projects, including one being built by the RNC with help from Crossroads. And Restore Our Future argued to the donor class that it was the best investment for ensuring a White House victory because it was the only big-money group devoted exclusively to helping Romney.

The power struggle between Restore Our Future and Rove was particularly fierce, and for good reason. If Romney won, the thinking in GOP money circles went, Charlie Spies and the Restore gang could displace Rove atop the shadow party. But it wouldn't be easy. Rove had constructed his throne on a foundation of relationships with the biggest GOP donors. Rove reinforced his status with donors by coaxing his competitors—including those associated with the Kochs and various business and social conservative groups—into his Weaver Terrace coalition to coordinate spending. That was no small accomplishment, and when Rove informed donors of this feat, which he did often, they were impressed. *They are part of my coalition, not the other way around,* was the message the donors heard. At the same time, though, in conversations with donors Rove was privately undercutting his rivals just as aggressively as they were coming at him. Among his main arguments was that Crossroads was making the most effective use of donor dollars because of its low overhead. He touted a green-eyeshade culture overseen by Mike Duncan, which included annual audits, lower-than-standard commissions on ad buys, and even a reluctance to reimburse taxicab receipts. Rove contrasted that to suggestions that Restore Our Future, in particular, was paying too much to its fund-raising consultants.

In nearly constant private briefings and phone calls with megadonors, Rove reinforced the message of Crossroads's effectiveness. Several donors regarded him as their personal consultant. He'd debrief them on the latest developments, explain how their money was being spent, and take donor advice on how to proceed. "I think they listen to all of us," the Minnesota media mogul Stan Hubbard told me at the beginning of the general election. A day earlier, Hubbard and the billionaire venture capitalist Ken Langone, traveling on business together in the Bahamas, had a long phone call with Rove to discuss the race. "I don't think Karl would want me to tell you what it was about. But obviously it's not about how to reelect Obama," Hubbard said jovially. It was all part of a donor persuasion strategy flawlessly executed by Rove down the home stretch of the 2012 campaign. Whether or not Rove in fact idolized Mark Hanna, the operative behind the robber barons who funded William McKinley's presidential campaigns, Hanna would likely be in awe of Rove's performance. Flattery, exclusivity, pressure, passion—Rove coddled the donors with artful precision.

The Republican National Convention in Tampa was the perfect stage for his dance, giving him a stage in front of an audience full of mega-donors. On the final morning of the convention, after Hurricane Isaac had passed, Crossroads convened a breakfast briefing attended by some of the biggest whales in GOP politics, including Wall Street billionaires John Paulson and Wilbur Ross. Crossroads staff had worked hard to keep the briefing private. But a reporter from *Bloomberg Business Week* named Sheelah Kolhatkar had surreptitiously gained access and recorded the event[11] by presenting herself as the guest of an invited donor. I learned later that the donor in question was a big-talking hedge fund manager named Anthony Scaramucci, who had revealed during an interview on another subject with Kolhatkar the preceding night that he had been invited to the breakfast, as well as a major-donor panel later that day organized by hedge fund billionaire Paul Singer. While Kolhatkar was removed from the Singer event by operatives who recognized her as a journalist, her stories on the Crossroads breakfast caused headaches for Rove and Scaramucci. They also showed Rove to be a master atop his game.

The breakfast briefing started with a testimonial from Florida senator Marco Rubio, a Crossroads favorite, who told the wealthy audience that they should be proud to donate to Crossroads. "This is a patriotic endeavor," he said. Then Rove laid it on thick. He suggested that Crossroads was the lead dog in the big-money pack, but implied that he was generous and inclusive to the other groups, with which he shared the results of Crossroads's comprehensive focus group testing and polling. "As many of you know, one of the most important things about Crossroads is: we don't try and do this alone. We have partners," he said. "The Kochs—you name it."[12]

Thanks to efforts by Crossroads and its partners, Rove suggested, Republican control of the Senate was in reach. That would require the GOP to maintain all the seats already in its possession, and to pick up four seats held by Democrats. While the odds of that had seemed good months earlier, by around the time of the convention even Republicans were conceding it was increasingly less likely.[13] Rove was still bullish, though, and he suggested other donors were, too. Sounding like a stockbroker coaxing an investment out of reluctant clients by informing them that everyone else is buying, Rove confided that an unnamed "benefactor" had recently pledged $10 million to Crossroads, money that would be spent in Florida helping Romney and the GOP Senate candidate there. But there were two conditions, he said. The gift had to be matched by other donors, and former Florida governor Jeb Bush had to join the Crossroads fund-raising effort. Well, Rove told the donors, "Jeb's making phone calls for us!"[14] Another donor had made a similar $6 million matching challenge for Ohio, Rove said. "Bob Castellini, owner of the Cincinnati Reds, is helping raise the other $3 million for that one."[15] And in a testament to Rove's perceptions of both his sway with the rich activists and their sway in the new big-money politics, he urged his donors to pressure Rep. Todd Akin to drop out of the Missouri Senate race. Akin had won the GOP nomination but was seen as having blown his chances by asserting in a television interview that victims of "legitimate rape" rarely get pregnant. "We should sink Todd Akin. If he's found mysteriously murdered, don't look for my whereabouts!" Rove cracked.[16] Rove, not known for his humility, later felt compelled to call Akin and apologize for the murder crack.[17] But the episode may have actually helped Rove's cachet with his big donors, since few of them hailed from their party's social conservative wing, where Akin still had some dwindling support. Most were business-minded fiscal conservatives appalled by Akin's comments.

Crossroads had arrived in Tampa two-thirds of the way to its $300 million goal, and as the breakfast was coming to a close, former Mississippi governor Haley Barbour took the mound to deliver the closing pitch to the assembled donors. Their donations, he argued, were at least as important as any contributions they might make to hospitals or cancer research. "You all give so unbelievably generously. But you know what, I don't have any compunction about looking you in the eye and asking for more," said Barbour. A savvy operative who had done stints as Ronald Reagan's political director and as chairman of the RNC before running for governor of his home state, Barbour had emerged as a sort of back-slapping big-money éminence grise since leaving office in January 2012, and Crossroads had been one of the main beneficiaries of his fund-raising prowess. "The consequences are greater than any election, and I know everybody in here wants their children and grandchildren to inherit the same country we did," he implored at the breakfast.[18] The pep talk seemed to work. Over the course of the next two weeks, American Crossroads raised $4.5 million, most of which came in the form of big checks from a few new contributors. Crossroads GPS likely raised much more, but it's impossible to know precisely how much, because it does not disclose the givers or dates of its donations. By Election Day, the groups had raised a combined $325 million, $25 million more than their target.

The breakfast—and the final fund-raising sprint that began there—showcased Rove's formula for success in big-money fund-raising. He made donors feel like part of an elite club, partly by providing intimate access to a marquee politician or two, who provided testimonials. Then he presented an analysis of the political landscape that was intended to make the donors feel like they were getting inside dope not available to regular activists or even political junkies. Next, he'd explain to them how their cash was being used to shape that landscape. Finally, he'd make the case that just a few million dollars more would be pivotal in allowing the donors to reach their goal of tipping the election. Scaramucci, though he caused drama for Rove in this case, fairly well typified the mind-set of the GOP big-money donor class for whom this approach seemed tailor-made. The publicity-loving Long Island native, who favors pink shirts, Italian silk ties, and custom-made Loro Piana suits,[19] couldn't get enough of the perks, status, and access provided to major donors by the Rove and Romney operations. (On Wall Street, Scaramucci is known as "the Mooch," though he enjoys pointing out that George W. Bush also dubbed him "Gucci Scaramucci.") Just a few years back, he supported mostly Democrats, including Obama, with whom Scaramucci makes a point of saying that he played basketball while the two were students together at Harvard Law School. But, like many in finance, Scaramucci began souring on Obama once he became president and turned into a populist anti–Wall Street crusader.

Scaramucci latched on early to the Romney campaign, earning a spot on the national finance committee. He boasted of scoring an invitation to Romney's eleven-acre estate on New Hampshire's Lake Winnipesaukee,[20] where the candidate and his wife, Ann, hosted donors for boat rides and policy chats over lunch,[21] with Mitt serving cookies baked by Ann.[22] "People love being able to say they went to Romney's house," he once confided to a reporter.[23] He basked in the glory of being a convention big fish, boasting to another reporter that the millions he'd bundled for Romney made him "one of the top raisers" for the campaign[24] and tweeting scores of photos and updates broadcasting his insider access, often in a dialect that merged the unique lingo of Twitter with that of the Mooch's hyper-machismo Wall Street fraternity. "@HaleyBarbour is the man, great seeing you today Governor, and thanks for all that you are doing," he tweeted at Haley Barbour soon after the Crossroads breakfast.[25] Barbour, a much less active tweeter, did not respond. About an hour later, the Mooch tweeted from a reception for Romney's finance committee, revealing that the campaign had raised $100 million in August.[26] It was a huge sum that seemed to put Romney in excellent shape for the final push, but the Mooch's exuberance was tactless. Campaigns like to keep their fund-raising tallies under wraps until they've determined the moment when bragging about the figures provides maximum strategic benefit.

The afternoon of the Crossroads breakfast, just hours before Romney would accept his party's nomination in a speech that would mark the zenith of his political career, the candidate stopped by a reception with big donors including the Mooch, who of course tweeted a photo of him smiling broadly while embracing the soon-to-be GOP nominee. "Warm up for tonight's big speech!" Scaramucci wrote,[27] followed two minutes later by a tweeted photo of him clasping Ann Romney's arm, accompanied by a summary of his private conversations with the would-be First Couple. Apparently Mitt Romney predicted his convention speech wouldn't be as good as the one his wife had given a couple of days earlier, while his wife lovingly disagreed (of course, in the Mooch's Twitter feed, this translated to "Will .@MittRomney be as good as .@AnnDRomney he says no, she say yes. #lovematch").[28]

Scaramucci's bravado and high spirits vanished suddenly the next morning, when Kolhatkar's story was posted on Bloomberg's website. Though Kolhatkar did not identify Scaramucci in the story, she included a cryptic disclaimer hinting at the circumstances behind her surprising access. "I was invited as the guest of a financier who is a significant Republican donor. The financier knew that I was a journalist. At no point was I presented with, nor did I agree to, restrictions regarding the information I heard. Upon my arrival at the breakfast, I was not asked if I was a journalist. I gave my name, identified the person who had invited me, was handed a wristband, and ushered into the dining room. American Crossroads disputes this version of events, but a spokesman did not immediately return calls to elaborate."

As the story was dominating the political news cycle, Scaramucci called Rove to apologize, but also called Kolhatkar and lit into her. "She gained access when she knew that stuff was off the record. She used my name without permission and did not have permission from anyone to write about it. It was unethical," Scaramucci told me later.[29] Kolhatkar arrived at the Crossroads breakfast before he did, and, according to Scaramucci, "insinuated to the Rove people that she was one of my handlers, like a political operative. At which point, because I have a good relationship with them, they let her in." Kolhatkar disputed Scaramucci's account, telling me, "It had happened exactly as I reported it in *Bloomberg BusinessWeek*."[30] Regardless, two weeks after the incident, Kolhatkar sent Scaramucci an apology letter, hoping to repair their relationship. He did not respond. Instead, he urged his friends in politics and finance not to cooperate with Kolhatkar.* As for the effects on Scaramucci, he said the whole episode "embarrassed me in front of

---

*He suggested he'd do the same to me if I included the incident in this book. "I'm a pretty outspoken guy, I'm a pretty well-connected guy, and I'm a guy that people like. And when your sources start closing down on you and you're saying, 'Geez, I wonder why no one wants to talk to me anymore,' you'll have a sense for it," he said, calling journalism "an unsavory business."

Karl Rove and Paul Singer, and called into question my relationship with those two people."

Crossroads did not go through with a fund-raising event Scaramucci had been planning in New York City. But it did accept $100,000 from his hedge fund, SkyBridge Capital—albeit months after Election Day. If the donation was intended as an olive branch, it appears to have worked. Rove was among the big political names who appeared a few months later at the 2013 edition of the opulent hedge fund bacchanalia that Scaramucci hosts each year in Las Vegas, and the architect was on the agenda again for 2014. And if word of Scaramucci's indiscretion got out in GOP politics, it didn't seem to damage his standing. He maintained access to the elite sanctum of Romney's big-donor land, where he continued to be an active player right through Election Day. Thanks to the rise of the shadow party, the campaigns are pretty much forced to tolerate the big donors' antics, indiscretions, and advice. They can't afford not to.

Things were more orderly on the left. The Democratic donors were more disciplined about the message, and there was no obvious big-money rivalry. That may have been partly because the left's big-money operation was more modest in size. But it was also, as Paul Begala had gleefully pointed out to donors, because for once Democrats had their "shit together." The Democratic super PACs clearly delineated lines of responsibility and stuck to them—Begala's Priorities USA Action was the official pro-Obama super PAC, Majority PAC was the Senate super PAC, House Majority PAC was the House super PAC, and American Bridge was the opposition-research super PAC. The Democratic super PACs held fund-raisers together and even arranged it so donors could write a single check to an umbrella group, which would divide the money equally among them. The collaboration, combined with the continued push by Bill Clinton, House Democratic leader Nancy Pelosi, and other Democratic money masters, started opening wallets even more after the conventions. George Soros committed $1.5 million to the Democratic super PACs—announced by his political advisor, Michael Vachon, at a late September Democracy Alliance luncheon headlined by Clinton, Pelosi, and New York senator Chuck Schumer, another donor darling. In an email to invitees explaining his shift, Soros wrote

that he was "appalled by the Romney campaign, which is openly soliciting the money of the rich to starve the state of the money it needs to
provide social services."[31]

The polling numbers had started to look good for Obama. Statistical
models used to project elections, like the closely watched one produced
by stats guru Nate Silver, then of the *New York Times,* showed a high
likelihood of an Obama win. Conservatives rejected those projections
as biased, with Rove branding as "goofy" and "weird"[32] polls that had
Obama ahead. A month before Election Day, the headline on his *Wall
Street Journal* column was "Can We Believe the Presidential Polls?"[33] It
was followed a week later by one asserting that Romney's undisputedly
strong performance in the first presidential debate had "changed the arc
of the election—and perhaps its outcome."[34]

While Rove amped up the bombast and pushed donors with maximum force, Crossroads spent money with boundless determination.
Crossroads and a number of other big-money GOP groups played
shock politics by expanding their ad buys into states that seemed
safely in Obama's column. Perhaps the most audacious of those plays
came the week before Election Day, when Crossroads, the main Koch
groups, and the Romney campaign combined to spend $6 million on
ads in Pennsylvania. It was a state where Obama had a vastly superior ground game and, according to polls, a sturdy lead. But Rove,
in particular, was hitting up some of his top donors to pay for more
ads in the state. Houston home builder Bob Perry, who had already
donated $7.5 million to Crossroads's 2012 efforts, wrote another $1
million check on October 23. It was proof again of Rove's brazen tactics and hinted at the self-fulfilling nature of the shadow campaign's
big-money fund-raising.

Democrats puzzled aloud over the Pennsylvania play. Obama senior
advisor David Plouffe called it a desperate ploy. "My sense is Karl is
going to be at a crossroads himself on Tuesday when he tries to explain
to the people who wrote him hundreds of millions of dollars why they
fell up short," Plouffe mused on ABC News a couple days before the
election.[35]

That night, Rove was on Fox News defending the Pennsylvania
push. "We would not be spending it unless we sensed an opportunity

there. We could have taken that money and plunged it into the existing battleground states, but instead, ya know, there's a real opportunity there, and it moved without the benefit of campaign activity."[36] Once more, Rove sounded pretty sure of himself and his analysis, and how could he not be? He had convinced his donors to go all in, and because of that he was all in as well. Rove wasn't alone, of course. The Kochs and other conservative big-money operations also were projecting confidence down the home stretch that their donors' unprecedented investment was going to pay off. For the shadow party, it was the biggest bet yet. On the day before the election, the big-money tea party group FreedomWorks held a conference call in which one of its operatives told donors to expect a blowout for Romney and big gains in the Senate, according to the Minnesota mogul Stan Hubbard, who participated in the call. Rove was more precise and slightly less ambitious, predicting on his website on Election Day that Romney would win 285 electoral votes to Obama's 253. It was a good thing the architect didn't bet the house.

As polls closed on November 6 and state tallies trickled in, the unprecedented fund-raising and spinning and strategizing of the Republican big-money alliance went up in smoke. The networks started calling the election for Obama early, after their models showed him locking up Ohio and, with it, the electoral votes necessary for four more years. Soon it became clear that the Democrats would hold the Senate as well. Even Fox News's number crunchers made the call for Obama, which the anchors dutifully relayed to viewers.

Everything Rove had worked for disintegrated in a matter of minutes. He spiraled into an epic meltdown live on Fox's airwaves that left Democrats and rival conservative operatives positively giddy—and GOP mega-donors wondering about the man they'd just entrusted with so much cash. When Rove urged the network to stand down on its prediction of an Obama win, suggesting on air that the call was "premature," Fox News threw Rove—and his spin—under the bus. Network anchor Megyn Kelly marched, cameras trailing her every step, to the "decision desk" to interview the experts who had made the call for Fox News. The decision desk stood by the call, with a pollster telling Kelly on live TV, "We're quite comfortable with the idea that Obama will carry Ohio."

By the end of what was a nasty night for Rove, of the thirty-one races in which the Crossroads groups had aired ads, the Republican won in only nine. Fox News anchor Chris Wallace drove the point home later that night, after the dust had settled. "We spent billions of dollars," Wallace said to Rove, who was by now slightly calmer, if exhausted-looking. "Crossroads, which you helped found, spent—what?—$325 million, and we've ended up with the same president, the same Democratic majority in the Senate, and the same Republican majority in the House. Was it worth it?" The question would hang in the air for months to come.

But Rove responded right away. "Yeah," he said. "Look, if groups like Crossroads were not active, this race would have been over a long time ago." It came across as an uninspired effort to justify a big, lost bet.

The question at this point wasn't what Rove thought. It was what his donors thought, and the donors thought in the Koch network and all the other big-money groups. The answer would determine whether the shadow party would be back in 2014 and beyond—and who would be at its helm.

CHAPTER 10

The Autopsies

For most people, the 2012 election will be remembered for the reelection of the country's first African American president, for its first Mormon presidential nominee, and perhaps for one of the most theatrical Republican primaries in some time.

But a handful of stunning numerical milestones from 2012 provide a more methodological look at the direction of American democracy:

- *$7 billion:* the traceable amount spent by all the candidates, parties, and outside groups combined, a record figure[1]
- *$2.5 billion:* the amount spent by super PACs and other independent outfits[2]—the first time outside groups did more spending than the two major political parties themselves,[3] which together spent $1.6 billion[4]
- *$1.3 billion:* the amount paid to the five highest-grossing political consulting firms[5]
- *100:* the number of mega-donors it took to raise $470 million for the limit-free super PACs[6]
- *5,667,658:* the number of small donors it took to give a combined $370 million to President Obama and Mitt Romney[7]
- *6.6 percent:* the share of money spent by Karl Rove's Crossroads outfit in races where Republicans actually won,[8] out of a total of $175 million in traceable cash Crossroads poured into specific races

The numbers—which have a cartoonish quality to them—stand as incontrovertible proof of the arrival of big money in politics, ushering in an era in which billionaires reigned, party power waned, and consultants' payments grew insane. But even on Election Night 2012, as I started to process these numbers amid picked-over boxes of cold pizza at Politico's suburban Washington headquarters, it was obvious that we were just getting started—in 2016, those data points would seem quaint by comparison.

As it was becoming clear that Obama would win reelection, I could hear the disappointment in Foster Friess's voice. He was in Sheldon Adelson's Venetian casino in Las Vegas, where the state GOP was throwing its Election Night bash. "It's so heartbreaking, when you look at the political animal itself. It's so much effort, so much work, and then, in one night, it's all over," the Wyoming mega-donor told me. "I thought Romney was going to be able to really have a wide, wide margin." Friess would keep giving, he told me, but he wanted to redirect his money toward groups that copied Democrats by better coordinating their messages and investing more in grassroots organizing and social media. "I'm not a big fan of TV ads. They're just too quick. They are sound bites." Friess had invested more than $2.5 million in groups that focused primarily on just such sound-bite advertising, and had given still more to groups that didn't disclose their donors, though he admitted he couldn't remember many of them. "Everything happened so fast these last couple of months," he told me, his perpetually optimistic outlook seemingly wilting. "I'm kind of burned out right now. You know, with just how much effort and resources I put into it, but I think it's money well spent," he concluded feebly.

Republican Party loyalists were far less sanguine about the toppling piles of cash that big donors like Friess had poured into the election. Not long after Romney conceded, I got an email from a longtime RNC source who had put years into building the party's donor rolls and had spent the months before Election Day privately grumbling about the migration of cash away from the parties. The Republican Party had failed to convincingly make the case to big donors that it was a better steward of their cash than the outside groups, my source contended. And the outside groups were squandering their motherlode by pouring it into costly television ads that resulted in fat commissions for consultants while failing to change voters' attitudes. Summarizing the performance of the GOP's financial infrastructure, both in the official party committees and in the big-money sphere that had just produced this record spending orgy, my source's judgment was stark: "A disaster."

Democratic big-money types, meanwhile, were trumpeting the success of their effort, casting it as a triumph of brains over brawn, but also promising that next time they'd have more cash to go along with the superior coordination they had brought to bear in 2012.

"We hope it's a mutual disarmament, but if it's not, then we'll be back," Steve Mostyn bellowed into his phone from inside the boisterous Obama campaign victory party at Chicago's McCormick Place convention center. He and his wife, Amber, together with their firm, had donated $4.2 million to liberal super PACs. "The Democrats were slow to come to the super PAC idea and I think that, with the win tonight, you will see less reluctance, at least from the guys that I talk to about fund-raising, to do it next time," Mostyn told me.

Even before the confetti had been swept away, Democratic operatives were making it clear they would keep their foot on the gas pedal of their shiny new big-money machine. In the wee hours of Wednesday morning, Paul Begala offered me a preview of how the next round of mega-donor solicitations might sound: "Our super PAC was underfunded compared to the right, but we were more focused, more strategic, and much more effective," he said. "Our donors got a terrific return on their investment. I'm not sure donors to the right-wing super PACs feel the same way."

One reason the Democrats were more hopeful than the Republicans about their big-money future—quite apart from the outcome of the election, which sometimes seemed of secondary importance to the fund-raising competition—was their relative ideological unity. Even if a single billionaire or group of multimillionaires decided to spend big money pushing a given candidate or issue that bucked the Democratic orthodoxy, it was unlikely to seriously challenge the party. The biggest Democratic givers at that point were mostly on the same page as Obama, Nancy Pelosi, and Harry Reid.

The same could not be said of the Republicans. They faced a deep ideological rift, and big money was making it worse. Neither side—the business-backed country club set or the stridently ideological tea party wing—had emerged from Election Day with full control of the party. Both had access to backers willing to spend heavily to gain the upper hand, setting the stage for a lengthy and damaging shadow party civil war for the soul of the Republican Party.

The official Republican Party, weakened and searching, convened a special panel to study what had gone wrong in 2012 and how it could be fixed. The group's mission was ambitious, maybe even impossible—to figure out how the Republican Party could reclaim control and momentum in the big-money, *Citizens United* era. Officially, the panel and the report it was tasked with writing were called the "Growth and Opportunity Project." Around politics, though, it quickly became known as the "RNC Autopsy." Unless there were major changes to the campaign finance system or big donors decided on their own to abandon outside groups, the shadow party *was* the party. The Grand Old Party was just that, old, and clinging to relevance. Control of the shadow party would be determined not by anything the RNC did but by the conclusions donors drew from 2012 and their decisions about who could be trusted with their cash in the future. So, in the weeks after Election Day, nearly every conservative operative who had collected large checks in 2012 made the rounds of donors, outlining the analytics behind their spending, explaining where things had gone wrong, and pledging to learn the lessons of 2012. There were some tough questions from donors, not least about why there was such a disconnect between the election results and the metrics operatives had touted in the final weeks that showed Romney winning or at least in a deadlocked race. Some donors didn't seem entirely satisfied with some of the answers.

Mega-donor Stan Hubbard, referring to the pre-election prediction by a representative of FreedomWorks that there would be a blowout win for Romney and GOP gains in the Senate, called the organization "a bunch of knuckleheads."[9] FreedomWorks spent $45 million in 2012,[10] though it was unclear how much—if any—of that came from Hubbard, since a majority of the group's spending came through channels that are not subject to disclosure.

Frank VanderSloot, the Idaho businessman whose family and company donated $1.1 million to the pro-Romney Restore Our Future super PAC and at least $200,000 to Rove's Crossroads, said ominously that there "is going to be a sorting out of who got the job done. And I think there will be some who might lay claim to accomplishments that they maybe didn't personally accomplish. And that will get sorted out, I think, absolutely. And some of these organizations will gain in stature and some will probably fall by the wayside."

There was plenty of finger-pointing to go around. Rich Republicans were none too pleased with the super PACs, the RNC, Romney's campaign, and the campaigns of several GOP Senate candidates. Some establishment operatives blamed the RNC for lackluster ground organization, the tea party groups for supporting flawed candidates, and the candidates themselves for clumsy handling of divisive social issues. Tea partiers and social conservatives, in turn, blamed establishment super PACs for taking the grassroots for granted and pouring cash into worthless TV ads. Behind all the sniping was a single question that made many of the leading operatives very uncomfortable: where did all the money go?

For many donors and activists alike, the bull's-eye ultimately settled on a small group of publicity-averse Republicans who had reaped huge payments during the 2012 campaign despite their side's calamitous performance: professional political consultants. The ranks of this group were fed by operatives who mostly had come up through their party or its campaigns and then left in search of more influence and bigger paydays in the private sector consulting for the party, its candidates, and now the outside groups. The biggest prizes, then as now, were commission-based contracts for television ad buys, direct mail, and fund-raising. The consultants' firms usually got a cut of whatever the client raised and spent, sometimes as high as 15 percent. Plenty of vacation homes had been purchased over the years from such commissions.

Never before, though, had there been so much money pulsing into this consulting sphere. Not only was the sheer volume of cash being raised by the super PACs and the campaigns greater than ever, but much more political work was being contracted out to consultants. That included key functions that political campaigns and committees used to consider plum in-house gigs, with comfortable salaries and bountiful expense accounts. Across the board—in major campaign and party committees, but especially at the super PACs—positions such as those of political director, finance director, and digital director were either being contracted out to consultants or handled by employees on leave from consultancies who in turn oversaw the contracting out of much of the support work to their firms. The result was a privatization of politics that made good sense from the perspective of the client groups and campaigns, which benefited from economies of scale. But it also created an incredibly powerful, unelected brain trust of consultants who had great control over the shadow party—and politics as a whole. It was not dissimilar to the defense contractors that reaped billions each year from a federal government that ceded progressively more of its military functions and decision-making to the private sector. The political contractors were ultimately accountable only to those who wrote the checks. And unlike seasoned party or campaign officials—who knew how to spot when consultants were making decisions with the primary goal of increasing their commissions rather than ensuring success on Election Day—many of the donors didn't know whose advice was solid and who was merely calculating profit margins.

As questions mounted about the motives and performance of this well-compensated and influential, but low-profile, clique, they increasingly fell, as such attention often did, at Karl Rove's feet. Although he had made a point of insisting that he made no money from Crossroads (his critics consistently questioned the claim), he was a natural target. He was by far the best-known player in super PAC politics and he had come to personify the big-money shadow party. After all, he had imagined a network of independent deep-pocketed Republican groups even before *Citizens United* made them possible. He shaped new outfits like Crossroads, and the operatives and consultants running them were his protégés and allies. And it was he who convinced preexisting conservative groups to join up, won over the richest donors, and was credited with helping lift Republicans to landslide wins in the 2010 midterm elections.

Immediately after the 2012 debacle, Rove launched into damage control mode, directing blame in a variety of directions, none anywhere close to him. There was the bartender at a private fund-raiser who recorded the damaging video of Romney disparaging 47 percent of American voters; there was Hurricane Sandy, which interrupted Romney's surge and allowed Obama "to look presidential and bipartisan";[11] there were the Republican candidates who didn't connect with Hispanic voters the way they needed to. Plus the national and state Republican Party committees failed to match the Democrats' get-out-the-vote effort and allowed Obama to capitalize on that by "suppressing the vote"[12] among those who were dissatisfied with his leadership. Rove laid blame at the feet of specific Republican candidates, including Romney, asserting that his campaign had failed to respond adequately to Democratic efforts to brand him as an out-of-touch elitist. He also dropped more ordnance on the unfortunate political corpses of Republican Senate candidates like Missouri's Todd Akin, who Rove said should have abandoned the race after his claim that victims of "legitimate rape" rarely get pregnant. "He put his own personal ambitions above the best interests of the party," Rove tut-tutted.[13]

Crossroads's biggest donors got a chance to hear all this directly from Rove in an invitation-only conference call two days after the election. The call focused partly on Crossroads's strategy but also looked at Romney's campaign and those of GOP Senate candidates. "Everybody is disappointed who gave money, obviously," Stan Hubbard told me soon after hanging up from the call.[14] But, he added, when it came to the performance of the Rove-conceived Crossroads groups, "there were no recriminations. No blame. Nothing negative. It was all very factual: here's where we are, here's where we came from." Donors "weren't saying anything like 'Hey, you dumb son of a bitch,'" said Hubbard, who had donated to both the Rove-conceived American Crossroads super PAC and its secret-money nonprofit affiliate Crossroads GPS. "It was all very businesslike. It was as if you were in a business conference and you were a retailer and 'Why didn't this product sell better?'" Even if Rove had made some tactical errors, he had tried his best, Hubbard said: "Every quarterback, every coach doesn't call every play 100 percent right." When Hubbard gave his perspective, it sounded an awful lot like the conclusions that Rove wanted donors to reach: yes, there were problems, but Rove could solve them.

"You can't have candidates like we had in Indiana and Missouri who were nut cases. You can't have candidates like we had a couple years ago in Nevada. You know, it's craziness," Hubbard continued, referring to Akin as well as Senate candidates Richard Mourdock and Sharron Angle, who had won GOP primaries with support from tea party groups only to self-destruct in the general election. "Nominating people who are going to say, 'Well, if your daughter gets raped, it's God's will'—I mean, give me a break, will you? What kind of nonsense is that?" Hubbard huffed, referring to a Mourdock quote.

Hubbard wasn't showering praise on Mitt Romney, either. "Romney may have empathy, but he never showed it. The people have to have confidence in you and feel that you're one of them. Even I could do that better than he did." His conclusion: "I would absolutely be all for getting electable candidates. I'm a very conservative person, but I'd rather have somebody who is friendly to me than a fellow ideologue." He would resume giving to Rove's groups if he could find a way to avoid such candidates, Hubbard told me.

But Republican operatives had begun whispering that maybe it was the end of line for the architect—that he might be too toxic to be an effective player in the shadow party. If Rove didn't distance himself from Crossroads, he might just bring it down with him, Rove's rivals gleefully predicted.

Three weeks after Election Day, American Crossroads's founding chairman, Mike Duncan, met with its communications director, Jonathan Collegio, for an early breakfast at Washington's Madison Hotel to talk about reactions to the election and about the future of their group. Rove's role was a subject of conversation. In response to a question from Collegio, Duncan explained that about two-thirds of Crossroads's fund-raising could be credited to Rove, according to a source who happened to be seated at an adjacent table. While Crossroads in 2012 had come to be known as "Rove's group," Collegio and even the group's lawyers in its early days had tried to discourage that perception. And at their post-election breakfast Duncan said that when the group was formed, it was "not intended to be the Karl show," according to my source.

Duncan challenged that account, explaining he had "no recollection of a meeting like that," but stressing that he would never minimize

Rove's role at Crossroads.[15] "Since the beginning, Karl has been a senior advisor to the Crossroads groups and has raised significant resources in each cycle," Duncan asserted. While it would be difficult to measure how much fund-raising Rove accounted for, he said, "Crossroads wouldn't be what it is without Karl ... Karl is and always will be a key to the Crossroads efforts."

The centrality of Rove's role underscored a potentially pivotal threat for Crossroads. What would happen to the group if 2012 left Rove's reputation with donors damaged beyond repair? More broadly, the situation underscored a harsh reality in the new big-money politics: nothing was permanent. Unlike the political parties, which had an enduring and legally defined place in American politics, the big-money groups existed in a space that more closely resembled the free market. If a group didn't satisfy its customers—in this case, the donors—it could easily be replaced by another, and find itself out of business. But Crossroads wasn't planning on fading away. Quite the opposite. It was quietly preparing for an expansion. Not long after the election, it moved into new offices about half a mile from its old headquarters at 1401 New York Avenue, NW, where staff had been spread across two floors. In the new headquarters, at 1615 L Street, NW, everyone was on the same floor, allowing better communication regarding the ambitious plans the group was hatching. Nearly three months after Election Day, Crossroads publicly unveiled those plans—its answer to 2012. It was called the Conservative Victory Project. It would be run by the Crossroads team, and it was precisely tailored to meet the emerging demands of the new big-money political marketplace. The plan was to raise and spend large sums in Republican primaries through a super PAC and sister nonprofit group to ensure that the most viable general election candidates—from Crossroads's perspective, of course—won the party's nomination. In other words, the Conservative Victory Project would try to kill off candidates like Akin, Mourdock, and Angle before they could get going in GOP primaries and have the chance to lose to Democrats.

The project would open up an expansive new frontier. By wading into open Republican primaries, the biggest money would enter a domain that the party committees mostly tried to avoid. Both parties have generally shied away from entering primary fights, not wanting to pick one candidate over another unless there's an incumbent, or in rare other cases. The Conservative Victory Project, by contrast, could go so far as to oppose a sitting Republican lawmaker deemed problematic by the small handful of operatives who ran Crossroads. It was yet another way in which the unelected consultants and rich backers who constituted the shadow party had something of a competitive advantage over the official elected party apparatus. In fact, the new Crossroads play was motivated by an earlier move into primaries by the well-funded groups that represented the tea party wing of the shadow party, such as FreedomWorks, which had helped the subsequently unelectable Richard Mourdock defeat the centrist six-term sitting senator Richard Lugar in Indiana.

As Crossroads president and CEO Steven Law put it in an email to donors announcing the effort, the Conservative Victory Project would "weigh in on behalf of competitive, committed conservatives when they are attacked by outside groups attempting to boost a demonstrably flawed candidate who would forfeit the race."[16] But who would determine whether a candidate was flawed? Not the voters, but the donors and consultants to the Conservative Victory Project.

The underlying premise behind the new project was truly audacious: that despite its $325 million spending spree, Crossroads had bombed in 2012 because it hadn't spent enough money, and specifically enough early money in primaries, to shape the election. It seemed kind of like gambling away all your money at the blackjack table, then blaming your losses on the fact that you didn't have enough money to win back your savings. If donors were persuaded by that reasoning, then the Conservative Victory Project—and the Crossroads operation more broadly—was back on a path toward fund-raising success.

While Crossroads downplayed Rove's involvement in the new project, it had all the hallmarks of a Rove initiative. It was bold, ingenious, and perfectly attuned both to the political moment and—more important—to his donors' mind-set. His critics pounced on the project as a cynical rebranding effort by Rove and a cabal of well-connected operatives to protect themselves despite their failed 2012 effort. Rove did little to quash that speculation when, a few weeks after the unveiling, he confessed to a bit of self-preservational motivation. "My posterior was shredded a little bit by donors wondering why we are writing checks for people who then turn around and run such lousy campaigns," he said at an event in Dallas.[17] Likewise, the Crossroads team's assertions that the new project would adhere to "the 'William F. Buckley Rule' by supporting the most conservative candidate *who can win* in a given race"[18] did little to quell criticism from tea partiers. They saw the Conservative Victory Project as an effort by business interests and their consultant toadies to steer the Republican Party to the center by eradicating the tea party influence. It wasn't even three months after the 2012 election, and the big-money showdown had already begun ahead of the next election.

"The RINO project to beat conservatives in primaries is called 'Conservative Victory Project'???" tweeted[19] Koch World operative Phil Kerpen,[20] invoking the widely used acronym for despised moderate GOPers—Republican In Name Only. "Nothing says 'conservative victory' like defeating conservatives."[21]

The anti-establishment frustration took a more personal form with the public airing of long-simmering allegations that the circle of big-money consultants surrounding Rove were lining their pockets with donors' cash at the expense of the cause. Consultants from both parties had long whispered about rivals who charged more than the industry standard for advertising or fund-raising commissions, but this was different. Suddenly such charges were finding their way onto widely read blogs. And they were getting traction among everyone from grassroots activists who felt shut out of the party to politicians who felt like their campaigns were becoming mere consultant-enrichment vehicles and even some in the donor community itself. The money machine was turning on itself.

The influential conservative pundit Erick Erickson for months had been swiping obliquely at the consultants working for Romney, the RNC, and the leading super PACs. But after the election he launched a full frontal assault with a widely circulated blog post entitled "The Incestuous Bleeding of the Republican Party." Folks trying to decide where to lay the blame for the GOP's disastrous 2012 showing, he argued, should turn their gaze toward the fifth floor of a sprawling brick office complex on the banks of the Potomac River opposite Washington. That suite of offices, located at 66 Canal Center Plaza in Alexandria, Virginia, housed a handful of interlinked firms whose principles included Rove protégé Carl Forti and other top consultants who had helped steer the 2012 efforts of Crossroads, the RNC, Romney's campaign and super PAC, and other big-spending groups. Canal Center was where you'd find the nexus of power and cash in the new Republican shadow establishment, Erickson wrote. "Here, the top party consultants waged war with conservative activists and here they waged war with the Democrats. On both fronts, they raked in millions along the way with a more fractured, minority party in their wake. And they show no signs of recognizing just how much a part of the problem they are."[22] Erickson kept up the drumbeat, and major donors began reaching out to him, curious about his thoughts on whether it was possible to spend money in politics more effectively through other channels.

It was an uncomfortable development for the professional Republican class. And things got worse at the annual Conservative Political Action Conference in suburban Maryland's cavernous National Harbor convention center in March 2013. CPAC, as the forty-year-old conference is known, is sort of like Comic-Con for conservatives, where grassroots activists and operatives from across the conservative movement's disparate sects gather to network, party, and hear from top politicians. They enjoy open bars sponsored by various deep-pocketed groups as they try to chart the course for the Republican Party and the conservative movement. While there is always some tension among the factions—between fiscal and social conservatives, for instance—CPAC 2013 felt different. In the panels, there was a palpable strain of tea party anger at the GOP establishment, and it was directed most acutely at consultants like Rove, as opposed to the RNC.

Things boiled over during one of the side sessions where a packed crowd had gathered for a panel with a name that was anything but discreet: "Should We Shoot All the Consultants Now?" In a fiery speech that quickly generated buzz, erstwhile Democratic pollster Pat Caddell, enjoying a second professional life as a darling of the right, blasted a "racketeering" consultant class that put its bottom-line interests before the party's. "These people are doing business for themselves. They are a part of the Washington establishment. These people don't want to have change," thundered the excitable Caddell,[23] who looks a bit like an older, bespectacled version of Leonard Nimoy's Spock character. "They're in the business of lining their pockets, and preserving their power."[24] The system lacked accountability, Caddell went on. "I'll tell you who I blame—the donors who allow themselves to be played for marks," he said. Despite the fact that there was only a partial shaky recording, the speech became a rallying cry for a growing group of conservatives—from young activists to talk show king Rush Limbaugh—who were increasingly alarmed about what they saw as a big-money takeover of their party.

"The reaction I got to that speech was amazing," Caddell told me months later. Four former Republican presidential candidates, two sitting senators, and dozens of high-ranking operatives from both parties reached out privately to praise him for speaking truth to power, Caddell said. "The silence of the people I was attacking was deafening, and I get attacked by everyone for everything. They didn't want to have that debate. The dogs that don't bark I find most interesting."

Caddell dumped so much of the blame at the consultants' feet because he felt they had flipped the system on its head and were now exerting disproportionate control over it. It used to be that consultants mostly just spent the cash raised by their client campaigns and party committees to implement the strategies crafted by those clients. Now, though, they were actually setting the strategy, sometimes dealing directly with the donors who funded them. In the case of the big-money outside groups, the consultants frequently had nearly complete autonomy to spend as they saw fit, and in 2012 that meant huge ad buys that aggressively attacked Obama. While such ads often thrilled the donors, who were the ultimate authority to whom the consultants answered, they did little to build a positive narrative about Republicans that might win over swing voters. Caddell found it odd that the super PAC donors would bless—tacitly or directly—a strategy he found so ham-handed. "These are people for the most part who are quite successful in business and would never allow their businesses, their companies, to be taken for a ride the way they are in politics. But they are sold that politics is some kind of black magic."

Finding out what actually happens to the money once it leaves the big donors' wallets is easier said than done, since reports filed with the Federal Election Commission and the Internal Revenue Service only list what campaigns, parties, and some outside groups pay to various consultants, not the actual amounts pocketed by the consultants. Much of the money reflected in the federally reported payments is spent on things like airtime for ads, printing, and postage for mailers, and phone banks for polling. It's impossible to know with precision how much is cleared as profit. The operatives tend to prefer keeping this type of information a secret, both because it could fuel criticism like Erickson's and because it could give their rivals a competitive advantage in bidding on contracts or gaming out strategies. Among the only ways I know of to try to get a sense of how much the operatives are making is to examine their lives, to the extent that it's possible to assess what kinds of houses, cars, and boats they're buying. When I cross-referenced FEC records of top-earning big-money consulting fees with one key indicator of lifestyle, property records, I found a number of young operatives in their thirties and forties gobbling up million-dollar vacation getaways and Beltway-area homes.

These folks of my generation, who had cut their teeth inside the official party system—which happens to pay only slightly better than my chosen field, journalism—were suddenly upgrading their lifestyles. Not only that, they were doing it right in my neighborhood. My adopted hometown of Alexandria, Virginia, a historic little city across the Potomac River from Washington, was a hot spot for the political nouveau riche. Unexceptional $600,000 townhouses like mine were mixed in with stately old mansions, gleaming new homes built in a turn-of-the-century style, and a host of top consulting firm offices, including Canal Center. A trio of young operatives who were founding partners in firms headquartered at times on the fifth floor of 66 Canal Center, Michael Dubke, Carl Forti, and Zac Moffatt, had all settled into expensive new homes soon after Election Day. Of course, even the combination of real estate records and campaign payments offered only a partial snapshot of these consultants' lives. They wouldn't reveal if a parent recently left a large inheritance or a spouse had been putting in overnight shifts at a hospital to save up cash for a new house. Nor would they speak to the long hours that many of the operative class logged at Washington-area offices like Canal Center or in dingy campaign headquarters around the country, building their businesses and brands while providing valuable services to candidates and causes they believed in. And it's also possible that many of the consultants who cashed in on the 2012 election were making as much money or more from corporate work that wasn't subject to disclosure requirements.

Still, an assessment of the property records of the consultants tied to Canal Center seemed worthwhile, given the unprecedented stream of cash flowing into their firms, which served some of the biggest-spending efforts. One of the firms, Dubke's Crossroads Media, collected an astounding $248 million in payments during the 2012 campaign, with massive payments coming from the Crossroads groups, the RNC, and Restore Our Future, among others. Also on the fifth floor of Canal Center was another digital consultancy called TargetPoint, which reaped $5.1 million in payments from Romney's campaign, American Crossroads, Restore Our Future, and others in 2012. It was founded by Alex Gage, whose wife, Katie Packer Gage, was Romney's deputy campaign manager. She cofounded and was president of yet another consultancy located on Canal Center's fifth floor, WWP Strategies, which was paid $5.5 million for 2012 work by the Romney campaign and various state Republican Party committees. During the heat of the 2010 campaign, the Gages' firms combined to reap $1.5 million in payments from a list of overlapping clientele. They also got married around that time and bought a $1.1 million home in Alexandria.

Another firm with ties to the Canal Center brain trust was the direct-mail and phone-banking juggernaut FLS Connect, which was cofounded by Moffatt's mentor Tony Feather. FLS collected $68 million in 2012 from the RNC, Romney, American Crossroads, and others, while its founders and partners worked for the RNC and the Romney campaign. One such FLS partner, Rich Beeson, took a leave of absence to serve as Romney's political director. About a month after Election Day, Beeson bought a $935,000 getaway nestled against the border of Colorado's Rocky Mountain National Park. The front deck and windows of the four-bedroom home, which is built in a nouveau log-cabin style, overlook idyllic Shadow Mountain Lake and the majestic Rocky Mountains. Beeson, forty-five years old on Election Day, grew up in a trailer without indoor plumbing in eastern Colorado, the youngest of twelve children whose mechanic father never made more than $15,000 a year. Eight of his siblings have passed away—six from a debilitating hereditary disease—and Beeson has helped take care of their kids as well as his elderly parents. The Beesons' new getaway, a family retreat of sorts, was located about a two-hour drive from another house that Beeson owns in suburban Denver and a four-hour drive from a more modest cabin they owned in the southern part of the state. The Beesons had been saving for the new place throughout the stressful 2012 campaign, during which the couple and their kids relocated to Boston to be close to Romney campaign headquarters. Packer Gage and Moffatt also left their old lives behind to relocate to temporary digs near the campaign office, where they logged twenty-hour days seven days a week for two years.

Moffatt, who worked with Feather and Forti at Freedom's Watch, three years earlier had cofounded a digital strategy firm called Targeted Victory with the help of Feather, who served on the operating group and provided advice. It also was initially headquartered at 66 Canal Center. Drawing on connections to the Republican National Committee, Mitt Romney (for whom Moffatt took a leave from Targeted Victory to serve as digital director during the 2012 campaign), Crossroads, and other new super PACs, Targeted Victory exploded out of the gate. Its billings were unusually vigorous, reaching $114 million through February 2013. At the end of that month, Moffatt and his wife, who had not previously owned a home, spent $905,000 on a stately tan brick townhouse in Alexandria's showcase Potomac Yard development. The three-story home had four bedrooms and four and a half bathrooms, and—like the rest of Potomac Yards—was newly constructed. I'd watched the development rise in a formerly empty field, since my wife and I live less than two miles away.

About five miles south, Forti and Dubke, proud Buffalo, New York, natives and business partners, were moving into much more expensive homes located two miles from each other in the Fort Hunt neighborhood of Alexandria, one of the wealthiest census designations in the country. Forti and his wife bought their new home—a newly constructed six-bedroom, five-and-a-half-bath Craftsman-style house with tasteful stone masonry accents on the portico—for $1.7 million in January 2013, a few weeks after selling their old place for less than half that.

With all these members of the powerful and flush consulting class as neighbors, I figured I might as well take a driving tour to gauge for myself the lifestyles of the political rich and low-profile. So on a Sunday morning in the fall of 2013, I headed to the Forti, Dubke, Moffatt, and Gage estates. Where there were lawns, they were landscaped and immaculate. And even though it was two days before Virginia's off-year election, at none of those homes was there a yard sign or bumper sticker supporting the Republican candidates for governor (Ken Cuccinelli), lieutenant governor (E. W. Jackson), or attorney general (Mark Obenshain). That wasn't too much of a surprise, since the trio were aligned with the tea party wing of the Republican Party, which was locked in a battle with Crossroads and the other establishment groups and candidates that helped pay for those new homes. Instead of a Cuccinelli sticker, the SUVs in the driveways at chez Forti and Dubke had Buffalo Bills plate holders or trailer hitch emblems. In Dubke's driveway, a 2008 Range Rover Sport HSE, which he bought used, had a Virginia vanity plate reading "TAX CUT," while the late-model Mercedes in the Gages' driveway had plates from Vermont, where the couple owned a $1 million home set on thirty-six acres.

"No one got wealthy off the Romney campaign, and reporters and bloggers should do their homework before they attack the characters of honest, hardworking people," Katie Packer Gage told me.[25] She questioned whether it was "invasive to go digging up people's real estate holdings to try to make some connection between the money they made on the campaign and how much they spent on a home for their families."[26] Both her firm and her husband's actually did more corporate work than political. The same is true of Forti's.

More generally, Gage pointed out, political campaigns and committees are free to spend the money they raise from donors as they see fit, and they're wise to retain consultants they've worked with before and trust. "You're not going to get good people and pay a pittance for it," she said, noting how difficult it is to unseat an incumbent president and praising the Romney campaign team's effort. She questioned the political savvy of critics fixated on the fees collected by top Republican consultants in 2012. "I'm sure that Erick Erickson has opinions about all sorts of things that he has no experience with," she said.[27] But, she added, "people who haven't been through this, haven't been through it. And they have no idea what it's like. So I get pretty hostile when I see people sitting that far out of the arena suggesting how the game ought to be played." Her attitude toward them, she said, is, "What business is it of yours?"[28] Except for the screeds of people like Erickson and Caddell, consultants like the Gages, Zac Moffatt, Rich Beeson, Carl Forti, and Michael Dubke experienced little in the way of long-term consequences as a result of their parts in the 2012 letdown. The Republican National Committee's hundred-page post-election autopsy report did suggest it might be wise to audit future big contracts and also alluded to "a need for greater competition among vendors to spur more creativity and better outcomes." But the autopsy mostly focused elsewhere, and there was little indication that post-election analyses by Crossroads and other conservative big-money groups were any more critical of their consultants, though the Koch network was a bit tougher on some of its operatives.

The goal of these analyses seemed to be proving to donors that the groups had learned the lessons of 2012 and would get better results with donors' cash in the 2014 congressional elections and the 2016 presidential contest. The tone seemed to be a balance of remorse and self-affirmation, lest too-aggressive self-criticism hand an advantage to organizations competing for big-money donors.

In the official party autopsy, the RNC conceded it had lost control to the outside groups. With notable envy, it made a point of observing that the groups can

> use unlimited, and often unreported, amounts of the same money federal candidates and national parties are now prohibited from spending or raising. The result is an upside-down system where candidates and their parties no longer have the loudest voices in campaigns or even the ability to determine the issues debated in campaigns. Outside groups now play an expanded role affecting federal races and, in some ways, overshadow state parties in primary and general elections. As a result, this environment has caused a splintered Congress with little party cohesion so that gridlock

and polarization grow as the political parties lose their ability to rally their elected officeholders around a set of coherent governing policies.

The autopsy suggested that outside groups are less accountable than the parties and that they had spent way too much on television ads that weren't particularly effective. "Simply put, TV spending is out of control," the autopsy argued. "Despite the extraordinary amount of money that was invested in TV by outside groups in 2012, the final results of the election barely differed from the polls six months earlier." It even broached the possibility that the heavy focus on television spending may have been driven by some operatives' bottom-line interests, delicately noting that "the incentive system rewards expensive TV buys."[29] It took what many GOP insiders interpreted as a thinly veiled shot at the Rove and Koch camps, asserting, "The current campaign finance environment has led to a handful of friends and allied groups dominating our side's efforts. This is not healthy. A lot of centralized authority in the hands of a few people at these outside organizations is dangerous for our Party."[30]

The RNC called on its chairman, Reince Priebus, to put together "a command performance meeting of the leadership of our friends and allies and not allow anyone to leave the room until it's determined, to the extent allowed by law, who is doing what that can be divided legally," the report recommended.[31] "Without this sort of teamwork, there will be too much redundancy, turf battles, and waste. Lone wolf groups are more likely to waste their donors' money and act in a redundant, unhelpful manner."

Unsurprisingly, post-election analyses by the Koch political operation reached a different conclusion. Operatives at the brothers' April 2013 conference in Indian Wells applauded the campaign work of Koch-backed groups, suggesting it was superior to that of the RNC, Romney campaign, and Rove groups. There were plenty of veiled—and sometimes not-so-veiled—digs at the Rove operation. The mere presence of the conservative blogger Erickson, who by then had become known for his allegations that consultants in the Rove orbit had padded

their pockets, was seen by some as an implicit criticism of Rove's network, though the presentation Erickson delivered at the seminar dealt
mostly with basic campaign mechanics. During another presentation,
when talk turned to the fees being charged by Republican consultants,
a donor piped up, tongue firmly planted in cheek, to remind everyone
that Rove had been insisting he didn't make a dime in 2012 from Crossroads. The room burst into laughter.

While the Kochs didn't release their post-election audit publicly, there
were a number of changes in their political operation after the election
that seemed to be responsive to the 2012 disappointment. Americans for
Prosperity, the Kochs' main political outlet, parted ways with its chief
operating officer, most of the more than one hundred employees who
constituted its field staff, and several development associates. Generation Opportunity, a Koch-backed youth mobilization effort that fared
poorly in the post-election review, replaced its president. And the Koch
political network distanced itself from the consultant who had been its
lead operative during its political expansion in 2010 and 2012, Sean Noble. He repeatedly declined my interview requests. But his ignominious
marginalization coincided with an aggressive investigation by California
campaign finance regulators into a pair of secret-money nonprofits that
funneled $15 million into two state ballot campaigns just before Election
Day—one boosting a 2012 ballot measure to restrict union political activity and another opposing a separate ballot proposition to raise taxes.

The two nonprofits—the Center to Protect Patient Rights (CPPR)
and Americans for Responsible Leadership (ARL)—had close ties to
the Koch political operation. Noble served as president of CPPR, which
was funded by anonymous donations from Koch seminar attendees
and which acted as a conduit for that cash, directing it to a number of
Koch-backed nonprofits. Noble's allies ran ARL, which was the group
that tried to draft Chris Christie into the 2012 presidential race. CPPR
provided all but a tiny fraction of ARL's $25 million 2012 budget, ac-
cording to the groups' tax filings. The manner in which the two groups
steered cash into California ballot measure campaigns "was definitely
money laundering," Ann Ravel, who headed the California agency leading the investigation, told me. Her agency charged the two groups with
violating disclosure rules, and months after the election they agreed to

pay a $1 million fine to settle the case. The settlement stipulated that the violation "was inadvertent, or at worst negligent." Yet in announcing it, Ravel's agency trumpeted the nonprofits' ties to the "'Koch Brothers' Network' of dark money political nonprofit corporations," and bemoaned what Ravel called "the nationwide scourge of dark money nonprofit networks hiding the identities of their contributors."[32]

As part of its investigation, her agency obtained a fascinating email from a fellow Koch mega-donor who was seeking cash for the proposition to clamp down on unions. "I have committed an additional 2 million today making my total commitment of 7 million. It would be great if you could support the final effort with several million," the mega-donor wrote Charles Koch about a month before Election Day, after failing to get through on the phone. "I must tell you that Sean Noble from your group has been immensely helpful in our efforts," continued the donor, whose name and email address were redacted from the version of the email released by Ravel's commission. "I look forward to seeing you on a golf course—probably after the election." Koch spokesman Rob Tappan would not say whether Charles Koch responded to the email, but he did stress that neither brother gave to or was otherwise involved in either California effort.

The Kochs worked to distance themselves from the episode, with their company's general counsel, Mark Holden, telling me he wasn't sure whether the folks in the operation were aware during the election that Noble and CPPR were even working on the California issues— despite the friendly donor's email. "Sean worked on a lot of things. We don't know everything that he's doing," Holden explained. "I don't know that we tell Sean what he can and can't do. I mean, he's an independent contractor. He's a consultant." Holden added that the Koch operation didn't control CPPR, and he challenged the premise that the group was part of the Koch network of nonprofit groups. "There is not a Koch network in the sense of we control these groups. I don't understand what that means."[33] Whether Holden wanted to acknowledge it or not, there was a Koch network, and it was extremely deliberative in plotting its strategy, as Holden's own boss acknowledged in a letter inviting donors to a 2011 seminar. "Twice a year our network meets to review strategies for combatting the multitude of public policies that threaten to destroy America as we know it," Charles Koch wrote.[34] Their review of the 2012 disappointment was pointing toward a strategy of doubling down, like Rove. Americans for Prosperity established new full-time ground operations or beefed up existing ones in several states with 2013 and 2014 elections in which it was interested, including Louisiana, New Jersey, and South Carolina. Operatives affiliated with brothers' network were discussing starting an opposition research and candidate tracking effort—dark arts that had long been the terrain of the parties. Plus, the network blessed the creation of a new for-profit campaign consulting firm called Aegis Strategic. Founded in the summer of 2013 by a former high-ranking AFP official named Jeff Crank, it planned to both recruit and advise candidates who fit the Kochs' small-government, free-market mold—including helping them through competitive Republican primaries. The Koch network was clearly maneuvering to expand its footprint into the same space that Rove and an increasingly influential coalition of big-money tea party groups were moving. While the major axes of the conservative shadow party were reshuffling the decks, big-money donors and operatives were planning to steer more cash into boutique super PACS pushing narrow slates of causes or candidates. One started to build Republican support for immigration reform, while another launched an effort to bring social issues like opposition to abortion rights and gay marriage into the spotlight. Meanwhile, a big New York donor, hedge fund tycoon Paul Singer, said he would double down on his super PAC push to boost Republicans who support gay rights. And an outside group backed by the family of billionaire Ameritrade founder Joe Ricketts aired ads in a couple of 2013 races and appeared to be gearing up for a major 2014 push. Additionally, a motley array of big-money tea party nonprofits was pledging to spend big to fight Rove and his allies over any effort to steer the GOP to the middle. There was FreedomWorks (which split from AFP in 2004 in a bitter feud), the Senate Conservatives Fund (which was started in 2008 by then-senator Jim DeMint), and even the once-stodgy Heritage Foundation (which DeMint left the Senate to lead in 2013 and which now included an increasingly aggressive political arm called Heritage Action for America). While the groups liked to emphasize their small-donor base and present themselves as opponents of the

Washington establishment, they competed with one another and with establishment outfits for big checks from the richest donors. Heritage Action accepted $500,000 through the Koch network in 2012,[35] while FreedomWorks received more than $12 million through mysterious shell corporations from Dick Stephenson, the founder and chairman of the for-profit Cancer Treatment Centers of America.[36] While many groups were chasing the same big checks, they had very different ideas about how to spend them. "This is a little bit like gang warfare right now. It's not clear who is in charge," Matt Kibbe, president of Freedom-Works, told me. His tea-party-linked outfit spent more than $45 million in the 2012 cycle, including backing candidates like Richard Mourdock. "And you have this pushback from the empire, the guys who want to be in charge. And those are corporate interests. They're GOP lobbyists. They're the guys who fund groups like Rove's. They want to reestablish that they're in charge, and I just don't think they understand the inevitable decentralization and democratization of politics."

On the right, the shifting tactics seemed more about satisfying donors and controlling the conservative movement than about defeating Democrats. The jockeying marked the beginning of a new conservative civil war, one both motivated and fueled by rich Republicans against other rich Republicans. The party's big money, in other words, was shaping up as its own worst enemy. Sparring sects were positioning themselves to take control of the party by determining its nominees, shaping the issues, and electing the candidates. But there was a very real possibility that they would instead cancel each other out.

There was no such demolition derby on the left side of the aisle. At least not yet. Partly there were no razor's-edge ideological divides, and so there were fewer openings for competitive primaries in which rivals and their big-money supporters could battle over the direction of the Democratic Party. Also, the Democrats didn't have as many headstrong billionaires willing to write eight-figure checks to sway primary voters. In the few cases where there were high-profile primaries, the big spending didn't lift a weaker candidate to the nomination or weaken the eventual nominee. In the Democratic primary for the 2013 special election to fill a Massachusetts Senate seat vacated when its occupant, John Kerry, became secretary of state, San Francisco billionaire Tom Steyer

spent heavily on super PAC ads criticizing Stephen Lynch, a congressman who supported the Keystone XL oil pipeline, which Steyer and
other environmentalists opposed. While Lynch's opponent, Ed Markey,
a fellow congressman and the intended beneficiary of the ads, unsuccessfully urged Steyer to take them down, they didn't end up doing any
damage to Markey, who won the nomination and the seat.

A similar scenario played out when Michael Bloomberg, then New
York City's mayor, spent $2.2 million on television ads and direct mail
in a 2013 Democratic primary for a special congressional election in
Illinois. Bloomberg's Independence USA super PAC, which supports
stricter gun control measures, launched the campaign in support of a
candidate who was simpatico on the issue and was running against one
who was not. While Bloomberg's preferred candidate won the primary
and then the general election, that outcome seemed likely even without the billionaire's intervention, given the district's heavily Democratic
electorate. Still, it wasn't hard to envision circumstances in which efforts
like Bloomberg's or Steyer's might backfire. For instance, if they were to
wade into a red-state primary against a conservative Democrat who opposed gun control or supported the Keystone XL oil pipeline—positions
held by some of the party's Senate caucus—they could end up helping
elect a Republican who was, from their perspective, no better on their
respective pet issues, and worse on other liberal priorities. Bloomberg
seemed willing to tempt that prospect. In Arkansas, for instance, his
super PAC was promising to spend heavily against Democratic senator
Mark Pryor's 2014 reelection bid. Pryor had cast a 2013 vote against
a bill Bloomberg championed that would have expanded background
checks on gun sales in the wake of the December 2012 shooting that
killed twenty young children in Newtown, Connecticut. Of course, Pry-
or's Republican opponent, Rep. Tom Cotton, also opposed gun control.
Moreover, a victory by Cotton, who has been dubbed "the Republican
dream candidate,"[37] would decrease the prospects for action on other
liberal social policies that Bloomberg supports—including advancing
gay rights and combating climate change. With Democratic leaders urging Bloomberg to stand down,[38] he donated $2.5 million in 2014 to a
super PAC supporting the party's Senate candidates, including Pryor.

But Bloomberg, who had left the mayoralty in January 2014 pledging to spend down his estimated $31 billion fortune[39] on pet causes including politics, was still seen as something of a big-money wild card on the left, as was Steyer. Given the deeper bench of mega-donors on the Republican side, Democrats viewed it as critical to keep their big-money players on the same page.

After the 2012 election, the Taco Bell heir Rob McKay, who chaired the Democracy Alliance, sounded a cautionary note: Democrats could not count on being bailed out by Republican disarray next time. "We heard in state after state that the Romney campaign would be up with one ad, Rove's folks at Crossroads would be up with another, and the Koch brothers' groups would have a third message." Democrats, he said, had a more unified big-money messaging operation, "and it was out of necessity. We didn't have the luxury of having ten, fifteen multi-multimillion-dollar PACs. The dollars weren't there, so the discipline was enforced on all sides, both by the folks running the PACs [and] the donors."[40] The risk for Democrats was that Republicans would get their act together, just as Democrats started splintering. "They're in that place that we were in going into 2004, which is desperate," said McKay, who was an early donor to the Democrats' 2004 big-money push. "They lost a couple of elections at the presidential level, and I think they're going to try a lot of different things before they figure out what sticks. And they have the resources to do it."

Plus, it didn't take national message discipline to tip congressional elections, which are fought in individual states and districts. In those contests, a single big-money outside group's ads can be decisive, as Republicans showed in 2010. In order to avoid a repeat of that in the 2014 midterms, Democrats were moving to affirm the importance of big money on their side, and working to institutionalize it. One week after Election Day, at the annual winter meeting of the Democracy Alliance, donors convened at Washington's W Hotel to congratulate one another on their victories. They received the grateful thanks of top Democratic politicians, including Nancy Pelosi and Chuck Schumer, as well as the super PAC operatives whose groups raised an estimated $14 million from Democracy Alliance members.[41]

"There was a lot of back-slapping. Everyone was kind of congratu-
lating each other," one attendee told me. It struck me as the type of lavish spectacle that Team Obama would cluck their tongues at if it were
Republicans toasting their big donors. But Democrats were increasingly
shaking off the lingering effects of Obama's big-money moralizing and
were growing more comfortable with this type of donor maintenance,
so long as it was benefiting their candidates. And, as on the right, there
was also plenty of salesmanship, including presentations highlighting
the return on investment of Democrat-affiliated outside groups like the
pro-Obama Priorities USA, the opposition-research group American
Bridge, the Pelosi-backed House Majority PAC, the nonprofit America Votes, the Jonathan Soros–backed Friends of Democracy super
PAC (Jonathan is George Soros's son), and the abortion rights political
groups EMILY's List and Planned Parenthood Action.

The groups laid out plans for a more permanent presence in politics. Some were moving into state-level politics, some gravitated toward
policy fights, and some were even considering tentative forays into primaries. Unlike in the run-up to 2012, when the party was still conflicted
about super PACS, post-election Democrats were warming to the idea.
"They will be more willing to participate in super PACs early and more
than they did this time," Democracy Alliance member Steve Mostyn
confirmed soon after the election. "The lesson is: it takes some money
to beat big money. Big money outspent us. I was probably in the top
one or two Democratic funders. I wouldn't make the top ten on the
Republican side."

While 2012 was Mostyn's first foray into national politics, the Houston trial lawyer professes distaste for the idea of huge sums from just
a few people influencing elections. "I know there's some irony in me
giving a lot of money to super PACs in the hopes of eliminating them,
but that's what I hope happens. Do I think that's going to happen? No, I
don't." He predicted a several-month lull in the conservative big-money
flow before the spigot turned on again. "They will double down and
then we'll double down. These things get ridiculous."

Things were already getting kind of ridiculous. On a panel at the
Democracy Alliance's post-election meeting at the W Hotel, veteran
liberal activist-scholar Leonard Zeskind, who had made a career of

calling out right-wing extremism, warned donors about the prominence of the tea party in the South. But then he went off on a wild tangent that surprised even some of those in attendance, according to sources who were there. He compared Kansas governor Sam Brownback, a Christian conservative, to a Nazi, tagging him "Gov. Brownshirt," and called the liberal struggle against the tea party a "second civil war." Asked later about the irony of his own inflammatory rhetoric, he responded, "Oh, please!" but did not challenge this characterization of his DA presentation. If the goal was to keep the donors riled up, he at least held their attention. The conference also featured a presentation on Obama's second-term agenda from a White House official named Jon Carson. He would soon leave the administration to start a group called Organizing for Action, intended to put the infrastructure and donor network of the Obama campaign to use advancing Democratic priorities. The group would later win the backing of the Democracy Alliance. It was yet another sign that a president who once had blasted big money in politics was now aggressively playing the game alongside those he used to look down his nose at.

It didn't take long to make the pivot. While the Obama team publicly was giving credit for victory to its small-donor effort, it chose a different emphasis at a private closed-door gathering at Washington's glass-and-marble Newseum on Obama's inauguration weekend. Major donors were given tickets to the event, which had the feel of a celebration, featuring a combination of thanks for the 2012 cash and pitches for more from Carson, Obama campaign manager Jim Messina, and even Bill Clinton.[42]

"We raised over $1 billion for this campaign when no one thought we could," Messina bragged to the donors. "You all know that we were very metrically driven. I care very deeply about making sure we spent all the resources that we raised together in the states that mattered, and I think we can say to you, part of our board of directors, that we spent your time and money in a very smart way." The riff struck me as something that might just as easily have come out of the mouth of Romney finance chair Spencer Zwick. "We created a culture of fund-raising that was both fun and optimized people's time," Messina added. And then his competitive side surfaced. "We had two times the field offices as

Mitt Romney. This was a very big investment that you all made." The campaign also got more bang for its advertising buck than all the committees on the other side by buying airtime early, Messina said. "So the lowest cost per aired ad, OfA [Obama's campaign] won that. Priorities was second. Romney was third. I'd like to point out Karl Rove, down near the bottom."

Then he made the pitch for the new nonprofit fund-raising group his colleague Carson would oversee. "You have built the strongest political organization in the country. It would be really sad if we then said, 'Okay, let's put that away and build it in four years for the next presidential campaign.'" No, Messina said. "We're not going to shut this thing down."

Organizing for Action raised more than $26 million in 2013, from a mix of $50 donations and six-figure checks. But it didn't have much luck advancing Obama's top-line agenda items. Early in Obama's second term, compromises on gun control and immigration reform at various times appeared close, but both got bogged down in crippling partisan gridlock, which some liberals, perhaps ironically, blamed on the influence of big ideological money.

On the Republican side, things arguably looked worse. The party was suffering from low approval ratings, and their early embrace of big money hadn't proven to work out for the better. Instead of victory, the astonishing sums they raised had produced crippling infighting.

Within months of the 2012 election, it had become clear that a club of wealthy Americans was going to continue injecting money into the political system at an unprecedented rate, with an unprecedented impact on the process. What was not so clear was, in the end, what exactly was left for them to buy.

CHAPTER 11

The Civil Wars

By 6:30 p.m. on October 2, 2013, Washington was in the throes of an epic meltdown. Exactly forty-two and a half hours earlier, large swaths of the federal government had simply ceased operating when the House and Senate failed to reach an agreement to continue funding the government before a midnight deadline. The shutdown, as everyone was calling it, deprived hundreds of thousands of federal workers of paychecks and left millions of Americans, including low-income mothers and infants, at risk of losing their social services.

At that very moment, congressional leaders were meeting in the White House with President Obama to try to hammer out a deal that would end the uncertainty. As it became apparent that no deal was imminent, Obama pulled aside House Speaker John Boehner, who really just wanted to go outside to grab a smoke, and pressed him about how it had come to this.

"John, what happened?" wondered the president.

"I got overrun, that's what happened," Boehner responded.[1]

It was a concise explanation, but it didn't really do justice to the true forces behind the shutdown. The most obvious culprit—and the most immediate source of the Speaker's frustration—was a coalition of tea party lawmakers in Boehner's conference who were trying to use a traditionally noncontroversial appropriations process to undercut Obamacare, the president's signature health care overhaul law. But it didn't take much sleuthing to find the fingerprints of the conservative wing of the shadow party all over the shutdown. A loose coalition of outfits with hefty wallets—Americans for Prosperity, FreedomWorks, the Club for Growth, Heritage Action for America, and the Senate Conservatives Fund—were pressuring lawmakers against voting to fund the government. There were vague threats of primary challenges to any Republican who supported a so-called clean continuing resolution that simply appropriated more money, with Heritage Action and the Senate Conservatives Fund running ads in the weeks leading up to the shutdown attacking Republican congressmen and senators who wavered—including some who were already facing 2014 tea party challengers. Heritage Action spent $550,000 on Web ads urging a hundred GOP members of Congress to use the appropriations process to defund Obamacare.[2] The Senate's Republican leader, Mitch McConnell of Kentucky, came under particular fire. A month before the shutdown, the Senate Conservatives Fund spent $340,000 airing ads in his home state alleging that he "refuses to lead on defunding Obamacare. What good is a leader like that?"[3] Not long afterward, the group endorsed McConnell's tea party primary challenger, and its super PAC bought another $330,000 worth of Kentucky airtime for an ad opining that McConnell "let us down,"[4] as well as ads hitting Sens. Thad Cochran of Mississippi, Lindsey Graham of South Carolina, and Johnny Isakson of Georgia. As Rep. Greg Walden, chairman of the Republican Party's congressional campaign arm, reportedly explained to a group of centrist Wall Street donors during a private lunch at Manhattan's Le Cirque in the days leading up to the shutdown: "We have to do this because of the Tea Party. If we don't, these guys are going to get primaried and they are going to lose their primary."[5] The tea party wing wasn't going to be satisfied with merely symbolic gestures, though, as Walden himself would learn a few weeks later when, as one of seven congressman branded by the Club for Growth as a RINO,[6] he found himself facing his own tea party primary challenger back in his Oregon district.

At that moment, the official Republican Party—whether it was Boehner's Republican conference or Walden's National Republican Congressional Committee (NRCC)—seemed completely impotent. There was little the party could do on its own, either to reclaim control from the tea party wing of the shadow party or to reopen the government and prevent a disaster that could hamstring the party as it headed into 2014.

Nearly eleven months after an election in which the biggest of the big-money mostly failed to get its way at the ballot box, the shutdown battle was proof that the 2010 and 2012 spending sprees were having more impact than ever on the way American government functioned. Without the big money circulating outside the party system, some of the leaders of the GOP shutdown caucus—folks like Sens. Ted Cruz of Texas and Mike Lee of Utah—wouldn't have won their primaries. In such an environment, Speaker Boehner's best hope was the prospect that a rival shadow party would help him reassert control.

Just as Boehner was describing to the president the view from under the big-money bus that had run him over, the very folks who could form the Speaker's own cash cavalry were secretly convening a mile west of the White House at the Four Seasons hotel in Georgetown. Some of the richest Republican businessmen and most influential big-money operatives were set to gather over the next couple of days with the pols they hoped would lead the revival of the GOP's Chamber of Commerce centrist wing, including Walden, as well as a number of prospective 2016 GOP presidential candidates—Govs. Bobby Jindal of Louisiana, John Kasich of Ohio, and Scott Walker of Wisconsin, Sens. Rand Paul of Kentucky, Rob Portman of Ohio, and Marco Rubio of Florida—and a slew of centrist 2014 Senate candidates. The occasion was a closed-door summit organized by Karl Rove's American Crossroads and hosted by Rove and Crossroads president and CEO Steven Law. Among the donors, operatives, and politicians in the hotel there was an emerging consensus that in order to right the Republican ship, they needed to forcibly evict the tea party and its big-money backers from the controls. Whether the crew at the Four Seasons was ready for such a battle would go a long way toward determining the direction of the GOP—and American politics more broadly—over the next several years. This was where the real action was at six-thirty on that early October evening, not over at the White House.

The meeting agenda, branded with the Crossroads logo and a slogan, "The Republican Future," suggested that the organizers understood the moment's importance. The summit was both a grand display of Rove's recalibrated positioning as the would-be tea party slayer and his answer to the Kochs' long-running seminars. Like the Koch post-2012 seminars, it had presentations that seemed intended to show that Crossroads had learned from its 2012 bust and would do things differently. One of the panels featuring Rove, Law, and Carl Forti was called "A New Approach for the 2014 Cycle"; there was also a speech entitled "How Republicans Win the Future with Governor Scott Walker." It had high-octane donor-bait speakers like Jindal, Kasich, Rubio, and Paul. It included fancy receptions and dinners, like one at the majestic waterfront Swedish embassy where donors could mingle with a handful of "the top 2014 Senate candidates"—a group conspicuous for its lack of tea party representation. And, of course, there was the tight security, with warnings in the agenda that the event was "closed to all press," that recording devices were banned, and that "all presentations and discussions are off the record and confidential." Anyone "not displaying their personalized credential will be asked to leave the meeting area by Crossroads or Four Seasons staff," the agenda warned.

As the minutes ticked by, I grew skeptical that any of the high-profile politicians listed as expected guests at that evening's "Next Wave Republicans" reception "with the party's future leaders" would show. After all, I figured, it would look pretty bad for any Republican to be caught schmoozing big donors at the very moment that the party's congressional contingent was being blamed for an unpopular stalemate causing real pain for regular Americans. I couldn't imagine, for instance, that Mitch McConnell, who right then was in the White House meeting with Obama and Boehner, would drop by the following evening's "Renewing the Republican Vision with Senator Marco Rubio and Senator Mitch McConnell," as the agenda promised. Some chatter was suggesting that there might have already been a cancellation by one of the big names expected for the "Next Wave" reception: House majority whip Kevin McCarthy, whose job at that moment included counting votes for any deal to end the shutdown. Yet just after 7:00 p.m.—at the precise moment when Boehner was emerging from the White House to announce there was no deal in sight to end the shutdown—up to the Crossroads summit registration desk swaggered two of the very men whose support Boehner would need to pass any such deal.

"Congressman Cory Gardner and Congressman Duffy," Gardner proclaimed jauntily to the two pretty young female staffers working the registration desk, checking in guests and handing out official conference name tags emblazoned with "The Republican Future" and the Crossroads logo.

"Do y'all want any badges?" one of the registration staffers asked Gardner, a thirty-nine-year-old from Colorado, and Sean Duffy, a forty-one-year-old from Wisconsin. Both men were media-savvy rising stars (Gardner at that moment was being hotly recruited by party establishment types to run for Senate, while Duffy was still perhaps best known for his turn as a hard-partying flirtatious law student on the 1997 season of MTV's reality show *The Real World*)[7] who were first elected during the 2010 tea party wave. Both had shown some allegiance to the tea party, but also a willingness to work with the official party leadership. In other words, they were potential swing votes in the battle of the establishment versus the tea party. And here they were coming to kiss the ring of the establishment shadow party. Maybe there was hope that Boehner and the establishment would stop getting run over after all.

Greg Walden, the NRCC chair, showed up a few minutes later at the registration desk, which was set up on the lower-mezzanine-level lobby, near a staircase leading down to the lower-level lobby hosting the actual Crossroads reception. Walden, like Gardner and Duffy before him, declined a name tag, and proceeded downstairs to the reception followed shortly thereafter by Oklahoma state House speaker T. W. Shannon, who, like Gardner, was being groomed by the establishment for higher office. The registration staffers kibitzed among themselves about the self-important auras of the donors and dignitaries. "We only had one guy yell at us," one of the duo explained to a higher-level Crossroads staffer, who had been summoned to bestow middle-tier VIP treatment on one of the "Next Wave" Republicans—Will Weatherford, Speaker of the Florida state House of Representatives. "Mr. Speaker!" the more senior Crossroads staffer loudly declared for the entire lobby to hear. Another young man named Nelson proudly announced to the registration staffers that he was the lead for a congressman whose name I didn't catch. Mike McFadden, an investment banker running against a slew of tea party candidates for the 2014 GOP Senate nomination in

Minnesota, accepted a name tag from one of the registration staffers after she explained playfully, "I have a very special one for you."

At that point, former Mississippi governor Haley Barbour, who had used his considerable fund-raising clout to help Crossroads in 2012, emerged from a nearby elevator, drink in hand. Barbour ambled past the registration desk toward a hotel restaurant hosting a party for another group. One of the registration staffers snapped to action, briskly chasing him down, gently touching his arm, and softly informing him that the Crossroads event was downstairs. "Oh, we got off at the wrong floor," Barbour said, chuckling, as he made a U-turn.

Barbour had helped Crossroads amass its astounding 2012 fund-raising haul. And after the election, he lent his blessing and name to its Conservative Victory Project to wade into GOP primaries on behalf of mainstream Republicans fighting tea party challengers. "This is a bad idea whose time has come," he said—a quote the group used in its initial pitch to donors.[8] Since then, the former governor had gone even further, working to steer rich donors away from tea party groups like the Club for Growth[9] and the Senate Conservatives Fund,[10] which was targeting Mitch McConnell and other Republicans who weren't gung-ho about the Obamacare-defunding strategy that had caused the shutdown. "Politics can't be about purity. Unity wins in politics, purity loses," Barbour told the conservative *National Review* a few months after the election.[11]

The Club for Growth's president, Chris Chocola, a former Indiana congressman, quickly lashed back at Barbour, suggesting his group's mission is more ideologically consistent. "Haley wants every Republican to win, regardless of how they vote in office. The Club for Growth PAC helps elect candidates who support limited government and free markets. Unfortunately, the two goals coincide less often than the Republican Establishment cares to admit," Chocola said.[12] He added a bring-it-on coda, a challenge to the centrists: "The more Haley Barbour and Karl Rove attack the work of the Club for Growth PAC, the more it energizes and grows our membership."

I wanted to determine whether the Crossroads donors at the Four Seasons were ready for the battle ahead. So, rising from the armchair where I had been monitoring the registration desk, I rode the elevator down to the ballroom where the actual Crossroads reception was being held. I realized instantly that the jig was up when I was spotted by a handful of Crossroads staffers checking to make sure everyone had credentials. Feigning confusion, I looked around, got back in the elevator, and rode it up to the hotel's main lobby, where I was tracked down in short order by Crossroads communications director Jonathan Collegio, who apparently had been alerted that there was a possible intruder and set out on a search.

"Oh, it's Vogel," Collegio sighed upon spotting me. Collegio had always projected professional courtesy, and even now, after I had breached the secrecy his group had worked so hard to establish, he stayed calm but firm, making it clear I would have to leave. As I turned to walk down the Four Seasons hotel's long marble hallway toward the exit, though, I spotted Haley Barbour headed out to wait for his driver to come pick him up. So—to Collegio's chagrin—I took the opportunity to ask Barbour my question: was Crossroads ready to engage in a big-money war with the tea party groups that had encouraged the shutdown?

"This meeting is not about current affairs and the government," Barbour replied tactfully. Rather, "it's about long-term thinking for future elections." The event allowed "people that had helped try to elect people last time [to] get together, talk about what the 2014 election is going to be about, what's it gonna be like. But, I mean, this was planned long before [the shutdown] and so it was not really related to it."

I asked Barbour how it looked for members to be here while the shutdown loomed. "Never seemed to bother Obama, when he would go from fund-raiser to fund-raiser between crises," Barbour said as he speed-dialed his driver, Omar, to bring his town car around to the Four Seasons's circular driveway. "I mean, I don't remember [that] they canceled one right after Benghazi, did they?" Barbour was right—the president had attended a fund-raiser in Las Vegas the day after the 2012 attack on an American diplomatic compound in Benghazi, Libya, that killed four people.

Finally I asked what lesson Crossroads and other big-money groups could take from their 2012 failures. Barbour used this as an excuse to take a swing at a traditional bête noire of Republicans of all stripes. "The lesson is that the news media is going to criticize the Republicans for how much they spend no matter how much the Democrats and the labor unions outspend 'em. I mean, that's why we have a liberal media elite, right?" As a big security guard stepped in and ushered me to the sidewalk, where I stood waiting for the bus, I chuckled to myself at the irony of being called an elitist by Barbour as he was chauffeured away in his shiny black town car.

Whether Barbour wanted to admit it or not, the battle lines were clearly drawn for a brutal shadow party civil war in the 2014 Republican primaries and beyond. Fighting that battle, rather than taking on the Democrats, seemed to be the priority for all factions in the Republican shadow party. The Crossroads "Republican Future" summit had the feel of an effort to brace centrist donors for the fight ahead against the tea party. The talk between sessions turned to frustration with the tea party wing of the party and its leading role in pushing the government toward shutdown in an effort to derail Obamacare,[13] which many of the donors deemed futile at best and self-destructive at worst. The day after I got the heave-ho, the anti-tea-party bearing of the Crossroads sect was highlighted by an evening reception featuring a number of Senate candidates who had already drawn sharp tea party opposition. Representative Shelley Moore Capito of West Virginia had announced her candidacy for outgoing Democratic senator Jay Rockefeller's seat and promptly been lashed by the Club for Growth[14] and the Senate Conservatives Fund[15] as a big-government establishment Republican. Then there was Representative Bill Cassidy, the establishment choice to challenge Democratic incumbent Mary Landrieu for a Louisiana Senate seat. A few weeks after attending the Crossroads reception, Cassidy's relatively unknown tea party primary opponent would win the backing of the Senate Conservatives Fund.[16] North Carolina state House Speaker Thom Tillis had a foot in both worlds, with his strong ties to the Koch confidant Art Pope and his increasing ties to Rove, who hosted him at the Crossroads summit and then traveled to North Carolina not long afterward on a fund-raising swing for him.[17] But Tillis—who the preceding summer had accidentally called David Koch "Mr. Cock"—had been left off the invitation list for the Kochs' 2013 summer seminar in Albuquerque, New Mexico, and had found himself facing a surprisingly brisk challenge from the tea party in the primary.

Even as Cassidy and Tillis courted an establishment shadow party that might be able to help them stave off such primary challenges, their big-money backers were taking matters into their own hands. Operatives close to the two candidates established super PACs specifically and exclusively intended to support their 2014 campaigns. And they weren't alone. An increasing number of players on both sides of the aisle were funding their own, individualized big-money factions to boost specific candidates for down-ballot races, from mayor to Congress to governor. Why should they give to a national group like Crossroads or Americans for Prosperity or the Harry Reid–blessed Democratic Senate super PAC without any guarantees that the money would get spent on their favorite candidate? As one operative involved in a race with a candidate-specific super PAC put it to Nick Confessore of the *New York Times,* "You don't want someone playing God above you saying: 'You don't need any more money in your race. You can win by a few less points.'"[18]

Better, then, to write a check that's definitely going to be spent boosting the donors' preferred candidate, the reasoning went—even if that meant starting a new super PAC from scratch for the purpose. This development, which began in 2012 with a handful of super PACs funded by family[19] and close friends, meant that every Senate or gubernatorial primary had the potential to become a messy, expensive super PAC brawl like the 2012 GOP presidential primary. The prospect was adding to the big-money-induced ulcers of party elders, who feared losing even more control of their nominating processes to the whims of major donors and their super PACs. Any candidate could have a private political militia, and it seemed likely that many high-profile politicians running in 2014 would.

New groups had been formed to help incumbent Republican senators in Kentucky, South Carolina, and Texas[20] in their bids to stave off 2014 primary challengers backed by big-money tea party groups. In Kentucky, a super PAC backing McConnell was stockpiling cash from several Crossroads donors in preparation for both the primary challenge from a tea party candidate and the forthcoming general-election battle with a Democratic rival who had her own super PAC. In Alaska's hotly contested Senate race, a trio of candidates had their own super PACs with ambiguously benign names. Put Alaska First, which indicated it might play in primaries for both parties,[21] launched an early six-figure ad buy supporting the Democratic incumbent, Mark Begich. Two of the Republicans seeking the nomination to challenge Begich had their own super PACs, as did Michelle Nunn, one of the three Democrats seeking the party's nomination to run for Senate in Georgia.

While party loyalists and even candidates bemoaned the potential of candidate-specific super PACs to replicate the havoc that Sheldon Adelson wreaked on the 2012 GOP presidential primary, most conceded that the new vehicles were merely a reflection of the new political reality. Big-money outside support was now a prerequisite for being taken seriously as a candidate. Candidates had to figure out where they fit in this new system before they could know whether they had a realistic shot. Simply put, any candidate running in a hotly contested congressional race in 2014 had to have at least one major financial sponsor. The ability to unite multiple big-money sects was of course far better. And while having big-money backing was no guarantee that the candidate would be able to withstand a primary opponent who had more, candidates trying to go it alone—particularly on the Republican side—were probably going to get overrun, as John Boehner had put it.

"No matter what stance you're taking, there's always going to be people that rally behind you, want to provide support, and the support comes financially. It is welcomed and I don't think it differs whether you're Republican, Democrat, no party, whatever the case may be," said Joni Ernst,[22] an Iowa state lawmaker running in a contested GOP primary for the Hawkeye State's open Senate seat in 2014. I'd called her up to chat because I'd heard that she hadn't been invited to the Crossroads summit but had scored a coveted invitation to the Kochs' summer seminar in Albuquerque a couple of months earlier. She told me she didn't think her appearance at the Koch seminar would preclude her from winning support from other coalitions of GOP donors, and also professed that she wasn't really sure how she'd been tapped to appear before the Koch donors. "You know, truly, I don't know how my name came through those channels," she told me.

A blessed trio at the Crossroads summit had also attended the Koch brothers' Albuquerque seminar. One of them was the investment banker McFadden. He had drawn multiple tea party opponents, including a state senator who was already accusing him of being "more concerned about what's happening in Washington than he is with talking to Minnesota voters."[23] The others were representatives Tom Cotton of Arkansas and Steve Daines of Montana. Cotton and Daines seemed to have a knack for uniting deep-pocketed factions of the conservative movement, scoring invitations to a February 2014 meeting of Wall Street mega-donors organized by the socially liberal hedge fund billionaire Paul Singer. Cotton, a combat veteran who did tours in Iraq and Afghanistan, was particularly noteworthy, securing the support of neo-conservative hawks while also gaining entrée into Koch World, where anti-interventionism reigns. He was considered a top Senate candidate by the GOP's establishment Chamber of Commerce wing, but he also had the support of the fiscal purists at the Club for Growth.

Politicians like Cotton who could win and maintain the backing of multiple shadow party factions—or attract their own big-money donors—would be the ones to watch. It would be the big-money equivalent of the three-legged stool of Ronald Reagan's coalition of fiscal, national security, and social conservatives. But the shutdown highlighted just how difficult it could be to straddle the widening rift between the shadow party sects.

As the shutdown dragged on, the mighty US Chamber of Commerce, which had been a force in big-money politics in the pre–*Citizens United* era, signaled that it was considering wading into 2014 Republican congressional primaries in a major way, with the goal of ousting tea party conservatives and replacing them with more business-friendly pragmatists.[24] That would be a departure for the typically risk-averse group, which in previous years had only selectively engaged in primaries. Its involvement would be seen as a declaration of all-out war on elements of the tea party that had been challenging business's seat near the head of the Republican table. Chamber president Tom Donohue apparently believed such a risk was warranted, and was said to be "all in" on the strategy.[25]

On the other side, big-money tea party groups were expressing their opposition to the emerging contours of a bipartisan deal being crafted by Mitch McConnell with the White House and congressional Democrats that would fund the government and raise the debt ceiling, while doing little in the way of reining in spending. "It's outrageous that politicians would consider a debt limit increase without also carefully scrutinizing wasteful government spending," tweeted the Koch-backed Americans for Prosperity.[26] "All increases to the debt ceiling must be accompanied with dollar-for-dollar spending cuts that will help put the U.S. back on a path to balance within 10 years," demanded a letter to Congress from a coalition of tea party groups including Americans for Prosperity, FreedomWorks, and Heritage Action.[27]

It didn't happen. Sixteen days after the shutdown began, with the government only hours away from a default and Republicans getting most of the blame in public opinion polls, McConnell swooped in to forge a bipartisan agreement that was functionally indistinguishable from the Democrats' starting negotiating position. Tea party groups including the Senate Conservatives Fund, Heritage Action, and the Kochs' Americans for Prosperity denounced the deal, with AFP president Tim Phillips proclaiming ominously in the hours after the agreement passed that "we intend to hold politicians accountable for their promise to stop overspending."[28] In short order, the Senate Conservatives Fund endorsed a tea-party-backed Louisville businessman with virtually no political experience in his 2014 primary challenge to McConnell,[29] while the Club for Growth and another conservative group joined the Senate Conservatives Fund in endorsing a primary challenger to Sen. Thad Cochran of Mississippi, who also voted for the deal.[30]

The deal ultimately was supported by 61 percent of Republican senators and 38 percent of Republican House members. Among the Crossroads summit invitees there was an even split: eight supported the deal and eight opposed it. Supporters included McConnell and McCarthy—neither of whom attended the summit after all. Opponents included Paul Ryan, the chairman of the budget committee, who likewise canceled his scheduled summit appearance. McCarthy's spokeswoman told me he didn't attend "because of the shutdown," which seemed like the astute thing to do, at least from the standpoint of political optics. But all Crossroads's top 2014 Senate candidates attended, and all—except Bill Cassidy of Louisiana—supported the deal, as did Rob Portman and Cory Gardner, who months later would declare his 2014 Senate candidacy after a potential tea party rival was coaxed out of the race. Yet two Crossroads summit attendees prominently mentioned as potential 2016 presidential candidates, Sens. Rand Paul and Marco Rubio, both opposed the deal, as did Sean "*Real World*" Duffy. Even NRCC chair Greg Walden voted no, though that did little to satisfy his tea party primary challenger, who deemed Walden's vote a cowardly cover-up.[31]

Not long after the government reopened, Boehner during a press conference lashed out at the collection of deep-pocketed conservative groups that he said "pushed us into this fight to defund Obamacare and shut down the government." His comments eerily echoed Obama's during the shutdown, when the president blamed *Citizens United* for the stalemate. "You have some ideological extremists who have a big bankroll, and they can entirely skew our politics," Obama had said in a press conference of his own. "And there are a whole bunch of members of Congress right now who privately will tell you, 'I know our positions are unreasonable but we're scared that if we don't go along with the tea party agenda or some particularly extremist agenda that we'll be challenged from the right.'" Boehner didn't draw the direct link back to *Citizens United*, but he did allude to conservative groups that had taken advantage of the decision, accusing them of "pushing our members in places where they don't want to be, and frankly, I just think that they've lost all credibility."

Yet, those groups still represented a major threat to Boehner headed into 2014, one of the Speaker's key big-money allies told me. "I don't know how many defeats it's going to take, either in general elections or in debates like the government shutdown, for some folks to realize that building a majority takes making some compromise, while still holding to principle," said financier Fred Malek,[32] a Republican donor and fund-raiser who attended the Crossroads Summit. Malek had a hand in starting and steering the American Action Network and the Congressional Leadership Fund, big-donor-funded groups closely aligned with Boehner and other Republican Party leaders. American Action Network, a key early partner of Crossroads, in 2010 and 2012 aired ads backing establishment centrists in competitive Senate primaries against tea-party-supported candidates, with mixed results. Big donors at the Crossroads Summit, like those around the country, "were still really upset" that the GOP had been hamstrung by candidates with lower odds of winning, like Mourdock and Akin, Malek told me shortly after the summit. Still, he said that he'd been talking to big donors, laying the groundwork for 2014, and that American Action Network was ahead of its fund-raising pace from 2012, when it raised and spent $44 million. "From all my conversations, I have no question about the fact that they will be receptive and we will be able to attract large dollars," he predicted. "There is going to be more money flowing to the traditional candidates who believe that politics is a game of addition where we need to bring people together, rather than divide and take a hard stance, one way or another. And, therefore, there is going to be more support for groups like ours and candidates that believe as we do."

That advantage had not become evident by the end of 2013. Malek's Congressional Leadership Fund and three other unlimited-money groups affiliated with the Republican Party establishment—the Young Guns Action Fund, American Crossroads, and its nonprofit affiliate Crossroads GPS—combined to raise $7.7 million by the end of the year.[33] That haul was dwarfed by the $20 million raised by a quartet of tea-party-linked groups challenging the GOP establishment on congressional spending negotiations and likely later at the ballot box—Club for Growth Action Fun, FreedomWorks, Senate Conservatives Fund, and the Tea Party Patriots.[34] Of course, those figures don't include fund-raising by many groups that aren't required to regularly disclose their finances, which could easily shift the balance.

Whether or not Malek's prophecy ultimately would be borne out, Republicans were well positioned to capitalize on an emerging axiom of big-money politics in 2014: it's easier to keep rich donors and their super PACs in line when the target on the other side of the aisle is bigger than the one on their own. The botched implementation of Obamacare—complete with website crashes and a blatantly false promise from the president that people would be able to keep their existing health plan[35]—seemed to present Republicans with the perfect opportunity. Because there was no national race on the ballot in 2014, they didn't need to be united on a solution or even on a candidate to fix it, as long as they could agree on the problem. Americans for Prosperity and other groups in the Koch network quickly pivoted from the shutdown debate and began spending heavily on anti-Obamacare ads attacking vulnerable Democrats who supported the bill's passage, including Sens. Kay Hagen of North Carolina, Mary Landrieu of Louisiana, and Jeanne Shaheen of New Hampshire. Others followed suit, and polls showed Obamacare was becoming an albatross for Democrats.

The power struggle between the GOP's big-money establishment and the tea party wings represented an opportunity for another faction of the conservative movement: the religious right. It had mostly missed the boat on the explosion in unlimited outside group spending after *Citizens United.* As a result, its leaders felt their issues—namely, strident opposition to abortion rights and gay marriage—were being minimized in the conservative movement by deeper-pocketed factions that considered them repellants to attracting swing voters.* It was against that backdrop that dozens of the religious right's richest activists and most influential operatives gathered at a Ritz Carlton in the northern Virginia suburbs on a snowy Washington day a couple of weeks after the shutdown to plot their own foray into the big-money conservative civil war.

Social conservative groups, several Ritz conferees agreed, needed to spend big to defeat Republican primary candidates deemed insufficiently conservative on their issues. And, they needed to better coordinate their political efforts. But, before they could do any of that, they needed to seriously increase their fund-raising. A lot of the ideas seemed ripped directly from the Rove and Koch big-money playbooks, including luring mega-donors to elaborate retreats. One proposal being shopped by a wealthy South Dakota businessman named Bob Fischer called for separate donor conferences at the Reagan Ranch in California and in Normandy, France, tied to the 70th anniversary of the D-Day invasion.

The Ritz summit was organized by the Conservative Action Project, an initiative chaired by former Reagan Attorney General Ed Meese that brings together conservative leaders and donors to try to shape

---

*The Republican National Committee in its post-2012 autopsy report declared that the party "must change our tone—especially on certain social issues that are turning off young voters" and women.

the movement. It was held in a Ritz ballroom outfitted with long tables arranged in a U-shape to facilitate discussion, and it was by-invitation-only and closed to the press. But much of the big-money plotting occurred in informal breakout sessions in an adjacent lobby featuring a lunch spread of soups, salads, and roast turkey sliders with brie, arugula, vine-ripened tomatoes and spicy mustard on pretzel roll buns. I stood sentry by the dessert buffet, feigning interest in the bite-sized holiday-themed cheesecakes, as I eavesdropped on a meeting convened by Fischer where donors and operatives discussed how they might go about poaching mega-donor support from the Koch and Rove networks.

"A lot of those donors who believe in our issues believe that when they give to Karl, that that's how he's spending their money, but it's not," said the conservative religious leader Gary Bauer, who ran for the GOP presidential nomination in 2000. A fund-raiser named Richard Norman suggested donors might be less eager to give to groups in Rove's network or the Kochs' if they were made aware "that these organizations spent the vast majority of their money on media consultants." And a consultant named Pam Pryor—who had worked in 2012 for a firm run by Sean Noble, at the time a top operative in the Koch brothers' political network—suggested she might be able to recruit Koch network donors to help fund the social conservative resurgence. "My firm was the recipient of a large pass-through and I'm still very close to many of those donors," Pryor told the group,* explaining she would help in whatever way she could because "I'm just crazy about Jesus."

If socially conservative super PACs raise enough money to notch a couple key victories in 2014, it could be huge, argued wealthy hedge fund investor Sean Fieler after the Ritz meeting. "Nothing breeds success like success. If we can show that integrated conservatism which embraces a middle class and a resonant economic message as well as a pro-family socially conservative message is the winning formula, then I think there will be a lot of money for that," Fieler told me. In 2013,

---

*Pryor, who had left Noble's firm by this point, later criticized me for eavesdropping on the meeting and disputed the context of this comment, but declined to elaborate on what she meant.

he gave $394,000 to a new super PAC that attacked New Jersey Dem-
ocratic Senate candidate Cory Booker as a "pro-abortion extremist"
and Wyoming Republican Senate candidate Liz Cheney as a gay marriage supporter. Booker won his special election to the Senate easily,
but Cheney's poll numbers tanked after the misleading attack* and she
eventually dropped out of the race. All it would take, Fieler predicted,
is a handful of Republican mega-donors giving big to elevate social
issues, and the party, which had urged its candidates to de-emphasize
abortion and gay marriage after 2012, would be compelled to put those
issues front and center again.

Things can change fast in big-money politics—faster than through
the party system, with its rigid and slow-to-adapt hierarchies. Another
emerging trend that seemed to bode well for Republicans was the fis-
sures developing among Democrats. Some of these appeared to have
the potential to turn into major chasms given the right combination of
primary challenges and big money. There was the Michael Bloomberg
super PAC crusade targeting anti-gun-control Democrats and the Tom
Steyer pledge to spend heavily to defeat candidates he deemed insufficiently supportive of environmental measures. But there was a bigger
threat to Democratic unity starting to make itself apparent, one that
threatened to pit its leading figures against each other. It was a divide between the party's populist wing and its centrist, business-friendly wing.
In some ways the rift mirrored the one splitting the right, except instead
of the tea party's populist demand for less government and taxes, populist Democrats saw more of both as the solution. Democratic elites
worried such a movement could pull the party to the left in a way that
would jeopardize its chances of cobbling together a winning electoral
coalition—if not in 2014, then certainly in 2016. Their concerns coincided with the quiet swelling of a Democratic big-money tidal force that
was very much the antithesis of the populist trend. It was a force that
was both new, in that it would capitalize on the *Citizens United* era in a

*Cheney, the daughter of former vice president Dick Cheney, said she op-
posed gay marriage, causing a rift with her sister Mary Cheney, who is
married to a woman.

way that Obama never did, and also quite familiar and comforting to many of the rich Democrats who had yearned for Obama to do more in the big-money arena. It was the return of the Clinton cash machine.

The huge network of mega-donors fostered by Bill and Hillary Clinton, first in the White House and then during her Senate and presidential campaigns, had largely gone untended after Obama dispatched her in the long and brutal 2008 presidential primary. Many turned away from big giving dispirited, wondering if they'd seen the last of the political dynasty that, more than perhaps any other operation in American politics, knew how to inspire the wealthiest of supporters. While some eventually threw in with Obama, especially after he tapped Hillary to be his secretary of state, it just wasn't the same. There were none of the late-night bull sessions after fund-raisers that there had been with the Clintons, no White House sleepovers. There was no spark. But once Hillary stepped down from a mostly well-received tenure helming the State Department, the magic started to come back. Her richest supporters—many of whom the family counted among their close friends—were whispering in her ear, telling her that the White House would be hers to lose in 2016. She said nothing to discourage them, and that was signal enough for many of the donors and operatives to begin building a big-money network that they hoped would put even Bill's vaunted soft-money machine to shame. The gang was getting back together. And there was no gang in politics that seemed as uniquely prepared to cash in on the new *Citizens United* era as the Clintons—not even Mitt Romney's family and friends. If Mitt was the big-money prototype candidate, Hillary seemed more like the finished product.

In some ways, the Clintons' network never totally went away. It was just idling during Obama's first term, with some of its energy shifted toward a less electoral footing. But during Obama's reelection campaign there were signs it was coming back to life. While some Clinton skeptics saw Bill's aggressive work rallying his old big donors for Obama as a self-interested attempt to prime the pump for his wife in 2016, few questioned its impact. When Bill started raising for Obama's campaign or the supportive Priorities USA, the big checks really started flowing.

And the former president kept his foot on the gas even after the election, when many Democrats began quietly fretting about the 2014 midterms. The Clintons' allies and other big-money operatives knew that Democrats could not afford to rest easy just because Republicans were at one another's throats. Sure, some of those primaries might in GOP general election candidates who were either easily caricatured tea partiers or damaged mainstream candidates who had been weakened by primary battles. But, as Democrats learned in 2010, it's easier for a big-money push—even a fractious one—to produce major victories in a congressional midterm election, when consistency of message across media markets and states is less important than in a presidential year. Plus, in 2014, the Republican base figured to be more motivated, as was the case in 2010 and as typically happens with the party out of power.

That was what Bill Clinton warned big donors about at the ticketed private event held in Washington's Newseum on the weekend of Obama's 2013 inauguration. In a never-before-reported pitch, Clinton urged the donors who constituted Obama's national finance council to fund Organizing for Action, a nonprofit created from the president's campaign machinery, because, Clinton said, it could be a powerful force in the midterm elections.[36] "I want to talk about that today because all of you and the president have made a decision to try to use the unprecedented, distributed empowering approach of the campaign to see if we can apply it to a midterm election, which we have not been able to do," Clinton said. Clinton's characterization seemed to conflict with the official Obama line, which was that Organizing for Action was exclusively focused on issues, not elections. Regardless of the Obama spin, Clinton saw Organizing for Action as a way to use the expensive and expansive infrastructure built by the president's campaign to provide cover for Democratic members of Congress and governors. "This is a huge deal, this midterm election," said Clinton. "And I think even more important, the question is whether we can use the techniques that actually gave people the chance to debate health care, debate economic policy, understand what happened in the Recovery Act, all these things that were an issue last time, understand why the welfare reform act was wrong, and the Medicare Act was wrong. Can we use that to actually enact an agenda in the Congress and then go into the midterm and protect the people who voted for it?" Pointing out that Democratic presidential candidates won the popular vote in every election since 1992, except for 2004, Clinton said, "We've been doing fine in these presidential elections and we're getting better and better and better at it. . . . So now, the question is, can we apply that first to the midterm elections, so that members of Congress that we ask to support the president can be supported, and the governors?"

Organizing for Action and its high-profile pitchman Bill Clinton may have still been figuring out how they wanted to approach 2014. But the Democracy Alliance chairman, Rob McKay, and his cohort were further along, trying to scale their 2012 effort to a midterm election where voter enthusiasm—and donor cash flow—was likely to be harder to maintain. "We're all very concerned about the midterms because of the lower voter turnout and the questions about whose voting base is more motivated. In '10, that was an enormous problem," he told me as he prepared for the DA's November 2013 meeting in Washington.[37] "But going into '14, folks are well aware of how badly we stumbled in '10," he said. "Plans are being drawn up earlier. People are on their games," he said, explaining that the Democracy Alliance would continue to treat super PACs as "an important part of the progressive infrastructure that needs to be well-financed in order to create a more progressive America." Even as McKay and others in Democratic money circles prepared for 2014, they kept their eyes on 2016. That's when feared they could find themselves facing the same kind of civil war as Republicans were grappling with. Without the benefit of a sitting president at the top of the ticket, the party was going to be casting about for a new leader and a new direction. And that was when big donors could make a mess of things. As Sheldon Adelson and Foster Friess had demonstrated in the 2012 GOP presidential primary, all it took to split the party and damage its White House prospects were two rich donors backing rival candidates.

Increasingly, the Democratic big-money donors and operatives were arriving at the same solution to this potential problem: preempt a Democratic civil war by uniting behind a single standard-bearer whose coalition of fat-walleted supporters would be so intimidating to prospective rivals that they would simply back down before ever throwing their hat in the ring, essentially anointing that person the successor to

President Obama as the leader of the Democratic Party. It would have to be someone who could unite all phases of the Democratic coalition, including an environmentalist faction that felt neglected under Obama and an increasingly vocal economic populist wing—all while not alienating donors on Wall Street and in other traditional Democratic constituencies. It would have to be . . . Hillary Clinton? Her backers had tried a similar shock-and-awe approach to locking up the Democratic nomination in 2008, only to be foiled by Obama. This time they were determined to avoid the complacency that had allowed Obama to sneak up on Clinton. Then, they were so confident in the inevitability of her nomination that they failed to recognize the threat that Obama's small-donor-funded juggernaut would pose to Clinton's more traditional big-donor-powered campaign. They failed to quickly pull together a planned big-money support effort, and by the time they did, it was too late.

Clinton would surely face another brisk challenge from her left flank this time around. But the biggest advantage she and her supporters would have over 2008—bigger even than their earlier start and increased sense of urgency—was a development they had no control over. It was the same one that Romney's big-money allies used to push him from 2008 also-ran to 2012 nominee: *Citizens United.*

Clinton was in many ways the perfect Democrat for the *Citizens United* era, much like Romney was the perfect Republican. Ironically, the origins of the Supreme Court case were in a movie produced by the nonprofit group Citizens United that attacked Hillary Clinton ahead of her 2008 presidential campaign. The Federal Election Commission ruled that the movie ran afoul of the rules, so Citizens United sued in late 2007, challenging the constitutionality of the rules. Fast-forward seven years, to when Clinton's allies found themselves the best-positioned beneficiaries of *Citizens United,* ready to take advantage of the new big-money-dominated political landscape created by the decision. By 2014—before Clinton had given much of a hint of her 2016 plans, let alone formally blessed any kind of big-money effort on her behalf—a number of the biggest donors in Democratic politics had already publicly committed to supporting her in a campaign that didn't even exist yet. "I hope she will run. She would be a wonderful president," billionaire media mogul Haim Saban told an Israeli newspaper.[38] "If it happens, we will of course pitch in with full might. Seeing her in the White House is a big dream of mine," Saban said, calling Clinton "Obama's natural successor." Joining Saban in pledging support were George Soros and Esprit cofounder Susie Tompkins Buell, as well as newer Obama mega-donors like the Mostyns. It was a formidable big-money coalition.

The Clinton loyalists had a stream of big money out there for the taking in a new Wild West–like legal landscape in which anything went. They had an early start to collect it. They had a new sense of urgency. But could they avoid infighting—a regular feature of the Clintons' inner circle? Unlike Romney, whose financial operation had a tightly regimented hierarchy in which the inside-money game was run by Spencer Zwick and the outside effort was helmed by Charlie Spies, the Clintons had always had multiple aides jockeying for control at any given time.

At least at first, the Clinton money team seemed to have arrived at a big-money organizational structure with relatively clear lines of responsibility that would limit intramural skirmishes. Some of that organization was a holdover from the Democrats' well-coordinated 2012 big-money effort, but it all fed into a network of big-money groups unofficially supporting her still nonexistent candidacy. Two of those groups were transitions from 2012—the pro-Obama Priorities USA attack ad super PAC and the American Bridge opposition-research machine. A brand-new entry into the Hillary Clinton cash derby was specifically devoted to building grassroots support and an expensive voter data file for her noncampaign and was called, fittingly, Ready for Hillary. The idea was to build an infrastructure that would pave the way for her candidacy by rebutting attacks against her before she officially entered the race, building a rapid-response organization, and assembling a staff of loyalists and a network of big donors so she wouldn't have to start from scratch. Taken together, American Bridge, Priorities USA, and Ready for Hillary formed a sort of Clinton Shadow Campaign. The groups combined to raise more than $12 million in 2013—an unprecedented sum for a pre-presidential operation—including $525,000 from Soros. The whole arrangement epitomized the *Citizens United* era, in which having a big-money network had become the most important prerequisite for planning a presidential campaign—more important, perhaps, even than the candidate.

But not everyone was swooning at the prospect of a Hillary candidacy. Some liberal major donors were interested in finding a candidate to challenge Clinton from the left, and among the names most commonly bandied about were those of Massachusetts senator Elizabeth Warren, outgoing Maryland governor Martin O'Malley, former Vermont governor Howard Dean, and former Wisconsin senator Russ Feingold. If any of those politicians ran against Clinton, they would be foolish not to cast her as a stooge of Wall Street big money. It was a potential vulnerability for her—one that Warren, O'Malley, Dean, Feingold, and other potential liberal rivals could exploit, since they, unlike Clinton, had track records of economic populism and opposition to big money in politics. Ironically, a challenge on those grounds could really achieve lift-off in the *Citizens United* age if a handful of rich backers were willing to drop seven figures into an anti-Hillary campaign. After all, the super PAC attacks casting Romney as a greedy vulture capitalist picking working-class pockets were largely funded by a billionaire casino owner.

They might be ready for Hillary, but were Clinton's big-money allies ready for this line of attack? The first-ever meeting of Ready for Hillary's national finance council seemed a good place to try to answer that question. It took place at a fancy midtown Manhattan hotel in November 2013, just a couple of days after the *New Republic* published an article that set Democratic circles abuzz by making a case that Elizabeth Warren could pierce Clinton's inevitability just as Obama had done in 2008.[39] Back then, the issue inflaming the left was the Iraq War, and Obama capitalized on Clinton's support for it to rally liberals. "This time the debate will be about the power of America's wealthiest," the article predicted. And Warren was just the candidate to exploit Clinton's ties to a Democratic elite that "still fundamentally believe the economy functions best with a large, powerful, highly complex financial sector."

Slipping into the lobby of Le Parker Meridien, I hoped to gauge how Clinton's donors and operative allies might deal with such a challenge. The next day, at the winter meeting of the Democracy Alliance at the Mandarin Oriental in Washington, D.C., Warren was set to speak to donors, the majority of whom had supported Obama over Clinton in 2008. Despite the likelihood that a liberal challenger to Clinton could expect to win major support at the Democracy Alliance, the battle lines had yet to be rigidly drawn. There would be a good bit of overlap between the crowds at Le Parker Meridien and the Mandarin, as was evident by the presence in New York of two big-money operatives with deep ties to major donors both in Clinton World and at the DA—Harold Ickes and David Brock.

They had worked together on pro-Hillary efforts in the past, and both had an entrée into rich liberal circles in a way that few Obama insiders could match. But they weren't at the New York hotel together, and they were actually quite a mismatched pair. Ickes—profane, lanky, and rumpled, with a few wisps of brown hair and wire-rim glasses—was a former Bill Clinton White House aide in his seventies. With the help of major investments from Democracy Alliance members, he had started a cooperative called Catalist that became the preeminent voter database for Democratic campaigns, unions, and party committees. Brock—soft-spoken, short, and stylish, with a thick head of silver-streaked hair styled at the time in a sort of modern pompadour—was a former conservative journalist in his early fifties who once described himself as a "right-wing hit man"[40] before reinventing himself as a liberal avenger. Both Ickes and Brock had been involved in a failed effort to launch a major big-money operation to back Clinton's 2008 campaign. Ickes had not talked to me since the bitter Democratic primary that year, when I posted audio of him telling Clinton's big donors that Obama "is not going to be able to win the general election against John McCain," partly because Obama "doesn't have the general election electoral base that Hillary has" and also because "we don't know enough about him. There may well be an October surprise. There may not. But we don't have the luxury of taking a chance."[41]

In 2012, he and Brock both used their big-money touches to help Obama, with Ickes raising cash for the pro-Obama Priorities USA super PAC and Brock starting American Bridge, which spent $17 million mostly lambasting Romney and Republican congressional candidates. A Clinton run would put them at the epicenter of Democratic politics. Catalist, which had been pushed to the sidelines a bit by Obama allies who still harbored a grudge against Ickes, was angling to be the official data broker of Hillary Land. It had already won a contract to do an expensive direct mail campaign for Ready for Hillary featuring an image of Clinton's face on the envelope and a letter inside from a big-name supporter asking for cash.[42] Brock had already launched a new project, called Correct the Record, to defend prospective 2016 Democratic candidates against what it called "GOP smears." Many in Democratic politics saw it as a thinly veiled Clinton vehicle. Brock and other Clinton backers suggested that the infrastructure being built by American Bridge, Ready for Hillary, and Priorities USA wasn't geared toward attacking rival Democratic candidates in 2016 and could be easily transferred to whoever won the nomination. But that seemed disingenuous. In fact, not long after the donor meeting at Le Parker Meridien, Priorities USA officially declared its support for Clinton, announced that it would be chaired by Messina, and suggested that it expected to raise even more to help Clinton than it did to help Obama in 2012.[43]

Messina's new role, along with his leadership of Organizing for Action and his ties to some of the party's biggest donors, positioned him as a potential Rove-like figure in the left's increasingly robust big-money universe. He was not in attendance at Le Parker Meridien, but there were plenty of eager donors and operatives milling about. At the front of a conference room was a large blue "Ready for Hillary 2016" banner over a low stage; at the back, a small crowd was gathered around Craig T. Smith, a lawyer who had been a Clinton advisor since Bill's days as governor of Arkansas. Smith had left his job at the firm started by Clinton pollster Mark Penn, for which he advised campaigns around the world. He was now advising Ready for Hillary part-time while continuing to juggle work for international clients like a liberal party in the Czech Republic. At the Clinton donor meeting, he delivered a presentation entitled "The Need for Ready for Hillary." Smith, who was seen as the Clinton family representative at Ready for Hillary, also sat on a panel called "What It Will Take to Win in 2016."

Brock gave a lunchtime presentation called "Ready for the Right Wing," in which he made the case that Clinton routinely came in for egregiously unfair coverage from the media generally, and from the conservative media specifically. Brock talked about strategies for neutralizing questions about Clinton's age (she would be sixty-nine years old on Election Day 2016), the dynastic feel of a potential campaign, and ways to fight back against negative media coverage, presumably including his own Correct the Record project. Lately he had become fixated on combatting stories about what was shaping up as the main black mark on Clinton's tenure at the State Department: her handling of security at the American diplomatic compound in Benghazi before and during the attack that killed the US ambassador and three others. Republicans had accused the Obama administration of misleading the country about the attack, and called Clinton before Congress to interrogate her about it, seizing on her brusque dismissal of confrontational questioning by Republican senator Ron Johnson about when the State Department knew the attack was an orchestrated terrorist plot. "With all due respect, we had four dead Americans," an agitated Clinton told Johnson. "Was it because of a protest? Or was it because of guys out for a walk one night and decided they would go kill some Americans? What difference at this point does it make?"

The line was sure to wind up in 2016 Republican ads challenging Clinton's leadership if she was the Democratic nominee, and Brock saw it as his duty as part of the emerging Clinton shadow party to preemptively neutralize the attacks. He had written a book called *The Benghazi Hoax,* which attempted to debunk some of the criticisms of the administration's handling of the situation. It was being distributed for free to donors who attended the soiree at Le Parker Meridien. And in the days preceding the gathering, Brock had won a major victory in his Benghazi pushback—an apology and admission of error from CBS News over a blockbuster report on the subject that had been discredited. Using his big-money nonprofits, Brock had led the charge against CBS, and he was getting lots of credit from Democrats for derailing—at least temporarily—the mounting Benghazi criticism. It was no wonder Brock was such a hit among the big-donor class. The man had a knack for picking high-profile fights against big targets and getting results. On the very day of the Ready for Hillary conference, the need for Brock's efforts was underscored anew to the donors when Republican senator Rand Paul, teasing out possibilities for his own 2016 presidential run, had used a high-profile speech to reiterate the assertion that the handling of Benghazi "should preclude Hillary Clinton from ever holding high office again."[44]

Brock's presentation to the Hillary donors included a video that spliced together clips of critical television news reports about a concussion Clinton had suffered after a fall earlier in the year while she was preparing to testify about the Benghazi attack (some conservative pundits suggested she was faking), as well as her response to the attacks more broadly. One attendee told me, "By the time it was done, you could feel people in the room wanting to throw stuff" at the news personalities featured in the clips.

The presentation—like all the others at the donor event—was closed to the press, and the organizers didn't want attendees talking about the proceedings. "You know we're under a gag order?" an attendee named Risa Levine said to me. Levine, who was wearing a gold pendant shaped like Hillary's recognizable signature, opened up a bit nonetheless, professing she wasn't worried about the Elizabeth Warren boomlet ("It's just talk") and asserting that Ready for Hillary was "not a defensive thing" to ward off prospective rivals, nor was it a big-donor vanity vehicle. "There are bigger-dollar people in that room, but I'm not one of them," she insisted, asserting she'd only given $20. In fact, the buy-in for the event was $5,000 minimum, but Ready for Hillary had capped donations at $25,000 a person, which qualified donors to be finance council cochairs.

Ready for Hillary was more of a placeholder super PAC, less important for the amount of money it raised than for the voter data file and grassroots network it was building and the commitments from major donors it was collecting. Soros, for instance, had donated $25,000 a couple months before the conference, and his political advisor, Michael Vachon, was present.

Ready for Hillary was not indifferent to the need to treat its potential whales well. At the penthouse level of the hotel, the super PAC threw a donor cocktail party in a room that offered views of Manhattan from floor-to-ceiling windows on three sides.

Inside were many of the trappings betokening major donor maintenance, from the placards on certain tables indicating they were "reserved for Gold Pin and Green Pin holders"—that is, those who donated

$25,000 or $5,000, respectively—to the gold lapel pins embossed with the distinctive Hillary *H* logo[45] that were offered to donors. Most telling was the way the Ready for Hillary staff devoted extra-special attention to the deepest-pocketed donors—the ones with the capacity to give a hundred times the Gold Pin level without batting an eyelash.

By far the biggest fish at Le Parker Meridien were Steve and Amber Mostyn. The couple had actually divided their loyalties in the 2008 primary, with Amber supporting Clinton and Steve going for Obama. Steve was concerned about the risk that rich Democrats, in writing super PAC checks to boost their favored 2016 presidential candidates, could inadvertently lead the party into a "demolition derby"—a term he used often that aptly described the 2012 GOP presidential primary. And it sometimes was difficult to tell whether his pledge of support to Clinton stemmed from passionate support for her or from a more pragmatic desire to avert the demolition derby. In the new politics, it didn't really matter what motivated the check-writing, as long as the checks got written. And the Mostyns had established themselves as bellwether Democratic donors during the 2012 campaign.

Since then, they'd found themselves besieged by eager operatives making elaborate pitches for all manner of campaigns and groups. The succession of presentations at the Ready for Hillary conference seemed to bore Steve, who played hooky for much of the day. He'd taken the couple's young daughter to the famed FAO Schwarz toy store before depositing her with a babysitter at the hotel for the end of the conference. From a marital harmony perspective, that was a wise move, since his wife headlined the final conference presentation, entitled "Why I Am Ready for Hillary." At the cocktail party afterward, Ready for Hillary operatives anxiously lined up to talk to the Mostyns like courtesans seeking an audience with—and maybe a bag of cash from—the royals.

"Thank you for all your help," the super PAC's lead fund-raiser, Rafi Jafri, told Amber Mostyn. The Mostyns tended to put folks at ease, and the cocktail party seemed to be closer to Steve's natural habit than the panels that preceded it. With their big personalities, Texas drawls, and quick laughs, they were warm and easy to talk to. Jafri chatted up Amber about the 2014 Texas governor's race. Mostyn was a leading patron of Democratic candidate Wendy Davis, introducing the state senator to big-time liberal donors eager to write her fat checks after she took to the state Senate floor in June 2013 wearing pink running shoes for a high-profile eleven-hour filibuster of a Texas anti-abortion bill. Mostyn's eyes lit up at the chance to talk about Davis. Jafri had done his research, as any savvy fund-raiser would before an audience with a major donor.

Eventually the Mostyns adjourned to the bar downstairs, where they ended up by chance sitting at a table right next to 1980s superstar Rod Stewart, who was feeding finger foods to the attractive young lady sitting on his lap. Amber broke out in a decent rendition of the chorus from "Da Ya Think I'm Sexy," but Steve seemed unimpressed by "Rod the Mod."

The next evening, I ran into the Mostyns at another bar 270 miles to the south, in the lobby of Washington's Mandarin Oriental hotel, which was hosting a much more elite gathering of Democratic checkbooks— the winter meeting of the Democracy Alliance. Here donors had the cash, the strong-mindedness, and the liberal sensibilities to buck the Hillary coronation plan being hatched by supporters like the Mostyns. The Democracy Alliance had done it before. During the run-up to 2008, the majority of DA donors backed Obama, offending a smaller but very ardent pro-Clinton contingent. Several got upset and quit the Alliance entirely, including Susie Tompkins Buell, who was now active in Ready for Hillary.

Back then, the split hadn't erupted into the kind of damaging money-vs.-money presidential primary that Republicans endured in 2012. "There was sort of an uneasy détente," DA chair Rob McKay told me. "No one really wanted to go hard after the other, on the outside, anyway."[46]

But it seemed like it would be different in the run-up to 2016. One thing that hadn't changed was that the Democracy Alliance donors considered themselves the liberal wing of the Democratic Party. They loved identifying and boosting politicians who they felt represented that wing, and none more so than Elizabeth Warren, who was scheduled to make an appearance at the conference, and Nancy Pelosi, who was downstairs at an opening reception. Hillary Clinton, for all her attributes, impressive resume, and boundary breaking, was not a representative of the liberal wing.

Beyond the basic ideological differences, there were other developments afoot at the Democracy Alliance that seemed inhospitable to Clinton. The Mandarin conference would be the last one under the leadership of the group's longtime director, a Clinton loyalist named Kelly Craighead. She was handing over the reins to Gara LaMarche, a former foundation official who DA seemed more liberal and less likely to steer donors to groups that supported Clinton. The liberal billionaire Tom Steyer was scheduled to pitch donors[47] on efforts like his big-spending super PAC campaign boosting environmentally minded candidates who oppose the Keystone XL oil pipeline. Warren had signaled concern over Keystone,[48] cheering environmental activists, some of whom remained leery of Clinton.[49]

Meanwhile, prowling for donors in the Mandarin lobby bar was an operative named Adam Green, who had cofounded a group called the Progressive Change Campaign Committee (PCCC). It was widely credited with helping to coax Elizabeth Warren into running for the Senate in 2012 and then boosting her to victory, and now was working to do the same for her in the 2016 presidential race. Green and his PCCC cofounder had just finished having a drink with San Diego real estate mogul Lawrence Hess. Not that Hess needed much convincing to give to Green's group or other liberal causes. He and his wife, Suzanne Hess, are longtime DA members who had backed Obama over Clinton in 2008 and seemed like precisely the type of folks who could be convinced to support a liberal challenger to Clinton again in 2016. They had given more than $3 million over the years in traceable contributions to liberal candidates and causes, including $225,000 since 2011 to Green's group, PCCC. But Green was on the hunt for new donors to sponsor his group's ambitious 2014 efforts, through which he hoped to pull Democrats to the left as 2016 approached. He was eager to be introduced to Steve Mostyn.

But when Green began talking about his group, Mostyn looked bored and quickly begged off, explaining that he and his wife were headed out with Wendy Davis, who was waiting with Amber Mostyn by the hotel's main exit. The Mostyns planned to introduce Davis around to other big donors at the conference over the coming days. When I approached to ask whether Davis had a minute to chat about the increasing role of big money in politics, Steve Mostyn cut me off. "No," he said emphatically, laughing, as he and Amber escorted Davis out into the brisk night. I was told later that Davis was a hit with the donors and was expected to attract major support from the DA members. They were accustomed to having would-be rising stars paraded before them at the DA conferences. In addition to Davis, fellow 2014 gubernatorial candidate Mary Burke of Wisconsin was presented to the donors by Vermont governor Peter Shumlin, who was the chair of the Democratic Governors Association.

"It's like a dog and pony show," someone who attends the conferences told me. The donors all wear name tags (though Steve Mostyn was gently reprimanded at the Mandarin for not wearing his), allowing savvy politicians and operatives to quickly assess how much time and effort to spend schmoozing a given donor.

I asked Green whether he thought Democrats had gotten over their coolness to big money. He was unusually candid. "Democrats have never been against big money," said Green, whose group is in the second tier of DA recommendees (meaning cash to PCCC counts toward members' quota only once they've made the minimum donation to other groups). "There's always been a hope that there would be less money in politics," but that wasn't going to stop them from trying to elect candidates they thought would help America. "These people give out of the goodness of their hearts," he said, motioning to the packed bar. "They're never going to make money off of it."

That contention, which liberals often invoked when arguing that conservative donors were more self-interested than their own, was a gross over-simplification at best. After all, there were Republican donors who gave primarily to causes and candidates unrelated to their financial interests. And there were Democratic donors whose giving overlapped significantly with their financial interests. Case in point was Steyer, who had investments in green energy companies that could benefit from the policy he was advocating through his political efforts—on which he was set to pitch donors at the Mandarin later that very weekend.

Just then, another populist liberal champion ambled over to say hello to Green in the Mandarin lobby. Congressman Alan Grayson of Florida was an old-style liberal bomb thrower whom some progressives had floated as a dream Warren vice presidential pick[50] (though the chances of this happening struck me as next to none). Like Warren, he was a brisk small-donor fund-raiser who had also benefited from the efforts of Green's group. I put the same question to him about the Democratic evolution on big money. "I don't think there was ever a reluctance. Anybody who could raise $750,000 from one donor, would. We are the party of Tony Coelho, after all," Grayson said, referring to the former California congressman who, as chairman of the Democratic Congressional Campaign Committee in the 1980s, took soft-money fund-raising to new levels. At Coelho's DCCC, lobbyists could pay an annual fee to join something he called the "Speaker's Club" that would allow them and their clients to socialize with House leadership.[51]

Wealthy corporate executives are constantly being solicited by politicians asking how the levers of government can be manipulated to help the executives or their companies, Grayson told me. "I know because I was one of them," Grayson said, referring to wealthy business executives. Grayson accrued a personal fortune estimated at $17 million,[52] mostly during his time as president of IDT Corporation, a telecom company. "I'm the sixth-richest member of the House," Grayson boasted, explaining that he had joined Democracy Alliance as a member a couple of years earlier to help fund the liberal infrastructure. A mega-donor congressman who doled out $200,000 a year minimum in big checks to outside groups—all while bashing big money? That surprised me, but I guess it shouldn't have, given the way things seemed headed.

Nonetheless, Grayson reiterated his opposition to big money in politics and the *Citizens United* decision. "But that doesn't change the fact that we have to play within the rules that there are, and do the best to win and to represent people the best we can," he said before begging off to join Pelosi at the reception downstairs.

I followed Grayson down the long escalator to the lower-level ballroom hosting the conference. Projected on a couple of large screens at the front of the room were the words "Reclaiming Democracy"—presumably the conference theme, which was slightly ironic, given that in the new big-money era, these donors had little to reclaim. They were in control. There were about seven tables, each seating ten, in the middle of the room, at which DA members were enjoying dinner. I began circulating, trying to find Pelosi, who had been hinting at support for Clinton[53] even as she remained neutral in the fledgling race for her party's nomination.

I didn't get very far. A security guard and a volunteer were on me quickly, asking for my credentials. "This is a private gathering," the guard explained, grabbing my phone as I tried to take a photo of the scene, and escorting me out of the ballroom and back up the escalator. The next day my sources told me about Warren's appearance before the donors. After she introduced a panel focusing on judicial issues, a cluster of donors swarmed her to ask whether she was going to run. "If you are, I'm not going to get behind another possibility," one donor said. Warren looked the donor in the eye and emphatically said no. Talk at the conference soon moved to whether Howard Dean or Russ Feingold could capture the liberal energy—and money—to Hillary's left, I was told.

It was fitting, I thought. Here among the wealthy liberals who had helped launch Obama into the White House five years earlier was the realization of the president's quiet warning about the increasing power of big money in politics. As Obama had told Bill Gates and a handful of other rich donors on that drizzly Seattle day in February 2012: "You now have the potential of two hundred people deciding who ends up being elected president every single time." It was three years before the next presidential election, yet the deciding was well under way among the folks gathered at the Mandarin. The fates of whoever the candidates eventually turned out to be—whether Clinton, Warren, or someone else—would be shaped dramatically by the checkbooks of the folks at the Mandarin and others in their income bracket who gathered at the Koch seminars and super PAC fund-raisers across the country. These donors would likewise have a major say in the direction of the Democratic and Republican parties, helping to determine whether the

GOP establishment could put down the tea party uprising and whether Democrats would embrace a tax-the-rich approach to reducing income inequality. There was still plenty of uncertainty around all these questions, and there were potential changes afoot to the campaign finance system as well. Politics would continue to change, but big money was here to stay.

Epilogue

Back at the fund-raiser on the suburban Seattle shores of Lake Washington where I began this book, President Obama was reaching for a positive takeaway. He had spooked his audience of ultra-rich donors with his warning about folks in their income bracket taking advantage of the new big-money landscape to hijack future presidential elections.

That, Obama had said, is "not the way things are supposed to work." And he wasn't going to get an argument from the small crowd, which included Microsoft billionaires Bill Gates and Steve Ballmer. Like most pockets of big Democratic money, the suburban Seattle donors had a reformist bent and were worried about the outsized influence of money in politics—despite the paradox that some of them were among those writing the big checks. Now, like a salesman who had just laid out the dire need for his services, Obama moved in to close the deal. If he won reelection to a second term, he promised the donors, he would invest major political capital in ending for good the escalating big-money dominance of American politics by stoppering the volcano from which, he contended, the cash was flowing—the Supreme Court's *Citizens United* decision.

"The Supreme Court made a constitutional ruling that was absolutely wrong, and that I said was wrong in a State of the Union speech. In front of the Supreme Court justices," he said,[1] smiling slyly, as he recalled chastising the justices on live television a week after *Citizens United*. "Because I foresaw what was going to happen," he told the donors. "I mean, this just basically eliminated all the rules." He went on, "Because it's a constitutional ruling—a ruling on the First Amendment—we can't overturn it legislatively, and there are limits to what we can do administratively. There are some things that probably would comport with the ruling in terms of requiring disclosure." But, he added, referencing Charles and David Koch, "the disclosure is not a sufficient deterrent for a lot of these folks who are writing checks."

No, Obama continued, "the only way we're going to do it effectively, I think, is with a constitutional amendment." Since *Citizens United,* some of the goo-goos who opposed big money in politics had reached the same conclusion. "Now, I taught constitutional law," Obama continued to Gates et alia. "I don't tinker with the Constitution lightly. But I think this is important enough that citizens have to get mobilized around this issue, and this will probably be a multiyear effort. After my reelection, my sense is that I may be in a very strong position to do it."

Then the president recalled some wisdom shared with him by his onetime mentor, Abner Mikva, a former federal judge and congressman from Chicago. Mikva told Obama that "being friends with a politician is like perpetually having a kid in college. Every year, there's just more tuition," Obama remembered, gesturing as if he were doling out dollar bills. "But I'm finally graduating, and that may allow me to use the bully pulpit to argue forcefully for a constitutional amendment," he said.

A constitutional amendment would be incredibly difficult to pass. Even if it was successful, its potential impact was far from clear. The most popular proposed amendment would make clear that corporations are not guaranteed First Amendment rights and therefore could not spend unlimited sums on politics. But that might not curb the majority of big-money political spending, which was done by rich individuals through super PACs. Nonetheless, Obama's promise seemed to be a hit with the crowd in Medina, Washington. And, months after his reelection, when I told several advocates for stricter campaign rules about his pledge, they were surprised. While they had initially regarded Obama as a kindred spirit in their quest to reduce the role of money in politics, they had come to view him as a major disappointment—as an accomplice in the big-money hijacking of American politics.

Obama was hardly alone in bashing big money, even as he helped raise it. Democratic congressional leaders including Nancy Pelosi and Harry Reid were among the leading critics of the new big money, yet they were also among their party's leading super PAC fund-raisers. They had lent their deft touch with big donors to a pair of super PACs that aimed to elect Democrats to Congress, which in 2013 raised $16.4 million—about three times as much as their Republican counterparts.

Republican congressional leaders had a similarly schizophrenic approach to outside spending. House Speaker John Boehner and Senate Republican leader Mitch McConnell railed against the big-money tea party groups that continually challenged their authority and prevented them from rallying their respective members to support fiscal compromises like those raising the nation's debt ceiling and ending the government shutdown. "They're using our members and they're using the American people for their own goals," Boehner thundered in late 2013 after tea-party-aligned outside groups opposed a bipartisan budget deal. McConnell, facing his own tea party challenger in a 2014 primary, charged that the groups "mislead their donors" and are "giving conservatism a bad name."[2] Nonetheless, for Boehner and McConnell, the solution was not changing the laws to clamp down on big money raised outside their party infrastructure, but rather to answer back with super PACs of their own.

Public opinion polls show that voters overwhelmingly believe there is too much money in politics and that the money has a corrupting effect. But the issue tends to land low on their list of priorities, well below kitchen-table concerns about jobs and the economy. If history is any guide, it's unlikely that there will be any substantial reforms limiting or further regulating the flow of big money into politics without a louder and more sustained public outcry.

Such political will has tended to spike mostly as a backlash to major money-in-politics scandals that riveted the public consciousness. About a decade after Mark Hanna and the robber barons paved the way for William McKinley's 1896 presidential election, McKinley's successor Theodore Roosevelt—facing his own controversy over corporate donations to his 1904 campaign, as well as lingering public distaste over Hanna's fund-raising—signed the Tillman Act, which barred corporations from contributing to campaigns. The intense fallout from the Watergate break-in scandals, during which Nixon's 1972 reelection campaign was found to have accepted millions in illegal corporate contributions, spurred Congress to pass a host of new campaign rules in 1974, setting limits on how much individuals, political parties, and political committees could give to campaigns, and establishing the Federal Election Commission to enforce the rules and facilitate disclosure of campaign cash. The tawdry spectacle of Bill Clinton renting out the Lincoln Bedroom in exchange for huge contributions of so-called soft-money to the Democratic Party—combined with the massive accounting scandal that brought down the energy giant Enron, one of the leading soft-money donors in the country—supplied the political momentum for Congress to pass the 2002 McCain-Feingold campaign finance overhaul. It banned soft-money donations to the parties and restricted corporate- and union-funded political ads, though the latter provision was overturned by *Citizens United*. And it was the Jack Abramoff lobbying scandal that provided the impetus for the last major campaign finance reforms, a 2007 law that, among other things, required disclosure of campaign contributions gathered by lobbyists. That provision was partly the work of a young Illinois senator named Barack Obama, who considered it among his proudest accomplishments in the U.S. Senate,[3] much as he counted a campaign finance reform bill among his top achievements during his tenure in the Illinois state legislature.

Coincidentally, on the day the post-Abramoff reforms passed the U.S. Senate, Obama happened to be headed home from Washington to Chicago on the same flight as a leading Illinois state campaign finance reform advocate, a woman named Cynthia Canary, with whom he had worked closely years earlier on the state-level reforms. "I passed another one for you," Obama said, smiling, as he stopped by Canary's seat to exchange pleasantries.

After Obama's 2012 reelection, with campaign finance reformers relegated to playing defense against a flood of big money, I called Canary to ask about Obama's legacy on the campaign cash restrictions they once had championed together. "It has been extraordinarily disappointing—the lack of leadership that he has shown in these areas," Canary told me.[4] "It's one thing to give a State of the Union and scold the court for *Citizens United*. But it's another thing to actually try to start turning things around, as opposed to looking at these decisions and these loopholes to try to figure out how you can game them. The combination just rings a little hollow." Canary, who for fourteen years ran the nonprofit Illinois Campaign for Political Reform, said, "I'm not going to hold my breath" for any significant reforms in Obama's final years in office. "I think he still believes with his organizer's heart in an equality of voices. But my sense is that his pragmatic nature overtook his reformist nature. It's unfortunate. If everyone weren't so afraid that they would be pulverized by not playing it, you might actually redefine politics in this country."

That was just it. Whether Canary and other campaign finance reformers liked it or not, the new big-money politics was the way politics was played. And politicians who didn't play along did, in fact, risk being pulverized, as Obama and the Democrats found out the hard way after the 2010 midterm election. Of course, in 2012, Republicans found out the hard way that raising far more big money than your opponent doesn't guarantee victory, as the political operations fronted by the Koch brothers and Karl Rove combined to spend about $725 million attacking Democrats, only to watch Obama win reelection and Democrats hold the Senate.

Headed into the 2014 and 2016 elections, there was little pragmatic incentive for either side to invest political capital in a quixotic fight to change the law—let alone the Constitution—to limit the flow of contributions. Operatives on both sides were rapaciously soliciting six- and seven-figure checks from wider and wider pools of extremely wealthy supporters. And that only fueled the arms race, as donors were warned that they needed to give more, lest the other side gain an advantage. No one could afford to stand down.

To folks like Canary, this state of affairs—a completely legal hijacking of American democracy by the ultra-rich—was in and of itself a massive systemic scandal that should have alarmed voters and spurred them to demand change from their leaders. Canary's allies in the reform community tried to stoke that public outrage, working to connect dots between massive campaign spending and policies that favored deep-pocketed special interests.

But as the flow of massive checks into super PACs continued, and the parade of top politicians genuflecting before mega-donors lengthened, it seemed voters might be becoming inured to this new reality. What would it take to shock the electorate and shame the body politic into shutting off the big-money spigot? Would it require an explosive scandal involving a smoking-gun quid pro quo between a mega-donor and a politician? Or would a jaw-dropping amount of legal spending suffice, and if so, how much would it take to tip the indignation meter? If $400 million in anonymous cash spent by the Koch brothers' donor network to influence the 2012 election didn't do the trick, would $1 billion from a small cluster of donors help elect a 2016 presidential candidate—say, Hillary Clinton? The fact that such a prospect could not be dismissed out of hand—only four years after Sheldon Adelson's $20 million investment in Newt Gingrich's White House bid seemed unimaginable—showed just how much the new big money had changed American politics.

Acknowledgments

This book wouldn't have been possible without Politico, where I am proud to work.

The publication's founders, Robert Allbritton, John Harris, and Jim VandeHei, took a chance on me. Even as they were staking their own names to a bold new journalism experiment in the face of dire industry trends and abundant skepticism, they provided me the time, resources, and platform to explore the rapidly changing role of money in American politics. Robert, John, and Jim also allowed me to work alongside an amazing group of journalists from whom I have learned an immense amount about both politics and journalism—folks like Mike Allen, Jeanne Cummings, Maggie Haberman, and Ben Smith, just to name a few. A number of Politicos past and present have been particularly helpful in shaping my reporting, writing, and thinking about the subject of this book while also putting up with my idiosyncrasies, including Dan Berman, Craig Gordon, Bill Hamilton, Danielle Jones, Charlie Mahtesian, Laura McGann, Tarini Parti, Olivia Peterson, Abby Phillip, Rachel Smolkin, and Byron Tau.

My reporting for this book overlapped with my reporting for Politico, so if you recognize a few quotes or anecdotes, that's why. But the organization also supported me as I stepped back from the frenetic pace of the political news cycle it has come to dominate, in order to delve more deeply into the subject and craft this book out of what I learned.

I wouldn't have been able to make sense of the way big money was reshaping politics without the insight of my sources. I won't name them here, both because the list is long and because many would prefer to remain anonymous. You know who you are, though, and I appreciate your trust and insight. The American Political Science Association Congressional Fellowship Program gave me the grounding to understand how Washington really works by allowing me to work inside

Congress—where I met my wife! I'm indebted to all the folks who helped shape me as a reporter before I got to Politico, including Larry Cook at the *Journal Inquirer* in Manchester, Connecticut; Chuck Lewis at the Center for Public Integrity; Todd Meyers and Allison Walzer at the *Times Leader* in Wilkes-Barre, Pennsylvania; R. B. Swift in the Pennsylvania state capitol newsroom; and Peter Callaghan, Hunter George, and Joe Turner at the *News Tribune* in Tacoma, Washington.

I also continue to learn from, and be challenged by, the folks who cover the same fertile money-in-politics turf as me—kick-ass reporters like Julie Bykowicz, Nick Confessore, Ken Doyle, Matea Gold, Andy Kroll, and Peter Stone; outfits dedicated to following the money, like the Campaign Finance Institute, the Center for Responsive Politics, and the Center for Public Integrity; and the hardworking folks at the Federal Election Commission.

This book never would have happened without Howard Yoon, who served as my guide to book writing and publishing. And it would have been a mess without Liz Spayd, who helped impose narrative structure and flow, and Sue Warga, who fixed my typos. Thanks also to all the (very patient) folks at PublicAffairs—Peter Osnos, Susan Weinberg, Clive Priddle, Melissa Raymond, Collin Tracy, Maria Goldverg, and Jaime Leifer—who trusted in my ability to write this book and helped me make it a reality.

Most of all, I'm thankful for the love and support of my family, including my parents, Ruth and Morris, and my brother, Jon. I wish that my Bubby Ruth, whose toughness and kindness made our family possible, had lived to see this book published, but I'm grateful for having had as many years with her as I did. And I'm especially grateful for my wife, Danielle, who provided constant advice and encouragement throughout the book writing, even as she was in the midst of the incredibly difficult process of launching her business.

Notes

Preface

1. Barack Obama, Remarks Announcing Candidacy for President, Springfield, Illinois, February 10, 2007, www.presidency.ucsb.edu/ws /index.php?pid=76999.

2. Harold Jackson, "W. Clement Stone: Self-Made Billionaire Who Helped Fund Richard Nixon's Watergate Dirty Tricks," *Guardian,* September 16, 2002, www.guardian.co.uk/news/2002/sep/17/guardian obituaries.haroldjackson.

3. Statement of Federal Election Commission chairwoman Ellen L. Weintraub, January 31, 2013, www.fec.gov/members/weintraub /statements/weintraub_statement_20130131.pdf.

4. The $2.5 billion figure was calculated by adding $2.2 billion in total political action committee disbursements (per Federal Election Commission news release, "FEC Summarizes Campaign Activity of the 2011–2012 Election Cycle," April 19, 2013, www.fec.gov/press/press 2013/20130419_2012-24m-Summary.shtml) and $300 million in independent expenditures reported by persons other than political committees (per Federal Election Commission table "Independent Expenditure Table 1," April 19, 2013, www.fec.gov/press/summaries /2012/ElectionCycle/file/IEs/IE1_2012_24m.pdf).

Chapter 1: The Billionaires' Club

1. Email from Kevin Gentry to first-time Koch conference attendees, March 5, 2013.

2. *Forbes,* Billionaire Profiles 2013, "Charles Koch, No. 6," September 2013, www.forbes.com/profile/charles-koch; *Forbes,* Billionaire Profiles 2013, "David Koch, No. 6," March 2013, www.forbes.com/profile /david-koch.

3. Kenneth P. Vogel, "Karl Rove vs. the Koch Brothers," Politico, October 10, 2011, www.politico.com/news/stories/1011/65504.html.

4. In 2011 and 2012, Americans for Prosperity spent $140 million, while its sister group Americans for Prosperity Foundation spent $39 million, according to the organizations' tax filings.

5. Kenneth P. Vogel, "Social Conservatives Make Big Money Plans," Politico, January 2, 2014, www.politico.com/story/2014/01/social -conservatives-fundraising-101666.html.

6. Brad Friedman, "Exclusive Audio: Inside the Koch Brothers' Secret Seminar," *Mother Jones,* September 6, 2011, www.motherjones.com /politics/2011/09/exclusive-audio-koch-brothers-seminar-tapes.

7. Kenneth P. Vogel, "The Kochs Fight Back," Politico, February 2, 2011, www.politico.com/news/stories/0211/48624.html.

8. Conversation overheard by the author at the Renaissance Esmeralda, April 29, 2013.

9. Richard Lardner, "Blackwater Hires PR Giant in Image Siege," Associated Press, October 5, 2007, http://usatoday30.usatoday.com/news /washington/2007-10-05-2348857332_x.htm.

10. Koch Industries, "We Confront Reuters on Advocacy Journalism," KochFacts, Friday, July 1, 2011, www.kochfacts.com/kf /we-confront-reuters-on-advocacy-journalism.

11. David Weigel, "Dick Armey: Please, Koch, Keep Distancing Yourself from Me," *Washington Post,* April 15, 2010, http://voices .washingtonpost.com/right-now/2010/04/dick_armey_please_koch_keep _di.html.

12. Hamilton Nolan, "The Desperate Campaign to Discredit Jane Mayer," Gawker, January 5, 2011, http://gawker.com/480977015.

13. Email from Rob Tappan, October 21, 2013.

14. Koch Industries general counsel Mark V. Holden letter to American Society of Magazine Editors chief executive Sid Holt, "Objecting to *New Yorker* Magazine Recognition," KochFacts, April 25, 2011, www.kochfacts.com/kf/letter-to-american-society-of-magazine -editors-objecting-to-new-yorker-magazine-recognition.

15. Jane Mayer, remarks at award ceremony for the 2013 I. F. Stone Medal for Journalistic Independence, Nieman Foundation for Journalism, Harvard University, August 27, 2013, http://vimeo.com /76006534.

16. Philip Ellender, "Letter in Response to Kenneth Vogel's Piece 'The Battle to Define Charles and David Koch,'" KochFacts, March 29, 2011, www.kochfacts.com/kf/letter-in-response-to-kenneth-vogels.

17. Koch Industries, "Confronting Inaccuracy and Journalistic Misconduct by Politico's Ken Vogel," KochFacts, February 22, 2013, www.kochfacts.com/kf/inaccuracyandmisconduct.

18. David Weigel, "The Best Flacking the Kochs Can Buy?" Slate, May 20, 2013, www.slate.com/blogs/weigel/2013/05/20/the_best_flacking_the _kochs_can_buy.html.

19. Author tweet, "Thx for congrats on book! Celebrated last nite by getting escorted from Koch conf by Koch ofcls (incldg security chf), @RenaissanceEs guards," April 30, 2013, 1:21 p.m., https://twitter.com /kenvogel/status/329284509868650496; author tweet, "Politely escorted, I should add MT @kenvogel Celebrated last nite by getting escorted from Koch conf by Koch ofcls & @RenaissanceEs security," April 30, 2013, 1:21 p.m., https://twitter.com/kenvogel/status/329284949079363584.

20. Author telephone interview with Stan Hubbard, August 7, 2013.

21. Matea Gold, "Koch-Backed Political Coalition, Designed to Shield Donors, Raised $400 Million in 2012," *Washington Post,* January 5, 2014, www.washingtonpost.com/politics/koch-backed-political-network -built-to-shield-donors-raised-400-million-in-2012-elections/2014/01 /05/9e7cfd9a-719b-11e3-9389-09ef9944065e_story.html.

22. Koch Industries, *Discovery* newsletter, January 2013, www.kochind .com/files/DiscoveryJanuary2013.pdf.

23. Author analysis of IRS and FEC filings by top-raising outside groups that spent directly or indirectly on 2012 presidential race (Restore Our Future, American Crossroads, Crossroads GPS, Americans for Prosperity, Freedom Partners Chamber of Commerce, Priorities USA Action, Winning Our Future, Freedomworks for America, AFL-CIO Workers' Voices PAC, Club for Growth Action, Service Employees International Union, Ending Spending Action Fund, American Bridge 21st Century, United Auto Workers, Congressional Leadership Fund, Women Vote!, Planned Parenthood Votes, America Votes Action Fund, Make Us Great Again, Fair Share Action, Restore America's Voice PAC, Super PAC for America, Endorse Liberty, Environment America

Action Fund, Liberty for All Super PAC, Our Destiny PAC, League
of Conservation Voters, America's Next Generation, Government
Integrity Fund, Republicans for a Prosperous America, National Right
to Life Victory Fund, United Food and Commercial Workers Advocacy,
National Horizon, Cain Connections PAC, Local Voices, Texans for
America's Future, Black Men Vote, Revolution PAC, Americans for
a Better Tomorrow Tomorrow, Hardworking Americans Committee,
Working for Us PAC, Faith Family Freedom Fund, Crossroads
Generation) vs. Open Secrets, "Total Outside Spending by Election Cycle,
Excluding Party Committees," Center for Responsive Politics, accessed
September 12, 2013, www.opensecrets.org/outsidespending/cycle
_tots.php.

24. Contributions reported in IRS and FEC filings for four nonprofit
groups: Media Matters for America, Media Matters Action Network,
American Bridge 21st Century, and American Bridge 21st Century
Foundation.

25. Salary payments to Brock reflected in IRS and FEC filings by
Media Matters for America (which paid him $273,954 in 2012), Media
Matters Action Network ($20,846), American Bridge 21st Century
($104,346), and American Bridge 21st Century Foundation ($29,277).

26. Sheelah Kolhatkar, "Exclusive: Inside Karl Rove's Billionaire
Fundraiser," *Bloomberg BusinessWeek,* August 31, 2012, www.business
week.com/articles/2012-08-31/exclusive-inside-karl-roves-billionaire
-fundraiser.

27. Kenneth P. Vogel, "2016 Contenders Court Mega-Donors,"
Politico, December 3, 2012, www.politico.com/story/2012/12/2016
-contenders-courting-mega-donors-84497.html.

28. Analysis considered all donations to the main committees playing
in the presidential campaign that were required to disclose detailed
information about their finances to the Federal Election Commission:
the presidential campaign committees, national party committees, joint
fund-raising committees, Priorities USA Action, Restore Our Future,
and American Crossroads. Large donors were those who gave $50,000
or more. Small donors were those who gave less than $200, the threshold
for itemizing contributions on FEC reports. The number of unitemized
donors was based on a Campaign Finance Institute calculation that the

average unreported donation to Obama for America and the Obama Victory Fund was $60, while the average unreported donation to Romney for President and Romney Victory was $80 and the average unreported donation to the other committees was $70.

29. The total number of donors to the committees in question (based on FEC reports and the Campaign Finance Institute's calculation of average unitemized donations) was 11,860,665.

30. According to FEC and IRS records, in 2011 and 2012, Simmons donated $25.8 million to Republican candidates and causes, his companies donated $4.7 million, and his wife, Annette Simmons, donated $1.3 million.

31. Karl Rove, "In Appreciation of Remarkable Lives," *Wall Street Journal*, January 1, 2014, http://online.wsj.com/news/articles/SB10001424 05270230413730457929223421403034.

32. C. J. Ciaramella, "Getting Its 'ACT' Together," Washington Free Beacon, February 24, 2012, http://freebeacon.com/getting-its-act -together.

33. Hui Chen, David C. Parsley, and Ya-Wen Yang, "Corporate Lobbying and Financial Performance," November 23, 2012, http://papers .ssrn.com/sol3/papers.cfm?abstract_id=1014264.

34. Alicia Mundy, "Adelson to Keep Betting on the GOP," *Wall Street Journal,* December 4, 2012, http://online.wsj.com/news/articles/SB100014 24127887323717004578159570568104706.

35. *Forbes,* Billionaire Profiles 2013, "Sheldon Adelson, No. 15," September 2013, www.forbes.com/profile/sheldon-adelson.

36. Seth Hanlon, "Sheldon Adelson's Return on Investment," Center for American Progress, August 2012, http://images.politico.com /global/2012/09/hanlon_adelsonc4brief.html.

37. Mike Allen, "Sheldon Adelson: Inside the Mind of the Mega-Donor," Politico, September 23, 2012, www.politico.com/news /stories/0912/81588.html.

38. Author interview with Jack Abramoff, May 29, 2013.

39. Author interview with Brian Kraft and Keith Coplen, Palm Springs, CA, April 30, 2013.

40. Author email interview with Steve Mostyn, November 29, 2012.

41. Ibid.

Chapter 2: The Pony

1. Mike Duncan quotes from May 6, 2010, panel moderated by author at McKenna Long & Aldridge, LLP, in Washington, DC. Partial video: http://bcove.me/q8h9ptgg.

2. Richard Reeves, *President Nixon: Alone in the White House* (New York: Simon and Schuster, 2001), 462–463.

3. Timothy Crouse, *The Boys on the Bus* (New York: Random House, 2003), 244.

4. Articles of Impeachment against Richard M. Nixon: http://classes .lls.edu/archive/manheimk/371d1/nixonarticles.html. Article V, Charge 25: "Receiving Money Unlawfully Obtained. By the means specified in Counts 10–24 Richard Nixon received and obtained for his own use and benefit and did have the use and benefit, for the purpose of financing his campaign for reelection as President, of moneys illegally obtained as specified in Counts 10–24 to a total amount of $1,652,500, which he knew and/or had reason to know had been unlawfully obtained; in violation of article II, section 4 of the Constitution and sections 201, 241, 371, 872, 1503 and 1505 of the Criminal Code."

5. John Aloysius Farrell, "Bush Shuts Agency Under Investigation," *Boston Globe,* May 4, 1991.

6. Lee Mueller, "GOP Stalwart from Inez to Chair RNC," *Lexington* (KY) *Herald-Leader,* November 17, 2006.

7. "Who Runs Gov Profile; Mike Duncan," *Washington Post,* accessed September 14, 2013, www.washingtonpost.com/politics/mike-duncan /gIQApNXr9O_topic.html.

8. "Duncan Decides Against Gubernatorial Run," Associated Press, December 30, 1998.

9. Duncan quotes from May 6, 2010, panel.

10. Center for Responsive Politics, "Party Fundraising Totals by Cycle," OpenSecrets.org, accessed September 18, 2013, www.opensecrets .org/bigpicture/ptytots.php?cycle=2012. The 1992 election cycle was the first presidential cycle during which the FEC required the disclosure of soft money.

11. Duncan quotes from May 6, 2010, panel.

12. Ibid.

13. Ibid.

14. Ibid.

15. James V. Grimaldi and Thomas B. Edsall, "Super Rich Step into Political Vacuum; McCain-Feingold Paved Way for 527s," *Washington Post,* October 17, 2004, www.washingtonpost.com/wp-dyn/articles /A38722-2004Oct16.html.

16. Analysis of Internal Revenue Service records filed by MoveOn. org Voter Fund, America Coming Together, the Media Fund, and Joint victory Campaign 2004.

17. Duncan quotes from May 6, 2010, panel.

18. Thomas B. Edsall, "FEC Adopts Hands-Off Stance on '527' Spending," *Washington Post,* June 1, 2006, www.washingtonpost.com /wp-dyn/content/article/2006/05/31/AR2006053101999.html.

19. "2005 Party Fundraising Summarized," press release, Federal Election Commission, February 16, 2006, www.fec.gov/press/press2006 /20060216party/20060216party.html.

20. Alex Seitz-Wald, "RNC Chairman Candidate Mike Duncan: 'There Is Not Enough Money' in Politics," ThinkProgress, December 1, 2010, http://thinkprogress.org/politics/2010/12/01/132862/duncan -more-money-politics.

21. Campaign Finance Institute, "All CFI Funding Statistics Revised and Updated for the 2008 Presidential Primary and General Election Candidates," January 8, 2010, www.cfinst.org/press/releases_tags/10-01-08 /Revised_and_Updated_2008_Presidential_Statistics.aspx.

22. Mike Allen and Kenneth P. Vogel, "Karl Rove, Republican Party Plot Vast Network to Reclaim Power," Politico, May 6, 2010, www .politico.com/news/stories/0510/36841.html.

23. Duncan quotes from May 6, 2010, panel.

24. Author interview with Michael Steele, August 22, 2011.

25. Ibid.

26. Author interview with Erick Erickson, September 2010.

Chapter 3: The New Boss

1. President Obama, State of the Union address, January 27, 2010: "With all due deference to separation of powers, last week the Supreme Court reversed a century of law that I believe will open the floodgates for special interests—including foreign corporations —to spend without limit

in our elections. I don't think American elections should be bankrolled by America's most powerful interests, or worse, by foreign entities." www.whitehouse.gov/the-press-office/ remarks-president-state-union-address.

2. Paul Gigot, "The Mark of Rove," *Wall Street Journal,* August 13, 2007, http://online.wsj.com/article/SB118697458949295744. html?mod=Politics-and-Policy.

3. Mike Allen, "Pro-War Group Launches $15 Million Ad Blitz," Politico, August 22, 2007, www.politico.com/news/stories/0807/5479.html.

4. "New Group, Freedom's Watch, to Launch Major Advertising Campaign in Support of Victory in Iraq," news release, PR Newswire, August 22, 2007, www.prnewswire.com/news-releases/new-group -freedoms-watch-to-launch-major-advertising-campaign-in-support -of-victory-in-iraq-58512892.html.

5. Author interview with Republican operative who worked with Freedom's Watch, June 9, 2013.

6. Democratic Congressional Campaign Committee, "DCCC Files 3rd FEC Complaint Against Freedom's Watch," press release, May 8, 2008, http://dccc.org/newsroom/entry/dccc_files_3rd_fec_complaint _against_freedoms_watch.

7. John D. McKinnon and Dionne Searcey, "Donors to GOP Group Drew IRS Scrutiny," *Wall Street Journal,* May 31, 2013, http://online .wsj.com/article/SB10001424127887324682204578517563566848922.html.

8. Paul Scicchitano, "Blakeman: IRS Targeted Freedom's Watch and Its Donors," Newsmax, May 31, 2013, www.newsmax.com/Headline /blakeman-freadoms-watch-donors/2013/05/31/id/507458.

9. Josephine Hearn, "Lawmakers' Iraq Views Shift at Home," Politico, August 25, 2007, www.politico.com/news/stories/0807/5509.html.

10. Kenneth P. Vogel and Ben Smith, "Karl Rove's Karl Rove," Politico, October 18, 2010, www.politico.com/news/stories/1010/43731.html.

11. Freedom's Watch form 990, 2008, www.guidestar.org /FinDocuments/2008/260/540/2008-260540871-057920dc-9O.pdf.

12. Jon Ward, "Exclusive: Freedom's Watch to Close," *Washington Times,* December 8, 2008, www.washingtontimes.com/news/2008/dec/08 /freedoms-watch-shut-end-month/?page=all#pagebreak.

13. Michael Luo, "Great Expectations for a Conservative Group Seem All but Dashed," *New York Times,* April 12, 2008, www.nytimes.com/2008/04/12/us/politics/12freedom.html?pagewanted=all&_r=0.

14. "The World's Billionaires; #178 Sheldon Adelson," *Forbes,* March 11, 2009, www.forbes.com/lists/2009/10/billionaires-2009-richest-people_Sheldon-Adelson_ER9O.html.

15. Author interview with Republican operative who worked with Freedom's Watch, June 9, 2013.

16. Joe Hagan, "Goddangit, Baby, We're Making Good Time; With a New Master Plan for the GOP, Karl Rove Is Revving Up for a Comeback," *New York Magazine,* February 27, 2011, http://nymag.com/news/politics/karl-rove-2011-3/index1.html.

17. Ibid.

18. Karl Rove, *Courage and Consequence: My Life as a Conservative in the Fight* (New York: Threshold Editions, 2010).

19. Frank Bruni, "Behind Bush Juggernaut, An Aide's Labor of Loyalty," *New York Times,* January 11, 2000, www.nytimes.com/2000/01/11/us/behind-bush-juggernaut-an-aide-s-labor-of-loyalty.html.

20. "Karl Rove; The Architect; Chronology: Karl Rove's Life and Political Career," PBS's *Frontline* and *Washington Post,* accessed September 21, 2013, www.pbs.org/wgbh/pages/frontline/shows/architect/rove/cron.html.

21. Rove, *Courage and Consequence.*

22. Miriam Rozen, "The Man Who Would Be Kingmaker," *Houston Press*, June 17, 1999, www.houstonpress.com/1999-06-17/news/the-man-who-would-be-kingmaker/6.

23. Rove, *Courage and Consequence.*

24. Ibid.

25. Ibid.

26. Hagan, "Goddangit, Baby."

27. Todd S. Purdum, "Karl Rove's Split Personality," *Vanity Fair,* December 2006, www.vanityfair.com/politics/features/2006/12/rove200612.

28. Author interview with Pat Caddell, June 7, 2013.

29. Kenneth P. Vogel and James Hohmann, "Karl Rove Unbowed," Politico, October 26, 2010, www.politico.com/news/stories/1010/44175.html.

30. Author interview with Ken Van Doren of the Campaign for Liberty, January 15, 2011.

31. Kenneth P. Vogel, "Tea Party Group Pictures Rove in Nazi Uniform," Politico, February 19, 2013, www.politico.com/story/2013/02/tea-party-group-pictures-karl-rove-in-nazi-uniform-87793.html.

32. Hans Hoyng and Marc Hujer, "*Spiegel* Interview with Karl Rove: 'Obama Has Turned Out to Be an Utter Disaster,'" *Der Spiegel,* October 19, 2010l, www.spiegel.de/international/world/spiegel-interview-with-karl-rove-obama-has-turned-out-to-be-an-utter-disaster-a-723880.html.

33. Andy Barr, "Karl Rove: Christine O'Donnell Said 'Nutty Things,'" Politico, September 15, 2010, www.politico.com/news/stories/0910/42205.html.

34. Author interview with Sheldon Adelson, December 15, 2011.

35. Monica Langley, "Texas Billionaire Doles Out Election's Biggest Checks," *Wall Street Journal,* January 22, 2013, http://online.wsj.com/article/SB10001424052702303812904577291450562940874.html.

36. Author interview with source familiar with meeting.

37. Peter H. Stone, "Campaign Cash: The Independent Fundraising Gold Rush Since 'Citizens United' Ruling," Center for Public Integrity, October 4, 2010, www.publicintegrity.org/2010/10/04/2470/campaign-cash-independent-fundraising-gold-rush-citizens-united-ruling.

38. District of Columbia property records.

39. Hagan, "Goddangit, Baby."

40. Ibid.

41. Ibid.

42. Thomas J. Josefiak letter to Shelia Krumholz, executive director of the Center for Responsive Politics, August 20, 2010, www.politico.com/static/PPM143_100929_holtzman_vogel_092910.html.

43. Jonathan Collegio email to Weaver Terrace Group attendees with subject line "Ken Vogel/Weaver Terrace," urging them not to divulge details and referencing "Fight Club," March 23, 2012, http://images.politico.com/global/2012/03/120323_weaver_collegio_email.html.

44. Ibid.

45. Kenneth P. Vogel, "New GOP 527 Far Short of $52M Goal," Politico, June 21, 2010, www.politico.com/news/stories/0610/38825.html.

46. Author conversation with Karl Rove on sidewalk outside of 400 N. Capitol St., NW, Washington, DC, February 27, 2012.

47. Dan Eggen and T. W. Farnam, "Pair of Conservative Groups Raised $70 Million in Midterm Campaign," Washington Post, December 2, 2010, www.washingtonpost.com/wp-dyn/content/article/2010/12/02 /AR2010120205667.html.

48. Carl Forti Q&A at Annenberg Public Policy Center panel, "Cash Attack: Political Advertising in a Post–Citizens United World," December 13, 2010, Holeman Lounge, National Press Club, http://factcheck.org /UploadedFiles/2011/01/rep_panel.pdf.

49. Kenneth P. Vogel and Steve Friess, "Karl Rove Hits Big: The Birth of a Mega-Donor," Politico, July 13, 2012, www.politico.com/news/stories /0712/78466.html.

50. Ibid.

51. Kenneth P. Vogel, "Crossroads: The ATM of the Right," Politico, April 18, 2012, www.politico.com/news/stories/0412/75283.html.

52. David Axelrod, "The Election Campaigners We Can't See," Washington Post, September 23, 2010, www.washingtonpost.com /wp-dyn/content/article/2010/09/22/AR2010092204665.html.

Chapter 4: The Barrel of a Gun

1. Author interview with Democracy Alliance Chairman Rob McKay, October 29, 2013.

2. Jane Mayer, "Schmooze or Lose," New Yorker, August 27, 2012, www.newyorker.com/reporting/2012/08/27/120827fa_fact_mayer.

3. A January 20, 2011, Gallup poll found that 80 percent of adults wanted Obama to pursue policies that were either more conservative (50 percent) or about the same (30 percent) as in his first two years. Lydia Saad, "Americans More Optimistic than Not About Obama, Economy," Gallup, January 20, 2011, www.gallup.com/poll/145694/Americans -Optimistic-Not-Obama-Economy.aspx.

4. Author interview with Art Lipson, August 5, 2013.

5. Scott Harris, "Rob McKay: Looking for Voters," *California Journal,* September 2002, 34–37, www.unz.org/Pub/CalJournal-2002sep-00034.

6. Carla Marinucci and Joe Garofoli, "Disappointed Democrats Protest Obama's SF visit," *San Francisco Chronicle,* October 25, 2011, www.sfgate.com/politics/article/Disappointed-Democrats-protest -Obama-s-SF-visit-2325626.php.

7. Luisa Kroll and Kerry A. Dolan, "The Forbes 400: The Richest People in America, 2011," *Forbes,* September 21, 2011, http://finance .yahoo.com/news/pf_article_113541.html.

8. Sewell Chan, "Soros: I Can't Stop a Republican 'Avalanche,'" *New York Times,* October 11, 2010, http://thecaucus.blogs.nytimes. com/2010/10/11/soros-i-cant-stop-a-republican-avalanche.

9. Author interview with Michael Vachon, April 27, 2011.

10. Sam Stein, "George Soros Tells Progressive Donors Obama Might Not Be the Best Investment," Huffington Post, November 17, 2010, www.huffingtonpost.com/2010/11/17/george-soros-obama_n _785022.html.

11. Author interview with Art Lipson, August 13, 2013.

12. Rob Stein, "The Conservative Message Machine's Money Matrix," 2004, http://agendaproject.org/History_of_the_Conservative_Movement .pdf.

13. Matt Bai, *The Argument: Billionaires, Bloggers, and the Battle to Remake Democratic Politics* (New York: Penguin Press, 2007).

14. Ibid.

15. Josh Burek, "Left Moves to Boost Its Intellectual Bulwark; Well-Heeled Democrats Rally to Craft a Network of Think Tanks—A Message Machine to Counter Conservatives," *Christian Science Monitor,* August 18, 2005, www.csmonitor.com/2005/0818/p02s02-uspo.html.

16. Author interview with Guy Saperstein, February 29, 2012.

17. Author interview with Guy Saperstein, September 28, 2012.

18. Joe Frolik, "A Newcomer to the Business of Politics Has Seen Enough to Reach Some Conclusions About Restoring Voters' Trust," Cleveland *Plain Dealer,* August 3, 1996.

19. Barack Obama, Remarks Announcing Candidacy for President, Springfield, Illinois, February 10, 2007, www.presidency.ucsb.edu/ws /index.php?pid=76999.

20. Kenneth P. Vogel, "W.H. Aide: Cash Race Had Spirit of 1776," Politico, May 8, 2009, www.politico.com/news/stories/0509/22266.html.

21. Obama for America, amended July 2007 quarterly report to the Federal Election Commission, filed August 22, 2008, http://query .nictusa.com/cgi-bin/dcdev/forms/C00431445/359395.

22. Hillary Clinton for President, amended July 2007 quarterly report to the Federal Election Commission, filed December 29, 2008, http://query.nictusa.com/cgi-bin/dcdev/forms/C00431569/392796.

23. Carla Marinucci, "Obama Blasts Shadow Fundraising Group," *San Francisco Chronicle,* August 8, 2007, www.sfgate.com/politics/article /Obama-blasts-shadow-fundraising-group-2512073.php.

24. Obama for America general counsel Robert F. Bauer letter to Vote Hope chairman Steve Phillips, December 28, 2007.

25. Federal tax filings for PowerPAC.org, PowerPAC Foundation, and Vote Hope.

26. Leslie Wayne, "In Aiding Poor, Edwards Built Bridge to 2008," *New York Times,* June 22, 2007, www.nytimes.com/2007/06/22/us/politics /22edwards.html.

27. Ben Smith, "Obama: Don't Fund Independent Groups," Politico, May 13, 2008, www.politico.com/news/stories/0508/10315.html.

28. Ben Smith, "Progressive Media to Fold into Media Matters, CAP," Politico, June 6, 2008, www.politico.com/blogs/bensmith/0608 /Progressive_Media_to_fold_into_Media_Matters_CAP.html.

29. Obama for America, amended June 2008 monthly report to the Federal Election Commission, filed August 18, 2008, http://query .nictusa.com/cgi-bin/dcdev/forms/C00431445/358076.

30. Hillary Clinton for President, June monthly report to the Federal Election Commission, filed June 20, 2008, http://query.nictusa.com /cgi-bin/dcdev/forms/C00431569/346097.

31. John McCain 2008, Inc., amended June monthly report to the Federal Election Commission, filed September 24, 2008, http://query.nictusa.com/cgi-bin/dcdev/forms/C00430470/364148.

32. Securities and investment: $15,798,904; misc. finance: $6,704,316; commercial banks: $3,409,194, according to Center for Responsive Politics, "Top Industries; Barack Obama; 2008," OpenSecrets

.org, accessed October 1, 2013, www.opensecrets.org/pres08 /indus.php?cycle=2008&cid=N00009638.

33. Elizabeth Williamson, "Obama Slams 'Fat Cat' Bankers," *Wall Street Journal,* December 14, 2009, http://online.wsj.com/article /SB126073152465089651.html.

34. Glenn Thursh, *Obama's Last Stand: Politico Playbook 2012* (New York: Random House, 2012).

35. Ibid.

36. Mark Halperin and John Heilemann, *Double Down: Game Change 2012* (New York: Penguin Press, 2013).

37. Mike Duncan comments at FreedomWorks RNC chairman forum, December 10, 2010, www.youtube.com/watch?v=3nZVgl3iDxI.

38. Jeanne Cummings, "New Democratic Money Group to Take On Republicans," Politico, April 29, 2011, www.politico.com/news /stories/0411/53905.html.

39. Andy Kroll, "Meet the New George Soros," *Mother Jones,* May 28, 2013, www.motherjones.com/print/223016.

40. Sandy Cohen, "Governors Awards 2012: Ceremony Honors Katzenberg, Pennebaker, and Stevens Among Others," Associated Press, December 2, 2012, www.huffingtonpost.com/2012/12/02/governors -awards-2012-ceremony-honors-katzenberg-pennebaker-stevens_n _2227317.html.

41. White House print pool report by Cynthia Gordy of *The Root.*

42. White House press office, Obama remarks at St. Regis, 7:05 p.m., January 31, 2012.

43. NBC News Transcripts, "Barack Obama Speaks to Matt Lauer Before Super Bowl," *Today,* February 6, 2012.

Chapter 5: The Political Fantasy Camp

1. Author telephone interview with Sheldon Adelson, December 15, 2011.

2. Connie Bruck, "A Multibillionaire's Relentless Quest for Global Influence," *New Yorker,* June 30, 2008, www.newyorker.com /reporting/2008/06/30/080630fa_fact_bruck?currentPage=all.

3. Nicholas Confessore and Jim Rutenberg, "Group's Ads Rip at Gingrich as Romney Stands Clear," *New York Times,* December 30, 2011, www.nytimes.com/2011/12/31/us/politics/restore-our-future-attack-ads-harm-gingrich-in-iowa.html.

4. James V. Grimaldi, "Sheldon Adelson and Newt Gingrich: One Gained Clout from Friendship, the Other Funding," *Washington Post,* January 19, 2012, http://articles.washingtonpost.com/2012-01-19/news/35439951_1_sheldon-adelson-speaker-newt-gingrich-mitt-romney.

5. Mike McIntire and Michael Luo, "The Man Behind Gingrich's Money," *New York Times,* January 28, 2012, www.nytimes.com/2012/01/29/us/politics/the-man-behind-gingrichs-money.html.

6. IRS data show Adelson donated $7.65 million from 2007 through 2011 to a Gingrich-led 527 group called American Solutions for Winning the Future.

7. According to the US Census Bureau, the population around the time of Adelson's call was about 312 million.

8. Mark Halperin and John Heilemann, *Double Down: Game Change 2012* (New York: Penguin, 2013).

9. Evan McMorris-Santoro, "Buying Iowa: Pro-Romney Forces Keep Up Unprecedented Battle for Hawkeye Airwaves," Talking Points Memo, December 20, 2011, http://2012.talkingpointsmemo.com/2011/12/buying-iowa-pro-romney-forces-keep-up-unprecedented-battle-for-hawkeye-airwaves.php.

10. Gabriella Schwarz and Paul Steinhauser, "Gingrich: I Was 'Romney-Boated,'" CNN Political Unit, January 1, 2012, http://politicalticker.blogs.cnn.com/2012/01/01/gingrich-i-was-romney-boated.

11. Tommy Christopher, "Newt Gingrich Hilariously Tells Chuck Todd He's No Victim of Citizens United," Mediaite, January 4, 2012, www.mediaite.com/tv/newt-gingrich-hilariously-tells-chuck-todd-hes-no-victim-of-citizens-united.

12. Halperin and Heilemann, *Double Down.*

13. Mitt Romney interview on MSNBC's *Morning Joe,* December 20, 2011.

14. Monica Langley, "Texas Billionaire Doles Out Election's Biggest Checks," *Wall Street Journal,* March 22, 2012, http://online.wsj.com /news/articles/SB10001424052702303812904577291450562940874.

15. Matea Gold and Melanie Mason, "Gov. Rick Perry's Big Donors Fare Well in Texas," *Los Angeles Times,* August 16, 2011, http://articles .latimes.com/2011/aug/16/nation/la-na-0816-perry-donors-20110816.

16. Real Clear Politics, 2012 poll tracker, Iowa Republican Presidential Caucus, www.realclearpolitics.com/epolls/2012/president/ia/iowa _republican_presidential_primary-1588.html.

17. "Christian Leaders Threaten to Abandon Republicans," World Net Daily, September 30, 2007, www.wnd.com/2007/09/43788.

18. Author interview with Foster Friess, November 6, 2012.

19. Author telephone interview with Foster Friess, January 12, 2012.

20. Foster Friess, "I Just Returned from the Iowa Caucus. Wow, Truly Americana!" FosterFriess.com (blog), January 6, 2012: "It was like being with a rock star as we entered the five town hall gatherings. Myriads of TV cameras and microphones blocked our way into the events. Unbridled enthusiasm rippled through the rooms in which people were sardined wall-to-wall." http://fosterfriess.com/blog/2012/01/06/i-just-returned -from-the-iowa-caucus-wow-truly-americana.

21. Author telephone interview with Foster Friess, January 12, 2012.

22. Public Policy Polling, poll of 597 likely voters, December 16–18, 2011 (Romney 20 percent, Paul 23 percent, Santorum 10 percent, Gingrich 14 percent), www.publicpolicypolling.com/pdf/2011/PPP _Release_IA_1218925.pdf; Rasmussen Reports poll of 750 likely voters, December 19 (Romney 25 percent, Paul 20 percent, Santorum 10 percent, Gingrich 17 percent), www.rasmussenreports.com/public_content /politics/elections/election_2012/election_2012_presidential_election /iowa/2012_iowa_republican_caucus.

23. Shannon Travis, "Santorum: Vander Plaats Said 'He Needed Money to Promote the Endorsement,'" CNN, December 22, 2011, http://politicalticker.blogs.cnn.com/2011/12/22/santorum-vander -plaats-said-he-needed-money-to-promote-the-endorsement.

24. Leaders for Family Values Super PAC, Inc. letter to Federal Election Commission accompanying statement of organization,

December 23, 2011, http://query.nictusa.com/pdf/936/11030700936
/11030700936.pdf.

25. Federal Election Commission independent expenditure data.

26. Alex Altman, "Under the Cowboy Hat: Foster Friess, Santorum's Controversial Benefactor," Time.com, February 17, 2012, http://swampland.time.com/2012/02/17/under-the-cowboy-hat-foster -friess-santorums-controversial-benefactor.

27. Maggie Haberman, "Sununu: Adelson Investors Will 'Remember' Gingrich Boost," Politico, January 11, 2012, www.politico.com /blogs/burns-haberman/2012/01/sununu-adelson-investors-will -remember-gingrich-boost-110461.html.

28. Kenneth P. Vogel, "Super PACs Echo Parodies," Politico, February 13, 2012, www.politico.com/news/stories/0212/72816.html.

29. Maggie Haberman, "Romney in the Hamptons with David Koch," Politico, August 16, 2010, www.politico.com/blogs/maggiehaberman /0810/Romney_raises_in_the_Hamptons_.html.

30. Author interview with Stan Hubbard, August 7, 2013.

31. Transcript: "Inside the Koch Brothers' 2011 Summer Seminar," Gov. Chris Christie's Keynote Address (Intro by David Koch), The Brad Blog, September 7, 2011 (recorded June 26, 2011), www.bradblog. com/?page_id=8702.

32. Author interview with Stan Hubbard, August 7, 2013.

33. Meredith Orban, "Christie Meets with Republican 'Heavy Hitters,'" FoxNews.com, July 19, 2011, http://politics.blogs.foxnews. com/2011/07/19/christie-meets-republican-heavy-hitters.

34. Author interview with Stan Hubbard, August 7, 2013.

35. David Weigel, "Christie the Redeemer: Is Rand Paul in a Fight with Chris Christie, or with the Entire GOP Mega-Donor Class?" Slate, July 26, 2013, www.slate.com/articles/news_and_politics/politics/2013/07 /chris_christie_is_the_favorite_for_the_gop_s_super_rich_the_gop_wants _the.html.

36. Lois Romano, "Dan Balz Book: Christie a Wanted Man in 2012," Politico, July 2, 2013, www.politico.com/story/2013/07/dan-balz-book -chris-christie-2012-93663.html.

37. Jonathan Martin, Maggie Haberman, and Alexander Burns, "Chris Christie Won't Run for President in 2012," Politico, October 4, 2011, www.politico.com/news/stories/1011/65094.html.

38. Maggie Haberman, "Sources: Adelson Met with Newt, then Romney Last Week," Politico, February 8, 2012, www.politico.com/blogs/burns-haberman/2012/02/sources-adelson-met-with-newt-then-romney-last-week-113929.html.

39. Maggie Haberman and Alexander Burns, "Adelson, Newt, Donors Convene at Venetian in Vegas," Politico, February 3, 2012, www.politico.com/blogs/burns-haberman/2012/02/adelson-newt-donors-convene-at-venetian-in-vegas-113469.html.

40. Nicholas Confessore and Jim Rutenberg, "Group's Ads Rip at Gingrich as Romney Stands Clear," New York Times, December 30, 2011, www.nytimes.com/2011/12/31/us/politics/restore-our-future-attack-ads-harm-gingrich-in-iowa.html; Julie Bykowicz, "Gingrich Seeks to Ease Fundraising Woes as Big Donations Slow," Bloomberg, February 10, 2012, www.bloomberg.com/news/2012-02-10/gingrich-seeks-to-ease-fundraising-woes-as-big-donations-slow.html.

41. Elizabeth Hartfield, "Meet Annette Simmons; Woman Put $1 Million Toward Rick Santorum," ABC News's The Note, March 21, 2012, http://abcnews.go.com/blogs/politics/2012/03/february-financials-good-for-romney-great-for-santorum.html.

42. Langley, "Texas Billionaire Doles Out Election's Biggest Checks."

43. Hartfield, "Meet Annette Simmons."

44. Kenneth P. Vogel, "Rick Santorum Speaks at Super PAC Fundraiser," Politico, February 24, 2012, www.politico.com/news/stories/0212/73262.html.

Chapter 6: The Big-Money Prototype Candidate

1. Reid J. Epstein, "Mitt Romney Reports He's Worth up to $255M," Politico, June 1, 2012, www.politico.com/news/stories/0612/76972.html.

2. Author interview with Frank VanderSloot, June 21, 2012.

3. Michael Barbaro, "Romney's Personal Touch Pays Off with Campaign Donors," New York Times, June 20, 2012, www.nytimes.com/2012/06/21/us/politics/romneys-personal-touch-pays-off-with-donors.html.

4. Scott S. Greenberger, "From Prankster to Politician, Romney Deemed a Class Act," *Boston Globe,* June 12, 2005. Archived version: http://web.archive.org/web/20091008050634/www.boston.com/news /education/k_12/articles/2005/06/12/ from_prankster_to_politician_romney_deemed_a_class_act.

5. Jeff Call, "The Fire Within," *BYU Magazine,* Winter 2002, http://magazine.byu.edu/?act=view&a=843.

6. Lisa Lerer, "Romney Aide Oversees Fundraising That Makes Him Cash, Too," Bloomberg News, June 12, 2012, www.businessweek.com /news/2012-06-11/romney-aide-oversees -fundraising-that-makes-him-cash-too.

7. The (BYU) Marriott School of Management Presents Morning Market Call, "Romney '08 Finance Director at Age 28—Spencer Zwick," October 1, 2010, http://youtu.be/m-i6in-MtFw.

8. David D. Kirkpatrick, "Romney Used His Wealth to Enlist Richest Donors," *New York Times,* April 6, 2007, www.nytimes.com/2007/04/06 /us/politics/06romney.html.

9. Author interviews.

10. Adam Nagourney, "Romney Makes It Official and Asks for '08 Cash in a Big Way," *New York Times,* January 9, 2007, www.nytimes .com/2007/01/09/us/politics/09romney.html.

11. BlueSwarm press release, "BlueSwarm Announces Groundbreaking Facebook Application for Social Fundraising," PR Newswire, April 8, 2010, www.prnewswire.com/news-releases /blueswarm-announces-groundbreaking-facebook-application-for -social-fundraising-90199122.html.

12. Glen Johnson, "Political Fundraising Tool Taps Social Networks," Associated Press, June 13, 2010, www.boston.com/news/local /massachusetts/articles/2010/06/13/political_fundraising_tool _taps_social_networks.

13. Fred Wertheimer, "A Democracy 21 Report: Leading Presidential-Candidate Super PACs and the Serious Questions That Exist About Their Legality," Democracy 21, January 4, 2011, www.democracy21 .org/uploads/Democracy_21_Super_PAC_Report__1_4_2012.pdf.

14. Marisa Schultz, "East Grand Rapids Native's Super PAC Fuels Romney's Rise," *Detroit News,* September 26, 2012, www.detroitnews

.com/article/20120926/POLITICS01/209260361#ixzz2bbgOEA4G
www.detroitnews.com/article/20120926/POLITICS01/209260361.

15. Andy Kroll, "Mitt Romney Would Be Toast Without This Man,"
Mother Jones, October 31, 2012, www.motherjones.com/politics/2012/10
/mitt-romney-charles-spies-super-pac-obama-presidential-election.

16. Paul Abowd and Alexandra Duszak, "Pennsylvania Governor
Benefited from Untraceable $1.5 Million Donation," Center for Public
Integrity, October 18, 2012, www.publicintegrity.org/2012/10/18/11498/
pennsylvania-governor-benefited-untraceable-15-million-donation.

17. Jonathan Martin, "Romney Returns to D.C., Fueling 2012 talk,"
Politico, February 25, 2009, www.politico.com/news/stories/0209
/19325.html.

18. Ari Werth, "Mitt's Matchmaker Looks Back and Ahead,"
JNS.org, November 26, 2012, www.jns.org/latest-articles/2012
/11/26/mitts-matchmaker-looks-back-and-ahead.html.

19. The Reliable Source, "Which 'Housewives' Will Make the Cut?
Lisa Spies and Edwina Rogers Drop Out of Show; Lynda Erkiletian,
Mary Amons, Michaele Salahi Still In," *Washington Post,* October 13,
2009, http://voices.washingtonpost.com/reliable-source/2009/10
/rs-housewives13.html.

20. Kenneth P. Vogel and Ben Smith, "When 'Coordinate' Is a Dirty
Word," Politico, May 31, 2011, www.politico.com/news/stories/0511
/55911.html.

21. Mark Halperin and John Heilemann, *Double Down: Game Change
2012* (New York: Penguin Press, 2013), ebook location 3655 of 9315.

22. Ibid., location 3672/9315.

23. Campaign Finance Institute, "Table 1: 2012 Presidential
Fundraising Receipts, Debts and Cash on Hand as of December 31,
2011," February 2, 2012, www.cfinst.org/pdf/federal/president/2012
/Pres12_YE_Table1.pdf.

24. Campaign Finance Institute, "48% of President Obama's 2011
Money Came from Small Donors—Better than Doubling 2007.
Romney's Small Donors: 9%," February 8, 2012, www.cfinst.org/Press
/PReleases/12-02-08/Small_Donors_in_2011_Obama_s_Were
_Big_Romney_s_Not.aspx.

25. Ibid.

26. Campaign Finance Institute, "Table 3: 2012 Presidential Candidate Super PACs Receipts, Cash on Hand, Independent Expenditures Reported," February 2, 2012, www.cfinst.org/pdf/federal/president /2012/Pres12_YE_Table3.pdf.

27. Schultz, "East Grand Rapids Native's Super PAC."

28. Romney Victory, National Finance Committee brochure, Romney campaign, and the RNC, May 18, 2002, http://images.politico.com /global/2012/05/120518_romneyvictorydonor.html.

29. Sara Murray, "Romney Specifies Deductions He'd Cut," *Wall Street Journal,* April 15, 2012, http://online.wsj.com/article/SB100014240 52702304432704577346611860756628.html.

30. Sam Youngman and Donna Smith, "Romney's Remarks on Limiting Tax Deductions Draw Fire," Reuters, April 16, 2012, www.reuters.com/article/2012/04/17/us-usa-campaign-romney-comments -idUSBRE83F1BU20120417.

31. David Corn, "Secret Video: Romney Tells Millionaire Donors What He Really Thinks of Obama Voters," *Mother Jones,* September 17, 2012, www.motherjones.com/politics/2012/09/secret-video-romney -private-fundraiser.

32. MoJo News Team, "Full Transcript of the Mitt Romney Secret Video," *Mother Jones,* September 19, 2012, www.motherjones.com /politics/2012/09/full-transcript-mitt-romney-secret-video.

33. Alexander Burns, "Priorities USA Keeps Hitting '47 Percent,'" Politico, September 27, 2012, www.politico.com/blogs/burns- haberman/2012/09/priorities-usa-keeps-hitting-percent-136797.html.

34. Seema Mehta, "Romney Defends 'Off the Cuff' Remarks on Obama Backers as Victims," *Los Angeles Times,* September 17, 2012, http://articles.latimes.com/2012/sep/17/news/la-pn-mitt-romney-victims -remarks-20120917.

35. MoJo News Team, "Full Transcript of the Mitt Romney Secret Video."

36. Stephanie Mencimer, "Pyramid-Like Company Ponies Up $1 Million for Mitt Romney," *Mother Jones,* February 6, 2012, www.motherjones.com/politics/2012/02/mitt-romney-melaleuca-frank -vandersloot.

37. Human Rights Campaign, "HRC Calls on Romney Campaign to Fire Virulently Anti-Gay National Finance Chair," press release, March 8, 2012, www.hrc.org/press-releases/entry/hrc-calls-on-romney-campaign -to-fire-virulently-anti-gay-national-finance-c.

38. Author interview with Frank VanderSloot, May 20, 2012.

39. Lisa Lerer, "Romney Donors Get Access, and Face Time, at Utah Retreat," Bloomberg, June 24, 2012, www.bloomberg.com/news/2012 -06-24/romney-donors-get-access-and-face-time-at-utah-retreat.html.

40. Ibid.

41. Ibid.

42. Ibid.

43. Ginger Gibson, "Mitt Romney Rewards Donors at Utah Retreat," Politico, June 24, 2012, www.politico.com/news/stories/0612/77757.html.

44. Michael Barbaro, "For Wealthy Romney Donors, Up Close and Personal Access," *New York Times,* June 23, 2012, www.nytimes .com/2012/06/24/us/politics/for-wealthy-romney-donors-up-close -and-personal-access.html.

45. Ibid.

46. Kenneth P. Vogel, "Sheldon Adelson Pledges $10M to Koch Effort," Politico. June 29, 2012, www.politico.com/news/stories/0612 /78005.html.

47. Eric Wolff, "High Security at Koch Conclave," BuzzFeed, June 24, 2012, www.buzzfeed.com/ericwolff/high-security-at-koch-conclave-6lzb.

48. Barbaro, "For Wealthy Romney Donors, Up Close and Personal Access."

Chapter 7: The Brothers Behind the Tea Party

1. Author interview with Americans for Prosperity chairman Art Pope, October 2, 2012.

2. Mike Allen and Jim VandeHei, "GOP Groups Plan Record $1 Billion Blitz," Politico, May 30, 2012, www.politico.com/news/stories /0512/76849.html.

3. Andy Kroll, "Americans for Prosperity Chief: We Don't Know if $27 Million in Anti-Obama Ads Has Any Effect," *Mother Jones,* September 3, 2012, www.motherjones.com/mojo/2012/09/americans -for-prosperity-chief-obama-ads-27-million.

4. Americans for Prosperity press release, "AFP Announces Details of Major Ad Buy," August 7, 2012.

5. Katrina vanden Heuvel, "The Third Koch 'Brother' Hits North Carolina," *Washington Post,* June 11, 2013, http://articles .washingtonpost.com/2013-06-11/opinions/39883018_1_koch-brothers -north-carolina-citizens-united.

6. Americans for Prosperity press release, "Obama's Failing Agenda Tour Travels 55,000 Miles," November 13, 2012 (accessed October 8, 2013), http://americansforprosperity.org/failingagenda/uncategorized /obamas failing-agenda-tour-travels-55000-miles.

7. Micheal Foley, "Americans for Prosperity Bus Tour to Stop in Hudson on June 1," *Hudson* (Wisc.) *Patch,* May 23, 2012, http:// hudson-wi.patch.com/groups/politics-and-elections/p/americans -for-prosperity-bus-tour-to-stop-in-hudson-on-june-1.

8. Themis Trust and Freedom Partners Chamber of Commerce form 990 tax returns filed with the IRS covering 2010, 2011, and 2012.

9. Interview of Anthony Russo by the California Fair Political Practices Commission and the California Attorney General's Office, July 17, 2013.

10. *Forbes,* Billionaire Profiles 2013, "Charles Koch, No. 6," September 2013, www.forbes.com/profile/charles-koch; *Forbes,* Billionaire Profiles 2013, "David Koch, No. 6," September 2013, www.forbes.com/profile /david-koch.

11. Under Charles Koch's stewardship, Koch Industries grew to more than 2,600 times the size it was in the early 1960s, according to Matthew Continetti, "The Paranoid Style in Liberal Politics; The Left's Obsession with the Koch Brothers," *Weekly Standard,* April 4, 2011, www.weekly standard.com/articles/paranoid-style-liberal-politics_555525.html.

12. Federal Election Commission records.

13. Rinker Buck, "The National Interest: How Those Libertarians Pay the Bills," *New York Magazine,* November 3, 1980.

14. Ibid.

15. Alexia Campbell, "Koch: 1996 Marks Beginning of National Efforts," July 1, 2013, http://investigativereportingworkshop.org /investigations/the_koch_club/story/Koch-1996_marks_beginning.

16. Author interview with Jack Abramoff, May 29, 2013.

17. David Koch remarks at Americans for Prosperity's "A Salute to Entrepreneurs Building America," Tampa, FL, August 30, 2012: "My brother and I provided the funding to create this wonderful organization about 10 years ago."

18. Continetti, "The Paranoid Style in Liberal Politics."

19. Ibid.

20. "The radical press is coming after me and Charles . . . using us as whipping boys." He kept a photocopy of a Greenpeace flyer in his office with the words "Wanted for Climate Crimes" above sketches of him and Charles. Shaking it in the air, he complained Greenpeace wanted "to put me and Charles in jail." Andrew Goldman, "The Billionaire's Party; David Koch Is New York's Second-Richest Man, a Celebrated Patron of the Arts, and the Tea Party's Wallet," *New York Magazine,* July 25, 2010, http://nymag.com/news/features/67285.

21. Continetti, "The Paranoid Style in Liberal Politics."

22. Patrick Cole, "David Koch Toasted by Caroline Kennedy, Robert DeNiro (Update1)," Bloomberg, May 17, 2010, www.bloomberg.com /news/2010-05-17/david-koch-toasted-by-michelle-obama-caroline -kennedy-at-n-y-ballet-gala.html.

23. Ibid.

24. Author interview with Steven F. Hayward, February 2010.

25. Continetti, "The Paranoid Style in Liberal Politics."

26. Lee Fang, "Exclusive: Polluter Billionaire David Koch Says Tea Party 'Rank and File Are Just Normal People Like Us,'" ThinkProgress, January 6, 2011, http://thinkprogress.org/politics/2011/01/06/137586 /koch-teaparty-us.

27. Goldman, "The Billionaire's Party."

28. Elaine Lafferty, "'Tea Party Billionaire' Fires Back," Daily Beast, September 10, 2010, www.thedailybeast.com/articles/2010/09 /10/billionaire-david-koch-fires-back-at-the-new-yorker.html.

29. Quarterly congressional salary data from Office of the Clerk, United States House of Representatives.

30. Kim Barker and Theodoric Meyer, "The Dark Money Man: How Sean Noble moved the Kochs' Cash into Politics and Made Millions," ProPublica, February 14, 2014, www.propublica.org/article/the-dark

-money-man-how-sean-noble-moved-the-kochs-cash-into
-politics-and-ma.

31. Author interview with Tim Phillips, September 27, 2011.

32. John Gapper, "Koch Ventures into the Brooklyn Lion's Den," *Financial Times,* December 24, 2010, http://blogs.ft.com /businessblog/2010/12/koch-ventures-into-the-brooklyn-lions-den.

33. Nikki Willoughby, "We Got Their Attention," Common Blog, February 1, 2011, www.commonblog.com/2011/02/01/we-got-their -attention.

34. Continetti, "The Paranoid Style in Liberal Politics."

35. Page Six, "Mitt: What Koch 'Problem'?" *New York Post,* July 10, 2012, www.nypost.com/p/pagesix/mitt_what_koch_problem_6f4DGUSy l55cSBIuG74yDL#ixzz20EDPXQ6L.

36. Keenan Steiner, "Access Denied: Koch Funded Group Bars Sunlight in Tampa," Sunlight Foundation, August 30 2012, http://reporting.sunlightfoundation.com/2012/access-denied-koch -funded-group-limits-press-access-tampa; Barry Yeoman, "RNC Day 5: Tossed from the Art Pope–David Koch Cocktail Party," Indy Week, August 31, 2012, www.indyweek.com/triangulator/archives/2012/08 /31/rnc-day-5-tossed-from-the-art-pope-david-koch-cocktail-party.

37. Benjy Sarlin, "David Koch Dines with Senator in Tampa," TPMLiveWire, August 27, 2012, http://livewire.talkingpointsmemo.com a/entry/david-koch-dines-with-senator-in-tampa.

38. Anthea Butler response to Matt Laslo tweet, "David Koch Judging Me for Taking Photos of Him While He Eats. #gop2012 http://instagr .am/p/O2iIRwEwA9/," August 27, 2012, https://twitter.com/MattLaslo /statuses/240248839850848256.

39. David Weigel, "David Koch Eats Out," Slate, August 28, 2012, www.slate.com/blogs/weigel/2012/08/28/david_koch_eats_out.html.

40. Author interview with Sen. Ron Johnson, January 2, 2014.

41. Lee Bergquist, "Latest Independent Ad Attacks Baldwin Spending," *Milwaukee Journal Sentinel,* October 3, 2012, www.jsonline .com/blogs/news/172484841.html; Don Walker, "Conservative Seniors Group Running Anti-Baldwin Ads," *Milwaukee Journal Sentinel,* August 24, 2012, www.jsonline.com/blogs/news/167310825.html & Kirsten Adshead, "WI: $500K Ad Buy Attacks Baldwin on Obamacare, Stimulus

Votes," *Wisconsin Reporter,* July 12, 2012, http://watchdog.org/36314
/wi-500k-ad-buy-attacks-baldwin-on-obamacare-stimulus-votes.

42. Author interview with David Koch, August 30, 2012.

43. Kenneth P. Vogel, "David Koch Breaks from GOP on Gay
Marriage, Taxes, Defense Cuts," Politico, August 30, 2012, www.politico.
com/news
/stories/0812/80483.html.

44. Trudy Ring, "Shocker: David Koch Supports Marriage Equality,"
Advocate.com, August 30, 2012, www.advocate.com/politics
/marriage-equality/2012/08/30/koch-brother-supports-marriage-equality.

45. Statement from David H. Koch on Reducing the Federal Deficit,
KochFacts, September 5, 2012, www.kochfacts.com/kf/reducing
thefederaldeficit.

Chapter 8: The Turnaround

1. Jim Messina presentation to Obama for America National Finance
Committee, January 19, 2013, at the Newseum: "A lot of you called
me up after the first debate and said 'Oh. My. God.' And I said, 'Deep
breath. We're okay, and this is why we were okay.'"

2. Campaign Finance Institute: "Table 1: 2012 Presidential
Fundraising Receipts, Debts and Cash on Hand as of April 30, 2012,"
May 23, 2012, www.cfinst.org/pdf/federal/president/2012/Pres12
_M5_Table1.pdf; "Table 7: National Party Committee Fundraising,
2012," May 23, 2012, www.cfinst.org/pdf/federal/president/2012/Pres12
_M5_Table7.pdf.

3. Jim Messina presentation to Obama for America National Finance
Committee, January 19, 2013, at the Newseum.

4. Lloyd Grove, "Exclusive: President Obama Asks Campaign Donors
to Send Him More Money," Daily Beast, June 30, 2012, www.thedaily
beast.com/articles/2012/06/30/exclusive-president-obama-asks-campaign
-donors-to-send-him-more-money.html.

5. Author interview with Don Peebles, July 9, 2012.

6. Maeve Reston, "Donors Arrive at Hamptons Fundraisers
with Advice for Mitt Romney," *Los Angeles Times,* July 8, 2012,
http://articles.orlandosentinel.com/2012-07-08/news/la-pn-romney

-hamptons-fundraiser-20120708_1_mitt-romney-president-obama
-fundraisers.

7. Kenneth P. Vogel and Tarini Parti, "Democratic Super PACs Get Jump on 2014, 2016," Politico, November 26, 2012, www.politico.com/news
/stories/1112/84205.html.

8. Michael Kranish, "Vital Asset Bill Clinton Back in Party Spotlight," *Boston Globe,* September 5, 2012, www.bostonglobe.com/news/nation
/2012/09/04/bill-clinton-and-president-obama-complicated-relationship
/cXAi452Yln5idr3bXnQN9N/story.html.

9. Maggie Haberman, "Clinton Pitches Obama, Clinton Donor Prospects for Super PAC," Politico, August 16, 2012, www.politico.com
/blogs/burns-haberman/2012/08/clinton-pitches-obama-clinton-donor
-prospects-for-132349.html.

10. Kranish, "Vital Asset Bill Clinton Back in Party Spotlight."

11. Author interview with attendee, who declined to be identified.

12. Ibid.

13. Noam Scheiber, "How I Got Ejected from a Super PAC Reception," *New Republic,* September 6, 2012, http://blogs.tnr.com/blog
/plank/106957/how-get-ejected-super-pac-reception.

14. Keenan Steiner, "At Democratic Super PACs Briefing, Strategists Ask for More Cash," September 4, 2012, http://reporting
.sunlightfoundation.com/2012/democratic-super-pacs-political-briefing
-strategists-ask-more-re.

15. Ibid.

16. Ibid.

17. Noam Scheiber, "How Obama's Biggest Donors Get Their Goodies in Charlotte," *New Republic,* September 5, 2012,
www.newrepublic.com/blog/plank/106961/how-obamas-biggest
-donors-get-their-goodies-in-charlotte.

Chapter 9: The Biggest Bet Yet

1. Author reporting from the Tampa Marriott Waterside Hotel and Marina.

2. Ibid.

3. Reince Priebus, "Chairman Priebus Memo Regarding RNC Convention," RNC Chairman's Blog, August 25, 2012, www.gop.com /news/chairmans-blog/chairman-priebus-memo-regarding-rnc-convention.

4. Romney Victory, "VIP Convention," August 18, 2012, http://images .politico.com/global/2012/08/120822_starsagenda.html.

5. Julie Hirschfeld Davis, "Obama Leads in Poll as Voters View Romney as Out of Touch," Bloomberg, June 20, 2012, www.bloomberg .com/news/2012-06-20/obama-leads-in-poll-as-voters-view-romney-as -out-of-touch.html.

6. Lisa Lerer, "Romney Donors Get Access, and Face Time, at Utah Retreat," Bloomberg, June 24, 2012, www.bloomberg.com/news/2012 -06-24/romney-donors-get-access-and-face-time-at-utah-retreat.html.

7. Campaign Finance Institute, "Money vs. Money-Plus: Post-Election Reports Reveal Two Different Campaign Strategies," "Table 2: Presidential Campaign, National Party, and Joint Committee Fundraising Through Nov. 26th, 2012 and Cumulatively," January 11, 2013, www.cfinst.org/pdf/federal/president/2012/Pres12_30G_Table2.pdf.

8. Transcript, Fox News Network, "On the Record with Greta Van Susteren," August 8, 2012, www.foxnews.com/on-air/on-the-record /2012/08/09/rove-obamas-making-it-easier-people-stay-welfare?page=1.

9. Karl Rove, "The Obama Ad Blitz Isn't Working," *Wall Street Journal,* August 1, 2012, http://online.wsj.com/news/articles /SB10000872396390443687504577563002812933574.

10. Ibid.

11. Hans Nichols, "Inside Karl Rove's Billionaire Fundraiser," Bloomberg TV, August 31, 2012, http://bloom.bg/TDYfCE#ooid =Q5c2pyNTqHKQPdn3EI42NB537mF498oP: "A colleague of mine at BusinessWeek identified herself as a journalist to one of the guests. She was working with this person on a story. The guest invited her to the briefing, she recorded it and so we have an actual transcript of what Rove says."

12. Sheelah Kolhatkar, "Exclusive: Inside Karl Rove's Billionaire Fundraiser," *Bloomberg BusinessWeek,* August 31, 2012, www.businessweek.com/articles/2012-08-31/exclusive-inside-karl-roves -billionaire-fundraiser.

13. David Catanese, "Forecast for GOP Senate Takeover: More Clouds," Politico, September 9, 2012.

14. Sheelah Kolhatkar, "Exclusive: How Karl Rove's Super PAC Plays the Senate," *Bloomberg BusinessWeek,* September 4, 2012, www.businessweek.com/articles/2012-09-04/exclusive-how-karl-roves -super-pac-plays-the-senate.

15. Kolhatkar, "Exclusive: How Karl Rove's Super PAC Plays the Senate."

16. Kolhatkar, "Exclusive: Inside Karl Rove's Billionaire Fundraiser."

17. Alexander Burns, "Akin Camp Says Rove Apologized for Murder Joke," Politico, August 31, 2012, www.politico.com/blogs/burns -haberman/2012/08/akin-camp-says-rove-apologized-for-murder -joke-134026.html.

18. Kolhatkar, "Exclusive: Inside Karl Rove's Billionaire Fundraiser."

19. Edward Robinson, "Scaramucci Schmoozes His Way into Funds," *Bloomberg Markets Magazine,* September 9, 2011, www.bloomberg.com /news/2011-09-09/-gucci-scaramucci-fired-by-goldman-schmoozes-his -way-into-top-hedge-funds.html.

20. Philip Elliott, "N.H. Home Gives Romney an Edge," Associated Press, July 10, 2007, http://usatoday30.usatoday.com/news/politics/2007 -07-10-1734462420_x.htm.

21. Lisa Lerer, "Romney Aide Oversees Fundraising That Makes Him Cash, Too," Bloomberg, June 12, 2012, www.bloomberg.com/news/2012 -06-12/romney-aide-oversees-fundraising-that-makes-him-cash-too.html.

22. Michael Barbaro, "Romney's Personal Touch Pays Off with Campaign Donors," *New York Times,* June 20, 2012, www.nytimes. com/2012/06/21/us/politics/romneys-personal-touch-pays-off-with -donors.html.

23. Ibid.

24. Alex Klein, "Meet Anthony Scaramucci, Mitt's Man on Wall Street," Daily Beast, August 30, 2012, www.thedailybeast.com/articles /2012/08/30/mitt-s-man-on-wall-street.html.

25. Anthony Scaramucci tweet, August 30, 2012, 10:42 a.m., https://twitter.com/Scaramucci/status/241184170783674368.

26. Anthony Scaramucci tweet, August 30, 2012, 11:52 a.m., https://twitter.com/Scaramucci/status/241201746721001472.

27. Anthony Scaramucci tweet, August 30, 2012, 3:55 p.m., https://twitter.com/Scaramucci/status/241262987262951424.

28. Anthony Scaramucci tweet, August 30, 2012, 12:57 p.m., https://twitter.com/Scaramucci/status/241263423856467969.

29. Author interview with Anthony Scaramucci, January 7, 2014.

30. Author interview with Sheelah Kolhatkar, January 9, 2014.

31. Nicholas Confessore, "Reversing Course, Soros to Give $1 Million to a Pro-Obama 'Super PAC,'" *New York Times,* September 27, 2012, http://thecaucus.blogs.nytimes.com/2012/09/27/soros-gives-1-million-to -democratic-super-pac.

32. Fox News Network transcript, "Hannity: Interview with Karl Rove," November 2, 2012.

33. Karl Rove, "Can We Believe the Presidential Polls?" *Wall Street Journal,* October 3, 2012,
     http://online.wsj.com/news/articles/SB1000087239639044376880457803 4341205066014.

34. Karl Rove, "The Dividends of Romney's Debate Victory," *Wall Street Journal,* October 11, 2012, http://online.wsj.com/news/articles/SB1 0000872396390443294904578048493477274544.

35. ABC News Transcript, *This Week with George Stephanopoulos,* interview with David Plouffe, November 4, 2012.

36. Real Clear Politics video of Fox News's *Hannity,* November 4, 2012, www.realclearpolitics.com/video/2012/11/04/karl_rove_predicts _romney_wins_by_2_margin_around_280_electoral_votes.html.

Chapter 10: The Autopsies

1. Federal Election Commission news release, "FEC Summarizes Campaign Activity of the 2011–2012 Election Cycle," April 19, 2013, www.fec.gov/press/press2013/20130419_2012-24m -Summary.shtml.

2. Ibid. Includes $2.2 billion in disbursements by political action committees combined with $300 million in independent expenditures reported by persons other than political committees (per Federal Election Commission table, "Independent Expenditure Table 1, April 19, 2013, www.fec.gov/press/summaries/2012/ElectionCycle/file/IEs/IE1_2012 _24m.pdf).

3. Statement of Federal Election Commission chairwoman Ellen L. Weintraub, January 31, 2013, www.fec.gov/members/weintraub /statements/weintraub_statement_20130131.pdf.

4. Federal Election Commission news release, "FEC Summarizes Campaign Activity of the 2011–2012 Election Cycle."

5. Author analysis of FEC and IRS filings for reported payments in 2011 and 2012 to GMMB ($419 million), Mentzer Media Service ($280 million), Crossroads Media ($248 million), American Rambler Productions ($241 million), and Targeted Victory ($112 million).

6. Center for Responsive Politics, "2012 Super PACs: How Many Donors Give?" Open Secrets, accessed November 1, 2013, www.opensecrets.org/outsidespending/donor_stats.php.

7. Analysis of Federal Election Commission data by the Campaign Finance Institute for the author.

8. Author analysis of Lindsay Young, "Outside Spenders' Return on Investment," Sunlight Foundation, December 17, 2012, http://reporting. sunlightfoundation.com/2012/return_on_investment. Of the $175 million in traceable advertising spending by the American Crossroads super PAC and the Crossroads GPS nonprofit group, 6.6 percent was for races won by the Republican candidate.

9. Author interview with Stan Hubbard, November 7, 2012.

10. FEC and IRS records show that FreedomWorks spent $15.6 million, FreedomWorks Foundation spent $7.6 million, and FreedomWorks for America spent $22 million.

11. Karl Rove, "The President's 'Grand Bet' Pays Off," *Wall Street Journal,* November 7, 2012, http://online.wsj.com/news/articles/SB100014 24127887323894704578105153335057318.

12. Dylan Byers, "Rove: Obama Won 'By Suppressing the Vote,'" Politico, November 8, 2012, www.politico.com/blogs/media/2012/11 /rove-obama-succeeded-by-suppressing-the-vote-149046.html.

13. *The Sean Hannity Show,* Clear Channel Communications, November 12, 2012.

14. Author interview with Stan Hubbard, November 8, 2012.

15. Author interview with Mike Duncan, January 10, 2014.

16. Steven Law email to donors, "Improving Candidate Quality," February 4, 2013.

17. Gromer Jeffers Jr., "Karl Rove Defends Move to Get Involved in GOP Primaries, Saying Republicans Can Rebound," *Dallas Morning News,* February 27, 2013, http://trailblazersblog.dallasnews.com/2013 /02/karl-rove-defends-move-to-get-involve-in-gop-primaries-saying -republicans-can-rebound.html.

18. Steven Law email to donors, "Improving Candidate Quality," February 4, 2013.

19. Phil Kerpen, Twitter, February 3, 2013, https://twitter.com /kerpen/status/298090452253560832.

20. Phil Kerpen, Twitter, June 6, 2013, acknowledging status as representing Koch World, https://twitter.com/kerpen/status /342863186724265984.

21. Phil Kerpen, Twitter, February 3, 2013, https://twitter.com /kerpen/status/298093771994828801.

22. Erick Erickson, "The Incestuous Bleeding of the Republican Party," Red State, November 28, 2012, www.redstate.com/2012/11/28 /the-incestuous-bleeding-of-the-republican-party.

23. Michael Patrick Leahy, "Caddell Unloads on 'Racketeering' GOP Consultants," Breitbart, March 14, 2013, www.breitbart.com /Big-Government/2013/03/14/Caddell-Blows-the-Lid-Off-CPAC-With -Blistering-Attack-on-Racketeering-Republican-Consultants.

24. Partial video of Pat Caddell CPAC speech, March 14, 2013, https://www.youtube.com/watch?v=2_MYVUc6Sas.

25. Katie Packer Gage email to author, January 6, 2014.

26. Author interview with Katie Packer Gage, January 4, 2014.

27. Katie Packer Gage email to author, January 6, 2014.

28. Author interview with Katie Packer Gage, January 4, 2014.

29. Republican National Committee, *Growth and Opportunity Project,* March 13, 2013, 46, http://growthopp.gop.com/rnc_growth_opportunity _book_2013.pdf.

30. Ibid., 51.

31. Ibid., 49.

32. California Fair Political Practices Commission press release, "FPPC Announces Record Settlement in $11 Million Arizona Contribution Case," October 24, 2013, www.fppc.ca.gov/releases pdf/2013-10-24.pdf.

33. Author interview with Mark Holden, November 21, 2013.

34. Charles Koch letter, September 24, 2010, obtained and posted online by ThinkProgress, http://images2.americanprogressaction.org /ThinkProgress/secretkochmeeting.pdf.

35. Freedom Partners Chamber of Commerce, Inc., a nonprofit funded by Koch seminar donors and controlled by Koch allies, donated $500,000 to Heritage Action for America at some point between November 2, 2011, and October 31, 2012, according to Freedom Partners tax filing covering that period.

36. Amy Gardner, "FreedomWorks Tea Party Group Nearly Falls Apart in Fight Between Old and New Guard," *Washington Post,* December 25, 2012, www.washingtonpost.com/politics/freedomworks -tea-party-group-nearly-falls-apart-in-fight-between-old-and-new -guard/2012/12/25/dd095b68-4545-11e2-8061-253bccfc7532_story.html.

37. Marin Cogan, video accompanying article: "Is This 36-Year-Old Veteran the Future of the GOP?" *National Journal,* December 6, 2013, www.nationaljournal.com/magazine/is-this-36-year-old-veteran -the-future-of-the-gop-20131206.

38. Noah Rothman, "At Democrats' Request, Even Mike Bloomberg Is Giving Up on Gun Control," Mediaite, January 7, 2014.

39. *Forbes,* "The World's Billionaires; Michael Bloomberg # 13," September 2013.

40. Author interview with Rob McKay, October 29, 2013.

41. Nicholas Confessore, "Reversing Course, Soros to Give $1 Million to a Pro-Obama 'Super PAC,'" *New York Times,* September 27, 2012, http://thecaucus.blogs.nytimes.com/2012/09/27/soros-gives-1-million -to-democratic-super-pac.

42. Transferrable tickets to the event were distributed among major donors to the Obama campaign and to big money groups. But one donor passed a ticket to my colleague Byron Tau, who recorded the event, which is how I am able to describe it here.

Chapter 11: The Civil Wars

1. John Bresnahan, Manu Raju, Jake Sherman, and Carrie Budoff Brown, "Anatomy of a Shutdown," Politico, October 18, 2013, www. politico.com/story/2013/10/anatomy-of-a-shutdown-98518.html.

2. Heritage Action for America press release, "Heritage Action for America Announces $550,000 Defund Obamacare Ad Campaign," August 19, 2013, http://heritageaction.com/press-releases/heritage -action-announces-550000-defund-obamacare-ad-campaign.

3. Senate Conservatives Fund press release, "SCF TV Ad Urges Mitch McConnell to Defund Obamacare," September 5, 2013, www.senateconservatives.com/site/post/2255/scf-tv-ad-urges-mitch -mcconnell-to-defund-obamacare.

4. Senate Conservatives Fund press release, "SCA TV Ad Exposes McConnell's Decision to Fund Obamacare," October 29, 2013, www.senateconservatives.com/site/post/2338/sca-tv-ad-exposes -mcconnells-decision-to-fund-obamacare.

5. David Freedlander, "GOP Donors Revolt Against Republican -Led Government Shutdown," Daily Beast, October 3, 2013, www.thedailybeast.com/articles/2013/10/03/gop-donors-revolt-against -republican-led-government-shutdown.html.

6. Kate Nocera, "Club for Growth Threatens NRCC Chairman Greg Walden Over 'Chained CPI,'" Politico, April 11, 2013, www.politico.com /story/2013/04/club-for-growth-threatens-nrcc-chairman-greg-walden -over-chained-cpi-89955.html.

7. Andrew Romano, "How 'Real World' Sean Duffy Morphed into the Shutdown Congressman," Daily Beast, October 10, 2013, www.thedailybeast.com/articles/2013/10/10/how-real-world-sean -duffy-morphed-into-the-shutdown-congressman.html.

8. Steven Law email to donors, "Improving Candidate Quality," February 4, 2013.

9. Robert Costa, "Barbour Goes to War with the Club for Growth," National Review, February 12, 2013, www.nationalreview.com /corner/340464/barbour-goes-war-club-growth-robert-costa.

10. Chris Cilliza, "Haley Barbour Blasts Senate Conservatives Fund and Club for Growth," Washington Post, September 24, 2013, www.washingtonpost.com/blogs/the-fix/wp/2013/09/24/haley-barbour -blasts-senate-conservatives-fund-and-club-for-growth.

11. Costa, "Barbour Goes to War with the Club for Growth."

12. Chris Chocola statement, "Club for Growth PAC Responds to Haley Barbour," Club for Growth press release, February 12, 2013, www.clubforgrowth.org/perm/pr/?postID=1191.

13. Tom Hamburger and Matea Gold, "Some Longtime Republican Donors Are Unnerved by the GOP's Shutdown Strategy," *Washington Post,* October 5, 2013, http://articles.washingtonpost.com/2013-10-05 /politics/42740424_1_federal-government-shutdown-donors-crossroads.

14. Chris Chocola statement, "Is Shelley Moore Capito the 'Right' Kind of Republican U.S. Senate Candidate? The GOP Establishment Says 'Yes,' but Recent History Says 'No,'" Club for Growth press release, November 26, 2012, www.clubforgrowth.org/perm/pr/?postID=1179.

15. Senate Conservatives Fund release, "SCF Won't Endorse Capito in WV," November 26, 2012, www.senateconservatives.com/site/post/1645 /scf-wont-endorse-shelley-moore-capito.

16. Alexis Levinson, "Maness Looks to Shake Up Louisiana Senate Race," *Daily Caller,* November 8, 2013, http://dailycaller.com/2013/11/08 /maness-looks-to-shake-up-louisiana-senate-race.

17. Paul Woolverton, "Karl Rove Visits Fayetteville to Raise Money for Thom Tillis," *Fayetteville* (N.C.) *Observer,* November 21, 2013, http://fayobserver.com/articles/2013/11/21/1297830?sac=fo.business.

18. Nicholas Confessore, "Upstart Groups Challenge Rove for G.O.P. Cash," *New York Times*, December 23, 2013, www.nytimes .com/2013/12/24/us/politics/upstart-groups-challenge-rove-for-gop-cash. html.

19. Kenneth P. Vogel, "Dawn of the Mommy and Daddy PACs," Politico, July 25, 2012, www.politico.com/news/stories/0712/78931.html.

20. Fredreka Schouten, "Super PACs Gear Up for Individual Senate Battles," *USA Today*, January 2, 2014, www.usatoday.com/story/news /nation/2014/01/02/ candidate-aligned-super-pacs-senate-races-midterm-elections/4289825.

21. Becky Bohrer, "New Super PAC Forms to Support Treadwell," Associated Press, August 20, 2013, www.newsminer.com/news/politics /new-super-pac-forms-to-support-treadwell/article_6918c778-09f0-11e3 -be3a-001a4bcf6878.html.

22. Author interview with Joni Ernst, October 15, 2013.

23. Corey Mitchell, "Star Tribune Morning Hot Dish; Ortman v. McFadden (v. Coleman)," November 20, 2013, http://dfl48.org/fyi -sparks-fly-messy-gop-primary-ortman-takes-whacks-sideswipes -mcfadden-coleman.

24. Laura Meckler, "Business Voices Frustration with GOP," *Wall Street Journal,* October 16, 2013, http://online.wsj.com/news/articles/SB1 0001424052702304384104579139903054309502.

25. Anna Palmer, "Business Looks to Challenge Tea Party in Primaries," Politico, October 21, 2013, www.politico.com/story/2013/10 /business-looks-to-challenge-tea-party-in-primaries-98582.html.

26. Americans for Prosperity, "It's outrageous that politicians would consider a debt limit increase without also carefully scrutinizing wasteful government spending #tcot," Twitter, October 16, 2013, 9:04 p.m., https://twitter.com/AFPhq/status/390644542539440128.

27. Americans for Prosperity press release, "Large Coalition to Congress: Path to Balance," October 11, 2013, http://americansfor prosperity.org/legislativealerts/large-coalition-to-congress-path -to-balance.

28. Americans for Prosperity, "AFP Statement on Budget Deal; Activists Want Meaningful Spending Cuts; Will Increase Pressure on Congress," October 17, 2013, http://americansforprosperity.org /newsroom/afp-responds-to-budget-deal.

29. Senate Conservatives Fund press release, "SCF Endorses Matt Bevin for U.S. Senate," October 18, 2013, www.senateconservatives.com /site/post/2325/scf-endorses-matt-bevin-for-u-s-senate.

30. James Hohmann, "Conservative Groups Back Thad Cochran Opponent," Politico, October 17, 2013, www.politico.com/story/2013 /10/chris-mcdaniel-thad-cochran-conservative-groups-98493.html.

31. Jeff Barnard, "Walden Gets Primary Challenge from Right," Associated Press, October 23, 2013, www.oregonherald.com/oregon /local.cfm?id=4977.

32. Author interview with Fred Malek, October 22, 2013.

33. Nicholas Confessore, "Fund-Raising by G.O.P. Rebels Outpaces Party Establishment," *New York Times*, February 1, 2014, www.nytimes .com/2014/02/02/us/politics/rebel-conservatives-lead-way-in-gop-fund -raising.html.

34. Ibid.

35. President Obama's repeated promise that "If you like your health care plan, you can keep it" was named "Lie of the Year" by Politifact. Angie Drobnic Holan, "Lie of the Year: 'If You Like Your Health Care Plan, You Can Keep It,'" Politifact, December 12, 2013, www.politifact .com/truth-o-meter/article/2013/dec/12 /lie-year-if-you-like-your-health-care-plan-keep-it.

36. Clinton's remarks were recorded by my colleague Byron Tau, who was given a transferrable ticket by a donor.

37. Author interview with Rob McKay, October 29, 2013.

38. Maggie Haberman, "Tycoon Vows 'Full Might' for Hillary Clinton," Politico, November 29, 2013, www.politico.com/story/2013/11 /tycoon-vows-full-might-for-hillary-clinton-100488.html.

39. Noam Scheiber, "Hillary's Nightmare? A Democratic Party That Realizes Its Soul Lies with Elizabeth Warren," *New Republic,* November 10, 2013, www.newrepublic.com/articlc/115509/ elizabeth-warren-hillary-clintons-nightmare.

40. David Brock, "Confessions of a Right-Wing Hit Man," *Esquire,* July 1997.

41. Ben Smith, "Ickes on Obama," Politico, June 3, 2008, www.politico.com/blogs/bensmith/0608/Ickes_on_Obama.html.

42. Kenncth P. Vogel, "With Eyes on Hillary Clinton, Democrats Fight to Maintain Digital Edge," Politico, December 16, 2013, www.politico.com/story/2013/12/2016-digital-campaign-101180.html.

43. Nicholas Confessore, "Huge 'Super PAC' Is Moving Early to Back Clinton," *New York Times,* January 23, 2014, www.nytimes. com/2014/01/24/us/politics/biggest-liberal-super-pac-to-fund-possible -clinton-bid.html.

44. Arlette Saenz, "Rand Paul: Benghazi Decisions 'Should Preclude Hillary Clinton' from Presidency," ABCNews.com, November 12, 2013, http://abcnews.go.com/blogs/politics/2013/11/rand-paul-benghazi -decisions-should-preclude-hillary-clinton-from-presidency.

45. Photo of Hillary lapel pin taken at Ready for Hillary sign-in table at Le Parker Meridien, posted to Twitter, November 12, 2013, 4:58 p.m., https://twitter.com/kenvogel/status/400382159237550081.

46. Author interview with Rob McKay, October 29, 2013.

47. Alicia Mundy, "Playing Green 'Hardball' in Coal Country," *Wall Street Journal,* November 15, 2013, http://blogs.wsj.com/washwire/2013/11/15/playing-green-hardball-in-coal-country.

48. Kate Sheppard, "Democrats Demand Clarity on Trade Representative's Position on Tar Sands Oil," Huffington Post, December 20, 2013, www.huffingtonpost.com/2013/12/20/trade-representative-tar-sands_n_4482133.html.

49. Bill McKibben, "Clinton's Environmental Failure," Daily Beast, December 9, 2012, www.thedailybeast.com/articles/2012/12/09/hillary-clinton-and-obama-s-dismal-record-on-the-environment.html.

50. Briandude, "Elizabeth Warren and Alan Grayson in 2016," Middle-Class Populist, November 11, 2012, http://middle-class-populist.com/elizabeth-warren-and-alan-grayson-in-2016.

51. Gregg Easterbrook, "The Business of Politics; Representative Tony Coelho Has Raised a Lot of Money for Congressional Democrats—and Roused a Lot of Debate," *Atlantic Monthly,* October 1986, www.theatlantic.com/past/politics/polibig/eastbusi.htm.

52. "50 Richest Members of Congress," Roll Call, September 13, 2013, http://media.cq.com/50richest/the-50-richest-members-of-congress-113th-2013.html.

53. Jennifer Bendery, "Nancy Pelosi: Hillary Clinton Would Be More Prepared for White House than Obama, Bush," Huffington Post, September 22, 2013, www.huffingtonpost.com/2013/09/22/nancy-pelosi-hillary-clinton_n_3971843.html.

Epilogue

1. Obama's remarks were detailed to me by a source familiar with the event.

2. David M. Drucker, "The Establishment Fights Back: Mitch McConnell Leads GOP's Battle Against Tea Party Insurgents," *Washington Examiner,* December 4, 2013, http://washingtonexaminer.com/the-establishment-fights-back-mcconnell-leads-gops-battle-against-tea-party-insurgents/article/2539778.

3. Kenneth P. Vogel, "Obama Blocked Own 'Top Senate Achievement,'" Politico, January 16, 2008, www.politico.com/news/stories/0108/7929.html.

4. Author interview with Cynthia Canary, July 10, 2013.

Index

Kenneth P. Vogel covers the confluence of money, politics, and influence for Politico. He's won awards from the Association of Capitol Reporters and Editors, the Society of Professional Journalists, and Investigative Reporters and Editors. He analyzes politics on national television and radio, and lives in Alexandria, Virginia, with his wife, Danielle, and their dog, Ali.

PublicAffairs is a publishing house founded in 1997. It is a tribute to the standards, values, and flair of three persons who have served as mentors to countless reporters, writers, editors, and book people of all kinds, including me.

I. F. STONE, proprietor of *I. F. Stone's Weekly*, combined a commitment to the First Amendment with entrepreneurial zeal and reporting skill and became one of the great independent journalists in American history. At the age of eighty, Izzy published *The Trial of Socrates*, which was a national bestseller. He wrote the book after he taught himself ancient Greek.

BENJAMIN C. BRADLEE was for nearly thirty years the charismatic editorial leader of *The Washington Post*. It was Ben who gave the *Post* the range and courage to pursue such historic issues as Watergate. He supported his reporters with a tenacity that made them fearless and it is no accident that so many became authors of influential, best-selling books.

ROBERT L. BERNSTEIN, the chief executive of Random House for more than a quarter century, guided one of the nation's premier publishing houses. Bob was personally responsible for many books of political dissent and argument that challenged tyranny around the globe. He is also the founder and longtime chair of Human Rights Watch, one of the most respected human rights organizations in the world.

• • •

For fifty years, the banner of Public Affairs Press was carried by its owner Morris B. Schnapper, who published Gandhi, Nasser, Toynbee, Truman, and about 1,500 other authors. In 1983, Schnapper was described by *The Washington Post* as "a redoubtable gadfly." His legacy will endure in the books to come.

Peter Osnos, *Founder and Editor-at-Large*